P9-DMV-608

Linux

P H R A S E B O O K

Scott Granneman

DEVELOPER'S LIBRARY

Sams Publishing, 800 East 96th Street, Indianapolis, Indiana 46240 USA

This Book Is Safari Enabled

The Safari® Enabled icon on the cover of your favorite technology book means the book is available through Safari Bookshelf. When you buy this book, you get free access to the online edition for 45 days. Safari Bookshelf is an electronic reference library that lets you easily search thousands of technical books, find code samples, download chapters, and access technical information whenever and wherever you need it.

To gain 45-day Safari Enabled access to this book:

- Go to http://www.samspublishing.com/safarienabled
- Complete the brief registration form
- Enter the coupon code N9LC-3J1M-GPLS-7LMX-TGYS

If you have difficulty registering on Safari Bookshelf or accessing the online edition, please e-mail customer-service@safaribooksonline.com.

Acquisitions Editor Jenny Watson	**Project Editor** George E. Nedeff	**Proofreader** Jessica McCarty	**Multimedia Developer** Dan Scherf
Development Editors Songlin Qiu Scott Meyers	**Copy Editor** Heather Wilkins	**Technical Editor** Timothy Boronczyk	**Book Designer** Gary Adair
Managing Editor Gina Kanouse	**Indexer** John Bickelhaupt	**Publishing Coordinator** Vanessa Evans	**Page Layout** Bronkella Publishing LLC

Table of Contents

Contents

Part II: Working with Files

Part III: Finding Stuff

Part IV: Environment

Contents

Part V: Networking

Contents

About the Author

Scott Granneman is an author, educator, and consultant. As a writer, he focuses on open source software, as shown by his first two books, *Don't Click on the Blue E!: Switching to Firefox* and *Hacking Knoppix*, and his contributions to *Ubuntu Hacks*. In addition, he is a monthly columnist for SecurityFocus, with op/ed pieces that focus on general security topics, and for *Linux Magazine*, in a column focusing on new and interesting Linux software, and he blogs professionally on The Open Source Weblog.

An Adjunct Professor at Washington University in St. Louis, Scott teaches a variety of courses about technology and the Internet. As an educator, he has taught thousands of people of all ages—from preteens to senior citizens—on a wide variety of topics, including literature, education, and technology. With the shift in focus over the last decade to Linux and other open-source technologies, Scott has worked to bring knowledge of these powerful new directions in software to people at all technical skill levels.

As a Principal of WebSanity, a website creation and hosting firm, he works with businesses and nonprofits to leverage the Internet's communication, sales, and service opportunities. He manages the firm's Unix-based server environment, thereby putting what he writes and teaches into practical use, and works closely with other partners and developers on the underlying WebSanity Content Management System (CMS) software and its extensions.

Dedication

*The book is dedicated to Linux users,
both old and new. Welcome!*

Acknowledgments

No one learns about the Linux shell in a vacuum, and I have hundreds of writers, working over the last several decades, to thank for educating me about the awesome possibilities provided by the Linux command line. Books, websites, blogs, handouts at LUG meetings: All helped me learn about `bash`, and they continue to teach me today. If I can give back just a fraction of what I have absorbed, I'll be satisfied.

In addition to that general pool of knowledgeable individuals, I'd like to thank the people (and animals) who gave me help and support during the writing of *Linux Phrasebook*.

My agent, Laura Lewin, who has been helpful in too many ways for me to recount.

My editors at Pearson, who gave me the opportunity to write this book in the first place and have encouraged me whenever I needed prodding.

Robert Citek provided invaluable help with RPM, and was always there if I had a question. That man knows Linux.

My business partner and lifelong buddy Jans Carton helped me focus when I needed it, and was a (mostly) willing guinea pig for many new commands and options. Looking back at that day in fifth grade when we met, who'da thunk it?

Jerry Bryan looked over everything I wrote and fixed all the little grammatical mistakes and typos I made. I promise, Jerry: One day I'll learn the difference between "may" and "might!"

My wife, Denise Lieberman, patiently listened to me babble excitedly whenever I figured out something cool, even though she had absolutely no idea what I was talking about. That's true love. Thanks, Denise!

Finally, I must point to my cute lil' Shih Tzu Libby, who always knew exactly the right time to put her front paws on my leg and demand ear scratches and belly rubs.

We Want to Hear from You!

As the reader of this book, *you* are our most important critic and commentator. We value your opinion and want to know what we're doing right, what we could do better, what areas you'd like to see us publish in, and any other words of wisdom you're willing to pass our way.

You can email or write me directly to let me know what you did or didn't like about this book—as well as what we can do to make our books stronger.

Please note that I cannot help you with technical problems related to the topic of this book, and that due to the high volume of mail I receive, I might not be able to reply to every message.

When you write, please be sure to include this book's title and author as well as your name and phone or email address. I will carefully review your comments and share them with the author and editors who worked on the book.

Email: opensource@samspublishing.com

Mail: Mark Taber
        Associate Publisher
        Sams Publishing
        800 East 96th Street
        Indianapolis, IN 46240 USA

Reader Services

Visit our website and register this book at www.samspublishing.com/register for convenient access to any updates, downloads, or errata that might be available for this book.

Introduction

Among key Linux features, the command-line shell is one of the most important. If you run a Linux server, your main interface is more than likely going to be the shell. If you're a power user running Linux on the desktop, you probably have a terminal open at all times. If you're a Linux newbie, you may think that you'll never open up the command line, but you will sometime ... and the more you use Linux, the more you're going to want to use that shell.

The shell in many ways is the key to Linux's power and elegance. You can do things with the command line that you simply can't do with whatever GUI you favor. No matter how powerful KDE or GNOME may be (or IceWM or XFCE or any of the other kajillion windowing environments out there), you will always be able to do many things faster and more efficiently with a terminal. If you want to master Linux, you need to begin by mastering the Linux command line.

The traditional method has been to use the Linux man pages. While man pages are useful, they are often not enough, for one simple reason: They lack examples. Oh, a few man pages here and there have a few examples, but by and large, examples are hard to come by. This presents a real problem for users at all experience levels: It's one thing to see options listed and explained, but it's another thing entirely to see those options used in real world situations.

This book is all about those missing examples. I've been using Linux for over a decade and I consider myself pretty knowledgeable about my favorite operating system. On top of that, I'm so addicted to the command line that I have KDE set up to automatically start Konsole, the KDE terminal, when I log in. But I'm always lamenting with other Linux users the dearth of examples found in man pages. When I was asked to write *Linux Phrasebook*, and told that it was to consist of hundreds of examples illustrating the most important Linux commands, I replied, "I can't wait! That's a book I'd buy in a heartbeat!"

You're holding the result in your hands: a book about the Linux commands you just have to know, with examples illustrating how to use each and every one. This is a reference book that will be useful now and for years to come, but I also hope you find it enjoyable as well, and even a little fun.

Audience for This Book

I've written this book to be useful both to beginners—the folks that show up to meetings of our Linux Users Group seeking guidance and a helping hand as they begin the adventure of using Linux—and to experienced users who use the shell for everything from systems administration to games to programming. If you've just started using Linux, this book will help teach you about the shell and its power; if you've been using Linux for years and years, *Linux Phrasebook* will still teach you some new tricks and remind you of some features you'd long ago forgotten.

There are many shells out there—csh, tcsh, zsh, to name but a few—but I use the default shell for virtually every Linux distro: bash, the Bourne Again Shell. The bash shell is not only ubiquitous, but also amazingly powerful and flexible. After you get comfortable with bash, you may choose to explore other options, but knowledge of bash is required in the world of Linux.

I wrote this book using K/Ubuntu, but the commands discussed should work on your distro as well. The only major difference comes when you run a command as root. Instead of logging in as root, K/Ubuntu encourages the use of the sudo command; in other words, instead of running lsof firefox as root, a K/Ubuntu user would run sudo lsof firefox.

In order to appeal to the widest number of readers out there, I showed the commands as though you have to run them as root, without sudo. If you see a # in front of a command, that's the shell indicating that root is logged in, which means you need to be root to run that command, or utilize sudo if you're using K/Ubuntu or a similar distro.

Conventions Used in This book

This book uses the following conventions.

- Monospace type is used to differentiate between code/programming-related terms and regular English, and to indicate text that should appear on your screen. For example:

The df command shows results in kilobytes by default, but it's usually easier to comprehend if you instead use the -h (or --human-readable) option.

```
It will look like this to mimic the way text
➡looks on your screen.
```

- An arrow (➡) at the beginning of a line of code means that a single line of code is too long to fit on the printed page. It signifies to readers that the author meant for the continued code to appear on the same line. Many of the code examples in this book have been truncated due to length.

- In addition to this, the following elements are used to introduce other pertinent information used in this book.

A Note presents interesting pieces of information related to the surrounding discussion.

A Tip offers advice or teaches an easier way to do something.

A Caution advises you about potential problems and helps you steer clear of disaster.

## 1

Things to Know About Your Command Line

Before you really dig in to your bash shell, you first need to understand a few things that will help you as you proceed throughout this book. These are some absolutes that you just gotta know, and, trickily, some of them are not obvious at all. But after you understand them, some of the ways in which your shell behaves will start making much more sense.

Everything Is a File

On a Linux system, everything is a file—everything, which may seem obvious at first. Of course a text document is a file, and so is an OpenOffice.org document, and don't forget a picture, an MP3, and a video. Of course!

But what about a directory? It's a file, too—a special kind of file that contains information about other files. Disk drives are really big files. Network connections are files. Even running processes are files. It's all files.

To Linux, a file is just a stream of bits and bytes. Linux doesn't care what those bits and bytes form; instead, the programs running on Linux care. To Linux, a text document and a network connection are both files; it's your text editor that knows how to work with the text document, and your Internet applications that recognize the network connection.

Throughout this book I'm going to refer to files. If it's appropriate, feel free to read that as "files and directories and subdirectories and everything else on the system." In particular, many of the commands I'll cover work equally well on documents and directories, so feel free to try out the examples on both.

Maximum Filename Lengths

People who can look back to using MS-DOS (shudder!) remember that filenames could be no longer than eight characters, plus a three-letter extension, giving you incredibly descriptive names such as MSRSUME1.DOC. Pre-OS X Macs, on the other hand, extended that limit to 31 characters, which might sound long but could still produce some odd-looking names.

Linux (and Unix) filenames can be up to 255 characters in length. That's an outrageous length for a filename, and if you're getting anywhere even close to that, your picture should appear next to *verbose* in the dictionary. You're given up to 255 characters, so feel free to be descriptive and accurate, but don't go nuts.

In fact, it's a good idea to keep filenames below 80 characters because that's the width of your average terminal and your filenames will appear on one line without wrapping. But that's just advice, not a requirement.

The freedom to describe a file in 200+ characters is yours; just use it wisely.

Names Are Case-Sensitive

Unlike Windows and Mac OS machines, Linux boxes are case-sensitive when it comes to filenames. You could find the three following files in the same directory on a computer running Linux:

- bookstobuy.txt

- BooksToBuy.txt

- BoOkStObUy.txt

To the Linux filesystem, those are three completely different files. If you were on Windows or Mac OS, however, you would be asked to rename or cancel your attempt to add BooksToBuy.txt to a directory that already contained bookstobuy.txt.

Case-sensitivity also means that commands and filenames must be entered exactly to match their real command names or filenames. If you want to delete files by running rm, you can't type in RM or Rm or rM. rm is it. And if you want to delete bookstobuy.txt and you instead enter rm BooksToBuy.txt, you just removed the wrong file or no file at all.

The lesson is twofold: Linux forces you to be precise, but precision is a good thing. At the same time, you're given a degree of flexibility that you won't find in other operating systems. That combination of required precision and flexibility is one of the things that makes Linux fun to use, yet understandably a bit confusing for new users.

Special Characters to Avoid in Names

Every operating system has certain no-no's when it comes to the characters you can use when naming files and directories. If you use Mac OS, the colon (:) isn't allowed; Windows users, on the other hand, can't use the backslash (\). Linux has its *verboten* characters as well. Before looking at those, however, here are the characters that are always safe: numbers, letters (either uppercase or lowercase), dots (.), and underscores (_). Other items on your keyboard might work perfectly, others might work but present complications due to the fact that your shell will try to interpret them in various ways, and some won't work at all.

/ is never an option because that particular character is used to separate directories and files. Let's say you want to keep a file listing books you want to buy. You somehow manage to name the file books/to_buy.txt (with a forward slash) to distinguish it from books/on_loan.txt and books/lost.txt. Now when you try to refer to your file at /home/scott/documents/books/to_buy.txt, your command isn't going to work because your shell thinks that a books directory is inside the documents directory, but it doesn't exist.

Instead of a forward slash, use an underscore (as I did for the to_buy part of the filename), or cram the words together (as in booksToBuy.txt or BooksToBuy.txt).

You could use a dash, forming books-to-buy.txt, but I find that underscores work nicely as word separators while remaining more unobtrusive than dashes. If you do use a dash, though, do not place it at the beginning of a filename, as in -books_to_buy.txt, or after a space, as in books - to buy. As you're going to see later, if you're using a command and you want to invoke special options for that command, you preface the options with dashes. As you're going to see in Chapter 2, "The Basics," the rm command deletes files, but if you tried typing rm -books_to_buy.txt, your shell would complain with the following error message:

```
rm: invalid option -- b
```

You can use spaces if you'd like, forming books to buy.txt, but you have to let your shell know that those spaces are part of the filename. Your shell usually sees a space as a separator between arguments. Attempts to delete books to buy.txt confuses the shell, as it would try to delete a file named books, then one named to, and finally one named buy.txt. Ultimately, you won't delete books to buy.txt, and you might accidentally delete files you didn't want to remove.

So how do you work with spaces in filenames? Or the * and ? characters, which you'll learn more about in the next section? Or the ' and " characters, which also have special meanings in your shell? You have several choices. Avoid using them, if at all possible. Or escape them by placing a \ in front of the characters, which tells the shell that it should ignore their special usage and treat them as simple characters. It can grow tiresome, however, making sure that \ is in its proper place all the time:

```
$ rm Why\ don\'t\ I\ name\ files\ with\ \*\?.txt
```

Yuck. A simpler method that's a bit less onerous is to surround the filename with quotation marks, which function similarly to the \:

```
$ rm "Why don't I name files with *?.txt"
```

This will work, but it's still a pain to have to use quotation marks all the time. A better solution is just not to use these characters in the first place. Table 1.1 has some characters and what to do about them.

Table 1.1   **How to Use Special Characters in Filenames**

Character	Advice
/	Never use. Cannot be escaped.
\	Must be escaped. Avoid.
-	Never use at beginning of file or directory name.
[ ]	Must be escaped. Avoid.
{ }	Must be escaped. Avoid.
*	Must be escaped. Avoid.
?	Must be escaped. Avoid.
'	Must be escaped. Avoid.
"	Must be escaped. Avoid.

Wildcards and What They Mean

Imagine that you have the following files—12 pictures and a text file—in a directory on your computer:

```
libby1.jpg
libby2.jpg
libby3.jpg
libby4.jpg
libby5.jpg
libby6.jpg
libby7.jpg
libby8.jpg
libby9.jpg
```

```
libby10.jpg
libby11.jpg
libby12.jpg
libby1.txt
```

You want to delete these files using the rm command (covered in Chapter 2) on your command line. Removing them one at a time would be tedious and kind of silly. After all, one of the reasons to use computers is to automate and simplify boring tasks. This is a job for wildcards, which allow you to specify more than one file at a time by matching characters.

There are three wildcards: * (asterisk), ? (question mark), and [ ] (square brackets). Let's take each one in order.

The * matches any character zero or more times. Table 1.2 has some uses of the * and what they would match.

Table 1.2   The Wildcard * and What It Matches

Command	Matches
rm libby1*.jpg	libby10.jpg through libby12.jpg, as well as libby1.txt
rm libby*.jpg	libby1.jpg through libby12.jpg, but not libby1.txt
rm *txt	libby1.txt, but not libby1.jpg through libby12.jpg
rm libby*	libby1.jpg through libby12.jpg, and libby1.txt
rm *	All files in the directory

The ? matches a single character. Table 1.3 has some uses of the ? and what they would match.

Table 1.3   The Wildcard ? and What It Matches

Command	Matches
rm libby1?.jpg	libby10.jpg through libby12.jpg, but not libby1.txt
rm libby?.jpg	libby1.jpg through libby9.jpg, but not libby10.jpg
rm libby?.*	libby1.jpg though libby9.jpg, as well as libby1.txt

The [ ] match either a set of single characters ([12], for instance) or a range of characters separated by a hyphen (such as [1-3]). Table 1.4 has some uses of the [ ] and what they would match.

Table 1.4   The Wildcard [] and What It Matches

Command	Matches
rm libby1[12].jpg	libby11.jpg and libby12.jpg, but not libby10.jpg
rm libby1[0-2].jpg	libby10.jpg through libby12.jpg, but not libby1.jpg
rm libby[6-8].jpg	libby6.jpg through libby8.jpg, but nothing else

You'll be using wildcards all through this book, so it's good to introduce them now. They make dealing with files on the command line that much easier, and you're going to find them extremely helpful.

Conclusion

You've learned the stuff about Linux that might not be obvious to the new user, but that will come in handy as you begin using your shell and its commands. The details in this chapter will save you headaches as you start applying the materials in later chapters. Wondering why you can't copy a directory with a space in it, how to delete 1,000 files at one time, or why you can't run RM bookstobuy.txt? Those are not fun questions. With a little up-front knowledge, you can avoid the common mistakes that have plagued so many others.

With that out of the way, it's time to jump in and start learning commands. Turn the page, and let's go!

## 2

The Basics

This chapter introduces the basic commands you'll find yourself using several times every day. Think of these as the hammer, screwdriver, and pliers that a carpenter keeps in the top of his toolbox. After you learn these commands, you can start controlling your shell and finding out all sorts of interesting things about your files, folders, data, and environment.

List Files and Folders

The `ls` command is probably the one that people find themselves using the most. After all, before you can manipulate and use files in a directory, you first have to know what files are available. That's where `ls` comes in, as it lists the files and subdirectories found in a directory.

NOTE: The `ls` command might sound simple—just show me the files!—but there are a surprising number of permutations to this amazingly pliable command, as you'll see.

Typing **ls** lists the contents of the directory in which you're currently located. When you first log in to your shell, you'll find yourself in your home directory. Enter **ls**, and you might see something like the following:

```
$ ls
alias Desktop    iso    pictures program_files todo
bin   documents music podcasts  src            videos
```

List the Contents of Other Folders

```
ls music
```

You don't have to be in a directory to find out what's in it. Let's say that you're in your home directory, but you want to find out what's in the music directory. Simply type the **ls** command, followed by the folder whose contents you want to view, and you'll see this:

```
$ ls music
Buddy_Holly  Clash  Donald_Fagen  new
```

In the previous example, a relative path is used, but absolute paths work just as well.

```
$ ls /home/scott/music
Buddy_Holly  Clash  Donald_Fagen  new
```

The ability to specify relative or absolute paths can be incredibly handy when you don't feel like moving all over your file system every time you want to view a list of the contents of a directory. Not sure if you still have that video of Tiger Woods sinking that incredible putt? Try this (~ is like an alias meaning your home directory):

```
$ ls ~/videos
Ubuntu_Talk.mpeg          nerdtv_1_andy_hertzfeld
airhorn_surprise.wmv      nerdtv_2_max_levchin
apple_navigator.mov       nerdtv_3_bill_joy
b-ball-e-mail.mov         RPG_Nerds.mpeg
carwreck.mpg              tiger_woods_just_did_it.wmv
```

Yes, there it is: `tiger_woods_just_did_it.wmv`.

List Folder Contents Using Wildcards

```
ls ~/videos/*.wmv
```

You just learned how to find a file in a directory full of files, but there's a faster method. If you knew that the video of Tiger Woods you're looking for was in Windows Media format (Boo! Hiss!) and therefore ended with `.wmv`, you could use a wildcard to show just the files that end with that particular extension.

```
$ ls ~/videos
Ubuntu_Talk.mpeg          nerdtv_1_andy_hertzfeld
airhorn_surprise.wmv      nerdtv_2_max_levchin
apple_navigator.mov       nerdtv_3_bill_joy
b-ball-e-mail.mov         RPG_Nerds.mpeg
carwreck.mpg              tiger_woods_just_did_it.wmv
$ ls ~/videos/*.wmv
airhorn_surprise.wmv      tiger_woods_just_did_it.wmv
```

There's another faster method, also involving wildcards: Look just for files that contain the word *tiger*.

```
$ ls ~/videos/*tiger*
tiger_woods_just_did_it.wmv
```

View a List of Files in Subfolders

`ls -R`

You can also view the contents of several subdirectories with one command. Say you're at a Linux Users Group (LUG) meeting and installations are occurring around you fast and furious. "Hey," someone hollers out, "does anyone have an ISO image of the new Kubuntu that I can use?" You think you downloaded that a few days ago, so to be sure, you run the following command (instead of `ls -R`, you can have also used `ls --recursive`):

```
$ ls -R ~/iso
iso:
debian-31r0a-i386-netinst.iso   knoppix   ubuntu

iso/knoppix:
KNOPPIX_V4.0.2CD.iso   KNOPPIX_V4.0.2DVD.iso

iso/ubuntu:
kubuntu-5.10-install.iso   ubuntu-5.10-install.iso
kubuntu-5.10-live.iso      ubuntu-5.10-live.iso
```

There it is, in ~/iso/ubuntu: kubuntu-5.10-install-i386.iso. The -R option traverses the iso directory recursively, showing you the contents of the main iso directory and every subdirectory as well. Each folder is introduced with its path—relative to the directory in which you started—followed by a colon, and then the items in that folder are listed. Keep in mind that the recursive option becomes less useful when you have many items in many subdirectories, as the listing goes on for screen after screen, making it hard to find the particular item for which you're looking. Of course, if all you want to do is verify that there are many files and folders in a directory, it's useful just to see everything stream by, but that won't happen very often.

View a List of Contents in a Single Column

```
ls -1
```

So far, you've just been working with the default outputs of ls. Notice that ls prints the contents of the directory in alphabetical columns, with a minimum of two spaces between each column for readability. But what if you want to see the contents in a different manner?

If multiple columns aren't your thing, you can instead view the results of the ls command as a single column using, logically enough, ls -1 (or ls --format=single-column).

```
$ ls -1 ~/
bin
Desktop
documents
iso
music
pictures
src
videos
```

This listing can get out of hand if you have an enormous number of items in a directory, and more so if you use the recursive option as well, as in `ls -1R ~/`. Be prepared to press Ctrl+c to cancel the command if a list is streaming down your terminal with no end in sight.

View Contents As a Comma-Separated List

```
ls -m
```

Another option for those who can't stand columns of any form, whether it's one or many, is the -m option (or --format=commas).

```
$ ls -m ~/
bin, Desktop, docs, iso, music, pix, src, videos
```

Think of the *m* in -m as a mnemonic for *comma*, and it is easier to remember the option. Of course, this option is also useful if you're writing a script and need the contents of a directory in a comma-separated list, but that's a more advanced use of a valuable option.

View Hidden Files and Folders

```
ls -a
```

Up to this point, you've been viewing the visible files in directories, but don't forget that many directories contain hidden files in them as well. Your home directory, for instance, is just bursting with hidden files and folders, all made invisible by the placement of a . at the

beginning of their names. If you want to view these
hidden elements, just use the -a option (or --all).

```
$ ls -a ~/
.                .gimp-2.2          .openoffice.org1.9.95
..               .gksu.lock         .openoffice.org1.9
.3ddesktop       .glade2            .openoffice.org2
.abbrev_defs     .gnome             .opera

.adobe           .gnome2_private    pictures
```

You should know several things about this listing. First,
ls -a (the *a* stands for *all*) displays both hidden and
unhidden items, so you see both .gnome and pictures.
Second, you'll always see the . and .. because . refers
to the current directory, while .. points to the directory above this one, the parent directory. These two hidden files exist in every single folder on your system,
and you can't get rid of them. Expect to see them
every time you use the -a option. Finally, depending
on the directory, the -a option can reveal a great number of hidden items of which you weren't aware.

Visually Display a File's Type

```
ls -F
```

The ls command doesn't tell you much about an item
in a directory besides its name. By itself, it's hard to tell
if an item is a file, a directory, or something else. An
easy way to solve this problem and make ls really
informative is to use the -F option (or --classify).

```
$ ls -F ~/bin
adblock_filters.txt       fixm3u*          pix2tn.pl*
```

```
addext*                 flash.xml*          pop_login*
address_book.csv        getip*              procmail/
address_book.sxc        homesize*
programs_kill_artsd*
address_book.xls        html2text.py*
programs_usual*
```

This tells you quite a bit. An * or asterisk after a file means that it is executable, while a / or forward slash indicates a directory. If the filename lacks any sort of appendage at all, it's just a regular ol' file. Other possible endings are shown in Table 2.1.

Table 2.1   Symbols and File Types

Character	Meaning
*	Executable
/	Directory
@	Symbolic link
		FIFO
=	Socket

Display Contents in Color

`ls --color`

In addition to the symbols that are appended to files and folders when you use the -F option, you can also ask your shell to display things in color, which gives an additional way to classify items and tell them apart. Many Linux installs come with colors already enabled for shells, but if yours does not, just use the --color option.

```
$ ls --color
adblock_filters.txt    fixm3u        pix2tn.pl
addext                 flash.xml     pop_login
address_book.csv       getip         procmail
```

In this setup, executable files are green, folders are blue, and normal files are black (which is the default color for text in my shell). Table 2.2 gives you the full list of common color associations (but keep in mind that these colors may vary on your particular distro).

Table 2.2   Colors and File Types

Color	Meaning
Default shell text color	Regular file
Green	Executable
Blue	Directory
Magenta	Symbolic link
Yellow	FIFO
Magenta	Socket
Red	Archive (`.tar`, `.zip`, `.deb`, `.rpm`)
Magenta	Images (`.jpg`, `.gif`, `.png`, `.tiff`)
Magenta	Audio (`.mp3`, `.ogg`, `.wav`)

TIP: Want to see what colors are mapped to the various kinds of files on your system? Enter **dircolors --print-database**, and then read the results carefully. You can also use the dircolors command to change those colors as well.

With the combination of --color and -F, you can see at a glance what kinds of files you're working with in a directory. Now we're cookin' with gas!

```
$ ls -F --color
adblock_filters.txt    fixm3u*        pix2tn.pl*
addext*                flash.xml*     pop_login*
address_book.csv       getip*         procmail/
```

List Permissions, Ownership, and More

You've now learned how to format the results of ls to tell you more about the contents of directories, but what about the actual contents themselves? How can you learn more about the files and folders, such as their size, their owners, and who can do what with them? For that information, you need to use the -l option (or --format=long).

```
$ ls -l ~/bin
total 2951
-rw-r--r--  1 scott scott  15058 2005-10-03 18:49
➥adblock_filters.txt
-rwxr-xr--  1 scott root      33 2005-04-19 09:45
➥addext

-rwxr--r--  1 scott scott    245 2005-10-15 22:38
➥backup

drwxr-xr-x  9 scott scott   1080 2005-09-22 14:42
➥bin_on_bacon
-rw-r--r--  1 scott scott 237641 2005-10-14 13:50
➥calendar.ics

-rwxr-xr--  1 scott root     190 2005-04-19 09:45
➥convertsize
```

```
drwxr-xr-x  2 scott scott    48 2005-04-19 09:45
➥credentials
```

The -l option stands for *long*, and as you can see, it provides a wealth of data about the files found in a directory. Let's move from right to left and discuss what you see.

On the farthest right is the easiest item: The name of the listed item. Want ls to display more about it? Then add the -F option to -l, like this: ls -lF. Color is easily available as well, with ls -lF --color.

Moving left, you next see a date and time. This is the time that the file was last modified, including the date (in year-month-day format) and then the time (in 24-hour military time).

Farther left is a number that indicates the size of the item, in bytes. This is a bit tricky with folders—for instance, the previous readout says that bin_on_bacon is 1080 bytes, or just a little more than one kilobyte, yet it contains 887KB of content inside it. The credentials directory, according to ls -l, is 48 bytes, but contains nothing inside it whatsoever! What is happening?

Remember in Chapter 1, "Things to Know About Your Command Line," when you learned that directories are just special files that contain a list of their contents? In this case, the contents of credentials consists of nothing more than the .. that all directories have to refer to their parent, so it's a paltry 48 bytes, while bin_on_bacon contains information about more than 30 items, bringing its size up to 1080 bytes.

The next two columns to the left indicate, respectively, the file's owner and its group. As you can see in the previous listing, almost every file is owned by the user scott and the group scott, except for addext and convertsize, which are owned by the user scott and the group root.

NOTE: Those permissions need to be changed, which you'll learn how to do in Chapter 7, "Ownerships and Permissions" (hint: the commands are chown and chgrp).

The next to last column as you move left contains a number. If you're examining a file, this number tells you how many hard links exist for that file; if it's a directory, it refers to the number of items it contains.

TIP: For more information about hard (and soft) links, see www.granneman.com/techinfo/linux/thelinuxenvironment/softandhardlinks.htm, or search Google for *linux hard links*.

And now you reach the final item on the left: The actual permissions for each file and directory. This might seem like some arcane code, but it's actually very understandable with just a little knowledge. There are 10 items, divided (although it doesn't look that way) into 4 groups. The first group consists of the first character; the second group contains characters 2 through 4; the third consists of characters 5 through 7; and the fourth and final group is made up of characters 8 through 10. For instance, here's how the permissions for the credentials directory would be split up:

d|rwx|r-x|r-x.

That first group tells you what kind of item it is. You've already seen that -F and --color do this in different ways, but so does -l. A *d* indicates that credentials is a directory, while a - in that first position indicates a file. (Even if the file is executable, ls -l still uses just a -, which means that -F and

--color here give you more information.) There are, of course, other options that you might see in that first position, as detailed in Table 2.3.

Table 2.3   Permission Characters and File Types

Character	Meaning
-	Regular file
-	Executable
d	Directory
l	Symbolic link
s	Socket
b	Block device
c	Character device
p	Named pipe

TIP: To view a list of files that shows at least one of almost everything listed in this table, try ls -l /dev.

The next nine characters—making up groups two, three, and four—stand for, respectively, the permissions given to the file's owner, the file's group, and all the other users on the system. In the case of addext, shown previously, its permissions are rwxr-xr--, which means that the owner scott has rwx, the group (in this case, also scott) has r-x, and the other users on the box have r--. What's that mean?

In each case, r means "yes, read is allowed"; w means "yes, write is allowed" (with "write" meaning both changing and deleting); and x means "yes, execute is allowed." A - means "no, do not allow this action." If that - is located where an r would otherwise show itself, that means "no, read is not allowed." The same holds true for both w and x.

Looking at addext and its permissions of rwxr-xr--, it's suddenly clear that the owner (scott) can read, write, and execute the file; the members of the group (root) can read and execute the file, but not write to it; and everyone else on the machine (often called the "world") can read the file but cannot write to it or run it as a program.

Now that you understand what permissions mean, you'll start to notice that certain combinations seem to appear constantly. For instance, it's common to see rw-r--r-- for many files, which means that the owner can both read and write to the file, but both the group and world can only read the file. For programs, you'll often see rwxr-xr-x, which allows everyone on the computer to read and run the program, but restricts changing the file to its owner.

Directories, however, are a bit different. The permissions of r, w, and x are pretty clear for a file: You can read the file, write (or change) it, or execute it. But how do you execute a directory?

Let's start with the easy one: r. In the case of a directory, r means that the user can list the contents of the directory with the ls command. A w indicates that users can add more files into the directory, rename files that are already there, or delete files that are no longer needed. That brings us to x, which corresponds to the capability to access a directory in order to run commands that access and use files in that directory, or to access subdirectories inside that directory.

As you can see, -l is incredibly powerful all by itself, but it becomes even more useful when combined with other options. You've already learned about -a, which shows all files in a directory, so now it should be obvious what -la would do (or --format=long --all).

```
$ la -la ~/
drwxr-xr-x   2 scott scott   200 2005-07-28 01:31
➥alias

drwx------   2 root  root     72 2005-09-16 19:14
➥.aptitude

-rw-r--r--   1 scott scott  1026 2005-09-25 00:11
➥.audacity
drwxr-xr-x  10 scott scott   592 2005-10-18 11:22
➥.Azureus
-rw-------   1 scott scott  8800 2005-10-18 19:55
➥.bash_history
```

NOTE: From this point forward in this chapter, if scott is the owner and group for a file, I will remove that data from the listing.

Reverse the Order Contents Are Listed

`ls -r`

If you don't like the default alphabetical order that -l uses, you can reverse it by adding -r (or --reverse).

```
$ ls -lar ~/

-rw-------  8800 2005-10-18 19:55 .bash_history
```

```
drwxr-xr-x    592 2005-10-18 11:22 .Azureus
-rw-r--r--   1026 2005-09-25 00:11 .audacity
drwx------     72 2005-09-16 19:14 .aptitude
drwxr-xr-x    200 2005-07-28 01:31 alias
```

NOTE: Keep in mind that this is -r, not -R. -r means
reverse, but -R means recursive.

When you use -l, the output is sorted alphabetically
based on the name of the files and folders; the addition
of -r reverses the output, but it is still based on the filename. Keep in mind that you can add -r virtually any
time you use ls if you want to reverse the default output of the command and options you're inputting.

Sort Contents by File Extension

`ls -X`

The name of a file is not the only thing you can use
for alphabetical sorting. You can also sort alphabetically
by the file extension. In other words, you can tell ls to
group all the files ending with .doc together, followed
by files ending with .jpg, and finally finishing with files
ending with .txt. Use the -X option (or --sort=
extension); if you want to reverse the sort, add the
-r option (or --reverse).

```
$ ls -lX ~/src
drwxr-xr-x       320 2005-10-06 22:35 backups
drwxr-xr-x      1336 2005-09-18 15:01 fonts
-rw-r--r--   2983001 2005-06-20 02:15 install.tar.gz
-rw-r--r--   6683923 2005-09-24 22:41 DuckDoom.zip
```

Folders go first in the list (after all, they have no file extension), followed by the files that do possess an extension. Pay particular attention to `installdata.tar.gz`—it has two extensions, but the final one, the `.gz`, is what is used by `ls`.

Sort Contents by Date and Time

```
ls -t
```

Letters are great, but sometimes you need to sort a directory's contents by date and time. To do so, use `-t` (or `--sort=time`) along with `-l`; to reverse the sort, use `-tr` (or `--sort=time --reverse`) along with `-l`.

```
$ ls -latr ~/
-rw-------   8800 2005-10-18 19:55 .bash_history
drwx------    368 2005-10-18 23:12 .gnupg
drwxr-xr-x  2760 2005-10-18 23:14 bin
drwx------    168 2005-10-19 00:13 .Skype
```

All of these items except the last one were modified on the same day; the last one would have been first if you weren't using the `-r` option and thereby reversing the results.

NOTE: Notice that you're using four options at one time in the previous command: `-latr`. You could have instead used `-l -a -t -r`, but who wants to type all of those hyphens? It's quicker and easier to just combine them all into one giant option. The long version of the options (those that start with two hyphens and consist of a word or two), however, cannot be combined and have to be entered separately, as in `-la --sort=time --reverse`.

Sort Contents by Size

```
ls -S
```

You can also sort by size instead of alphabetically by filename or extension, or by date and time. To sort by size, use -S (or --sort=size).

```
$ ls -laS ~/
-rw-r--r--  109587 2005-10-19 11:53 .xsession-errors
-rw-------   40122 2005-04-20 11:00 .nessusrc
-rwxr--r--   15465 2005-10-12 15:45 .vimrc
-rw-------    8757 2005-10-19 08:43 .bash_history
```

When you sort by size, the largest items come first. To sort in reverse, with the smallest at the top, just use -r.

Express File Sizes in Terms of K, M, and G

```
ls -h
```

In the previous section, the 15465 on .vimrc's line means that the file is about 15KB, but it's not always convenient to mentally translate bytes into the equivalent kilobytes, megabytes, or gigabytes. Most of the time, it's more convenient to use the -h option (or --human-readable), which makes things easier to understand.

```
$ ls -laSh ~/
-rw-r--r--  100K 2005-10-19 11:44 .xsession-errors
-rw-------   40K 2005-04-20 11:00 .nessusrc
-rwxr--r--   16K 2005-10-12 15:45 .vimrc
-rw-------  8.6K 2005-10-19 08:43 .bash_history
```

In this example, you see K for kilobytes; if the files were big enough, you'd see M for megabytes or even G for gigabytes. Some of you might be wondering how 40122 bytes for .nessusrc became 40K when you used -h. Remember that 1024 bytes make up a kilobyte, so when you divide 40122 by 1024, you get 39.1816406 kilobytes, which ls -h rounds up to 40K. A megabyte is actually 1,048,576 bytes, and a gigabyte is 1,073,741,824 bytes, so a similar sort of rounding takes place with those as well.

NOTE: In my ~/.bashrc file, I have the following aliases defined, which have served me well for years. Use what you've learned in this section to extend these examples and create aliases that exactly meet your needs (for more on aliases, see Chapter 11, "Your Shell").

```
alias l='ls -F'
alias ll='ls -lF'
alias la='ls -aF'
alias ll='ls -laFh'
alias ls='ls -F'
```

Display the Path of Your Current Directory

pwd

Of course, while you're listing the contents of directories hither and yon, you might find yourself confused about just where you are in the file system. How can you tell in which directory you're currently working? The answer is the pwd command, which stands for *print working directory*.

NOTE: The word *print* in *print working directory* means "print to the screen," not "send to printer."

The pwd command displays the full, absolute path of the current, or working, directory. It's not something you'll use all the time, but it can be incredibly handy when you get a bit discombobulated.

```
$ pwd
/home/scott/music/new
```

Change to a Different Directory

```
cd
```

It's possible to list the contents of any directory simply by specifying its path, but often you actually want to move into a new directory. That's where the cd command comes in, another one that is almost constantly used by shell aficionados.

The cd command is simple to use: Just enter **cd**, followed by the directory into which you want to move. You can use a relative path, based on where you are currently—cd src or cd ../../—or you can use an absolute path, such as cd /tmp or cd /home/scott/bin.

Change to Your Home Directory

```
cd ~
```

You should know about a few nice shortcuts for cd. No matter where you are, just enter a simple **cd**, and you'll immediately be whisked back to your home directory. This is a fantastic timesaver, one that you'll use all the time. Or, if you'd like, you can use cd ~ because the ~ is like a shortcut meaning "my home directory."

```
$ pwd
/home/scott/music
$ cd ~
$ pwd
/home/scott
```

Change to Your Previous Directory

```
cd -
```

Another interesting possibility is cd -, which takes you back to your previous directory and then runs the pwd command for you, printing your new (or is it old?) location. You can see it in action in this example.

```
$ pwd
/home/scott
$ cd music/new
$ pwd
/home/scott/music/new
$ cd -
/home/scott
```

Using cd - can be useful when you want to jump into a directory, perform some action there, and then jump back to your original directory. The additional printing to the screen of the information provided by pwd is just icing on the cake to make sure you're where you want to be.

Change a File to the Current Time

`touch`

The touch command isn't one you'll find yourself using constantly, but you'll need it as you proceed through this book, so it's a good one to cover now. Interestingly, the main reason for the existence of touch—to update the access and modification times of a file—isn't the main reason you'll be using the command. Instead, you're going to rely on its secondary purpose that undoubtedly gets more use than the primary purpose!

NOTE: You can only use the touch command on a file and change the times if you have write permission for that file. Otherwise, touch fails.

To simultaneously update both the access and modification times for a file (or folder), just run the basic touch command.

```
$ ls -l ~/
drwxr-xr-x    848 2005-10-19 11:36 src
drwxr-xr-x   1664 2005-10-18 12:07 todo
drwxr-xr-x    632 2005-10-18 12:25 videos
-rw-r--r--    239 2005-09-10 23:12 wireless.log
$ touch wireless.log
$ ls -l ~/
drwxr-xr-x    848 2005-10-19 11:36 src
drwxr-xr-x   1664 2005-10-18 12:07 todo
drwxr-xr-x    632 2005-10-18 12:25 videos
-rw-r--r--    239 2005-10-19 14:00 wireless.log
```

Thanks to touch, both the modification time and the access time for the wireless.log file have changed, although ls -l only shows the modification time. The file hadn't been used in more than a month, but touch now updates it, making it look like it was just...touched.

You can be more specific, if you'd like. If you want to change just the access time, use the -a option (or --time=access); to alter the modification time only, use -m (or --time=modify).

Change a File to Any Desired Time

```
touch -t
```

Keep in mind that you aren't constrained to the current date and time. Instead, you can pick whatever date and time you'd like, as long as you use this option and pattern: -t [[CC]YY]MMDDhhmm[.ss]. The pattern is explained in Table 2.4.

Table 2.4   Patterns for Changing a File's Times

Characters	Meaning
CC	First two characters of a four-digit year
YY	Two-digit year: • If 00–68, assumes that first two digits are 20 • If 69–99, assumes that first two digits are 19 • If nothing, assumes current year
MM	Month (01–12)
DD	Day (01–31)
hh	Hour (01–23)
mm	Minute (00–59)
ss	Second (00–59)

It's very important that you include the zeroes if the
number you want to use isn't normally two digits or
your pattern won't work. Here are a few examples of
touch with the -t option in action to help get you
started.

```
$ ls -l
-rw-r--r--   239 2005-10-19 14:00 wireless.log
$ touch -t 197002160701 wireless.log
$ ls -l
-rw-r--r--   239 1970-02-16 07:01 wireless.log
$ touch -t 9212310000 wireless.log
$ls -l
-rw-r--r--   239 1992-12-31 00:00 wireless.log
$ touch -t 3405170234 wireless.log
$ ls -l
-rw-r--r--   239 2034-05-17 02:34 wireless.log
$ touch -t 10191703 wireless.log
$ls -l
-rw-r--r--   239 2005-10-19 17:03 wireless.log
```

First you establish that the current date and time for
wireless.log is 2005-10-19 14:00. Then you go back in
time some 35 years, to 1970-02-16 07:01, and then forward a little more than 20 years to 1992-12-31 00:00,
and then leap way into the future to 2034-05-17 02:34,
when Linux computers will rule the world and humans
will live in peace and open-source prosperity, and then
finish back in our day and time.

You should draw a couple of lessons from this demonstration. You go back more than three decades by specifying the complete four-digit year (1970), the month
(02), the day (16), the hour (07), and the minute (01).
You don't need to specify seconds. After that, you never
specify a four-digit year again. 92 in 9212310000 is

within the range of 69–99, so touch assumes you mean 19 as the base century, while 34 in 3405170234 lies between 00 and 68, so 20 is used as the base. The last time touch is used, a year isn't specified at all, just a month (10), a day (19), an hour (17), and minutes (03), so touch knows you mean the current year, 2005. By understanding how to manipulate touch, you can change the date stamps of files when necessary.

Create a New, Empty File

`touch`

But that's not the main reason many people use touch. The command has an interesting effect if you try to use the touch command on a file that doesn't exist: It creates an empty file using the name you specified.

```
$ ls -l ~/

drwxr-xr-x  848 2005-10-19 11:36 src
drwxr-xr-x  632 2005-10-18 12:25 videos

$ touch test.txt
$ ls -l ~/

drwxr-xr-x  848 2005-10-19 11:36 src
-rw-r--r--    0 2005-10-19 23:41 test.txt
drwxr-xr-x  632 2005-10-18 12:25 videos
```

Why would you use touch in this way? Let's say you want to create a file now, and then fill it with content later. Or you need to create several files to perform tests on them as you're playing with a new command you've discovered. Both of those are great reasons, and you'll find more as you start learning more about your shell.

Create a New Directory

```
mkdir
```

The touch command creates empty files, but how do you bring a new folder into existence? With the mkdir command, that's how.

```
$ ls -l

drwxr-xr-x  848 2005-10-19 11:36 src
drwxr-xr-x  632 2005-10-18 12:25 videos

$ mkdir test
$ ls -l

drwxr-xr-x  848 2005-10-19 11:36 src
drwxr-xr-x   48 2005-10-19 23:50 test
drwxr-xr-x  632 2005-10-18 12:25 videos
```

NOTE: On most systems, new directories created by mkdir give the owner read, write, and execute permissions, while giving groups and the world read and execute permissions. Want to change those? Look in Chapter 7 at the chmod command.

It should make you happy to know that your shell takes care of you: Attempts to create a directory that already exists fail and result in a warning message.

```
$ mkdir test
mkdir: cannot create directory 'test': File exists
```

Create a New Directory and Any Necessary Subdirectories

`mkdir -p`

If you want to create a new subdirectory inside a new subdirectory inside a new subdirectory, this seems like a rather tedious task at first: create the first subdirectory, cd into that one, create the second subdirectory, cd into that one, and finally create the third subdirectory. Yuck. Fortunately, mkdir has a wonderful option that makes this whole process much more streamlined: -p (or --parents).

```
$ ls -l

drwxr-xr-x  848 2005-10-19 11:36 src

$ mkdir -p pictures/personal/family
$ ls -l
drwxr-xr-x   72 2005-10-20 00:12 pictures

drwxr-xr-x  848 2005-10-19 11:36 src

$ cd pictures
$ ls -l
drwxr-xr-x   72 2005-10-20 00:12
➟personal
cd personal
$ ls -l
drwxr-xr-x   48 2005-10-20 00:12
➟family
```

Find Out What mkdir Is Doing As It Acts

```
mkdir -v
```

Now isn't that much easier? Even easier still would be using the -v option (or --verbose), which tells you what mkdir is doing every step of the way, so you don't need to actually check to make sure mkdir has done its job.

```
$ mkdir -pv pictures/personal/family
mkdir: created directory 'pictures'
mkdir: created directory 'pictures/personal'
mkdir: created directory 'pictures/personal/family'
```

One of the best things about being a Linux user is that the OS goes out of its way to reward lazy users—the lazier the better—and this is a great way to see that in action.

Copy Files

```
cp
```

Making copies of files is one of those things that computer users, no matter the OS, find themselves doing all the time. One of the most venerable commands used by the Linux shell is cp, which copies files and directories. The easiest way to use cp is simply to type in the command, followed by the file you're wanting to copy, and then the copied file's new name; think of the command's structure as "cp file-you're-copying-from file-you're-copying-to." Another common way to express that relationship is "cp source target."

```
$ pwd
/home/scott/libby
$ ls
libby.jpg
$ cp libby.jpg libby_bak.jpg
$ ls
libby_bak.jpg   libby.jpg
```

This example is pretty simple: The picture is copied into
the same directory as the original file. You can also copy
files to another directory, or even copy files from a directory in which you're not currently located to another
directory located somewhere else on your file system.

```
$ pwd
/home/scott
$ ls ~/libby
libby_bak.jpg   libby.jpg
$ cp pix/libby_arrowrock.jpg libby/arrowrock.jpg
$ ls ~/libby
arrowrock.jpg   libby_bak.jpg   libby.jpg
```

The same filename, libby_closeup.jpg, is used in this
example, which is okay because the file is being copied
into another directory entirely. In the first example for
cp, however, you had to use a new name, libby_bak.jpg
instead of libby.jpg, because you were copying the file
into the same directory.

If you want to copy a file from another directory into
your working directory (the one in which you currently find yourself), simply use .. (Remember how you
learned earlier in this chapter that . means "the current
directory?" Now you see how that information can
come in handy.) Of course, you can't change the name
when you use . because it's a shortcut for the original
filename.

```
$ pwd
/home/scott/libby
$ ls
libby_bak.jpg  libby.jpg
$ cp pix/libby_arrowrock.jpg .
$ ls
arrowrock.jpg  libby_bak.jpg  libby.jpg
```

You don't need to specify a filename for the target if that target file is going to reside in a specific directory; instead, you can just provide the directory's name.

```
$ ls -l
drwxr-xr-x    224 2005-10-20 12:34 libby
drwxr-xr-x    216 2005-09-29 23:17 music
drwxr-xr-x   1.6K 2005-10-16 12:34 pix
$ ls libby
arrowrock.jpg  libby.jpg
$ cp pix/libby_on_couch.jpg libby
$ ls libby
arrowrock.jpg  libby.jpg  libby_on_couch.jpg
```

In the previous example, you need to be certain that a directory named libby already exists for libby_on_couch.jpg to be copied into, or you would have ended up with a file named libby in your home directory.

Copy Files Using Wildcards

`cp .*`

It's time for more laziness, namely, the capability to copy several files at one time into a directory using wildcards. If you've been careful naming your files, this can be a really handy timesaver because you can exactly specify a group of files.

```
$ pwd
/home/scott/libby
$ ls ~/pix
arrowrock.jpg  by_pool_03.jpg  on_floor_03.jpg
by_pool_01.jpg on_floor_01.jpg on_floor_04.jpg
by_pool_02.jpg on_floor_02.jpg
$ ls
arrowrock.jpg  libby.jpg  libby_on_couch.jpg
$ cp ~/pix/by_pool*.jpg .
$ ls
arrowrock.jpg   by_pool_02.jpg  on_couch.jpg
by_pool_01.jpg  by_pool_03.jpg  libby.jpg
```

You aren't limited to the * wildcard; instead, you can
more precisely identify which files you want to copy
using a bracket that matches any characters named
between the [and] characters. If you want to copy
the first three on_floor pictures but not the fourth,
that's easily done with cp.

```
$ pwd
/home/scott/libby
$ ls ~/pix
arrowrock.jpg  by_pool_03.jpg  on_floor_03.jpg
by_pool_01.jpg on_floor_01.jpg on_floor_04.jpg
by_pool_02.jpg on_floor_02.jpg
$ ls
arrowrock.jpg  libby.jpg  libby_on_couch.jpg
$ cp ~/pix/on_floor_0[1-3].jpg .
$ ls
arrowrock.jpg   libby_on_couch.jpg  on_floor_02.jpg
libby.jpg       on_floor_01.jpg     on_floor_03.jpg
```

Copy Files Verbosely

`cp -v`

Adding the -v option (or --verbose) shows you the progress of cp as it completes its work.

```
$ pwd
/home/scott/libby
$ ls ~/pix
arrowrock.jpg  by_pool_03.jpg  on_floor_03.jpg
by_pool_01.jpg on_floor_01.jpg on_floor_04.jpg
by_pool_02.jpg on_floor_02.jpg
$ ls
arrowrock.jpg  libby.jpg  libby_on_couch.jpg
$ cp -v ~/pix/on_floor_0[1-3].jpg .
'/home/scott/pix/on_floor_01.jpg'
➥-> './on_floor_01.jpg'
'/home/scott/pix/on_floor_02.jpg'
➥-> './on_floor_02.jpg'
'/home/scott/pix/on_floor_03.jpg'
➥-> './on_floor_03.jpg'
$ ls
arrowrock.jpg  libby_on_couch.jpg  on_floor_02.jpg
libby.jpg      on_floor_01.jpg     on_floor_03.jpg
```

The -v option does a nice job of keeping you abreast of the cp command's progress. It does such a good job that you really don't need to run that last ls command because the -v option assures you that the files you wanted were in fact copied.

Stop Yourself from Copying over Important Files

```
cp -i
```

The previous example demonstrates something important about cp that you need to know. In the "Copy Files Using Wildcards" example, you copied three libby_on_floor pictures into the libby directory; in the previous example, you copied the same three libby_on_floor images into the libby directory again. You copied over files that already existed, but cp didn't warn you, which is how Linux works: It assumes you know what you're doing, so it doesn't warn you about things like overwriting your files…unless you ask it to do so. If you want to be forewarned before overwriting a file using the cp command, use the -i option (or --interactive). If you tried once again to copy the same files but used the -i option this time, you'd get a different result.

```
$ pwd
/home/scott/libby
$ ls ~/pix
arrowrock.jpg   by_pool_03.jpg  on_floor_03.jpg
by_pool_01.jpg  on_floor_01.jpg on_floor_04.jpg
by_pool_02.jpg  on_floor_02.jpg$ ls
arrowrock.jpg   libby_on_couch.jpg  on_floor_02.jpg
libby.jpg       on_floor_01.jpg     on_floor_03.jpg
$ cp -i ~/pix/on_floor_0[1-3].jpg .
cp: overwrite './on_floor_01.jpg'?
```

Bam! The cp command stops in its tracks to ask you if you want to overwrite the first file it's trying to copy, libby_on_floor_01.jpg. If you want to go ahead and copy the file, enter **y**; otherwise, enter **n**. If you do choose n, that doesn't mean the cp stops completely;

instead, you're next asked about the next file, and the next, and so on. The only way to give an n to whole process is to cancel the whole process by pressing Ctrl+c. Similarly, there's no way to say yes to every question ahead of time, so if you want to copy 1,000 files over 1,000 other files with the same name and also intend to use the -i option, make sure you have plenty of time to sit and interact with your shell, because you're going to get asked 1,000 times if you really want to overwrite your files.

CAUTION: For normal users, -i usually isn't necessary. For root users, however, it's darn near essential, as a root user can errantly copy over a key system file, causing a disaster. For that reason, it's a good idea to create an alias in the root user's .bashrc file, making sure that cp is really cp -i instead.

```
alias cp='cp -i'
```

Copy Directories

`cp -R`

So far you've looked at copying files, but there are times you'll want to copy directories as well. You can't just enter **cp source-directory target-directory**, though, because that won't work as you expected; the directory will copy, but not the files inside it.

```
$ pwd
/home/scott
$ cp libby libby_bak
cp: omitting directory 'libby'
```

If you want to copy directories, you need to include the -R option (or --recursive), which you should recall from the ls command. The addition of -R means that the directory, as well as its contents, are copied.

```
$ pwd
/home/scott
$ ls -l
drwxr-xr-x   328 2005-10-17 14:42 documents
drwxr-xr-x   240 2005-10-20 17:16 libby

$ cp -R libby libby_bak
$ ls -l
drwxr-xr-x   328 2005-10-17 14:42 documents
drwxr-xr-x   240 2005-10-20 17:16 libby
drwxr-xr-x   240 2005-10-20 17:17 libby_bak
```

Copy Files As Perfect Backups in Another Directory

```
cp -a
```

You might be thinking right now that cp would be useful for backing up files, and that is certainly true (although better programs exist, and we'll take a look at one of them—rsync—in Chapter 15, "Working on the Network"). With a few lines in a bash shell script, however, cp can be an effective way to back up various files and directories. The most useful option in this case would be the -a option (or --archive), which is also equivalent to combining several options: -dpR (or --no-dereference --preserve --recursive). Another way of thinking about it is that -a ensures that cp doesn't follow symbolic links (which could grossly balloon your copy), preserves key file attributes such as owner and timestamp, and recursively follows subdirectories.

```
$ pwd
/home/scott
$ ls -l
drwxr-xr-x    216 2005-10-21 11:31 libby
drwxr-xr-x    216 2005-09-29 23:17 music
$ ls -lR libby
libby:
total 312
-rw-r--r--  73786 2005-10-20 12:12 arrowrock.jpg
-rw-r--r--  18034 2005-04-19 00:57 libby.jpg
-rw-r--r-- 198557 2005-04-19 00:57 on_couch.jpg
drwxr-xr-x    168 2005-10-21 11:31 on_floor

libby/on_floor:
total 764
-rw-r--r-- 218849 2005-10-20 16:11 on_floor_01.jpg
-rw-r--r-- 200024 2005-10-20 16:11 on_floor_02.jpg
-rw-r--r-- 358986 2005-10-20 16:11 on_floor_03.jpg
$ cp -a libby libby_bak
$ ls -l
drwxr-xr-x    216 2005-10-21 11:31 libby
drwxr-xr-x    216 2005-10-21 11:31 libby_bak/
drwxr-xr-x    216 2005-09-29 23:17 music
$ ls -lR libby_bak
libby:
total 312
-rw-r--r--  73786 2005-10-20 12:12 arrowrock.jpg
-rw-r--r--  18034 2005-04-19 00:57 libby.jpg
-rw-r--r-- 198557 2005-04-19 00:57 on_couch.jpg
drwxr-xr-x    168 2005-10-21 11:31 on_floor

libby/on_floor:
total 764
```

```
-rw-r--r-- 218849 2005-10-20 16:11 on_floor_01.jpg
-rw-r--r-- 200024 2005-10-20 16:11 on_floor_02.jpg
-rw-r--r-- 358986 2005-10-20 16:11 on_floor_03.jpg
```

NOTE: Yes, you've probably figured it out already, but let me confirm: Libby is my dog, a cute lil' shih-tzu who eventually ends up in some way in almost everything I write. To see her, check out http://www.granneman.com/go/libby.

Move and Rename Files

`mv`

So cp copies files. That seems simple enough, but what about moving files? In the similar vein of removing unnecessary vowels in commands, we have the mv command, short for *move*.

You're going to notice quickly that most of the options you learned for cp are quite similar to those used by mv. This shouldn't surprise you; after all, mv in reality performs a cp -a, and then removes the file after it's been successfully copied.

At its simplest, mv moves a file from one location to another on your file system.

```
$ pwd
/home/scott/libby
$ ls
libby_arrowrock.jpg  libby_bak.jpg  libby.jpg
➥libby_on_couch.jpg  on_floor
$ ls ~/pictures/dogs
libby_on_floor_01.jpg  libby_on_floor_03.jpg
libby_on_floor_02.jpg  libby_on_floor_04.jpg
```

```
$ mv ~/pictures/dogs/libby_on_floor_04.jpg
➥libby_on_floor_04.jpg
$ ls
libby_arrowrock.jpg libby.jpg
➥libby_on_floor_04.jpg
libby_bak.jpg           libby_on_couch.jpg on_floor
$ ls ~/pictures/dogs
libby_on_floor_01.jpg  libby_on_floor_02.jpg
➥libby_on_floor_03.jpg
```

Just as you did with cp, you can use a dot to represent the current directory if you don't feel like typing out the filename again.

```
$ pwd
/home/scott/libby
$ ls
arrowrock.jpg libby.jpg  on_couch.jpg  on_floor
$ ls ~/pictures/dogs
on_floor_01.jpg  on_floor_03.jpg
on_floor_02.jpg  on_floor_04.jpg
$ mv ~/pictures/dogs/on_floor_04.jpg .
$ ls
arrowrock.jpg  on_couch.jpg  on_floor_04.jpg
libby.jpg        on_floor
$ ls ~/pictures/dogs
on_floor_01.jpg  on_floor_02.jpg  on_floor_03.jpg
```

If you're moving a file into a directory and you want to keep the same filename, you just need to specify the directory. The filename stays the same.

```
$ pwd
/home/scott/libby
$ ls
arrowrock.jpg  on_couch.jpg  on_floor_04.jpg
libby.jpg        on_floor
```

```
$ ls on_floor
on_floor_01.jpg  on_floor_02.jpg  on_floor_03.jpg
$ mv on_floor_04.jpg on_floor
$ ls
arrowrock.jpg    on_couch.jpg    on_floor_04.jpg
libby.jpg        on_floor
$ ls on_floor
on_floor_01.jpg  on_floor_03.jpg
on_floor_02.jpg  on_floor_04.jpg
```

In order to visually communicate that on_floor is in fact a directory, it's a good idea to use a / at the end of the directory into which you're moving files, like this: mv libby_on_floor_04.jpg on_floor/. If on_floor is not a directory, your mv won't work, thus preventing you from accidentally writing over a file.

NOTE: The cp and mv commands use many of the same options, which work the same way for either command. For instance, -v copies and moves verbosely, and -i copies and moves interactively.

Rename Files and Folders

mv

As you'll soon see, however, mv does something more than move, something that might seem a bit counterintuitive, but which makes perfect sense after you think about it a moment.

At this point, it's a good idea to introduce the other cool feature of mv. Yes, mv moves files—that's its name, after all—but it also renames files. If you move a file, you have to give it a target name. There's no rule that the target name has to be the same as the source name, so shell users since time immemorial have relied on the mv command to rename files and directories.

```
$ pwd
/home/scott/libby/by_pool
$ ls -F
libby_by_pool_02.jpg   liebermans/
$ mv liebermans/ lieberman_pool/
$ ls -F
libby_by_pool_02.jpg   lieberman_pool/
```

When moving a directory using cp, you had to specify the -R (or --recursive) option in order to copy the actual directory itself. Not so with mv, which, as you can see in the previous example, happily moves or renames directories without the need for any extra option at all, a nice change from cp.

CAUTION: You need to know a very important, and unfortunately easy to overlook, detail about mv. If you are moving a soft link that points to a directory, you need to be extremely careful about what you type. Let's say you have a soft link named dogs in your home directory that points to /home/scott/pictures/dogs, and you want to move the link into the /home/scott/libby subdirectory. This command moves just the soft link:

$ mv dogs ~/libby

This command, however, moves the directory to which the soft link points:

$ mv dogs/ ~/libby

What was the difference? A simple forward slash at the end of the soft link. No forward slash and you're moving the soft link itself, and just the link; include a forward slash and you're moving the directory to which the soft link is designed to point, not the soft link. Be careful!

Delete Files

`rm`

The `rm` command (short for *remove*) deletes files. It really, really removes them. They're gone. There's no trash can or recycle bin on the Linux command line. You're walking a tightrope, baby, and if you fall you go splat!

Okay, that's a little extreme. It's true that the shell lacks an undelete command, but you're not completely hosed if you delete a file. *If* you stop working on your machine the second you realize your mistake, *if* the operating system hasn't overwritten the erased file's sectors, and *if* you can successfully use some rather complicated file recovery software, yes, it's possible to recover files. But it's no fun, and you'll be cursing the whole time. Better to just be careful in the first place.

TIP: Many folks have tried to provide some sort of safety net for `rm`, ranging from remapping or replacing the `rm` command to a temporary trash can (www.comwt.com/ open_source/projects/trashcan/); to adding a trash can onto the shell (http://pages.stern.nyu.edu/~marriaga/ software/libtrash/); to creating a new command, `trash`, to replace `rm` (www.ms.unimelb.edu.au/~jrlooker/shell. html#trash).

If, on the other hand, you want to make positively sure that no one can possibly recover your deleted files, even men in black working for shadowy U.S. government agencies, use the `shred` command instead of `rm`. The `shred` command overwrites the file 25 times so it is impossible to re-create it. Before using `shred`, however, read its `man` page, as its success rate is highly dependent on the type of filesystem you're using.

Using rm is easy. Some would say almost too easy.

```
$ pwd
/home/scott/libby/by_pool/lieberman_pool
$ ls
pool_01.jpg        pool_03.jpg
pool_01.jpg_bak    pool_03.jpg_bak
$ rm pool_01.jpg_bak
$ ls
pool_01.jpg    pool_03.jpg    pool_03.jpg_bak
```

Remove Several Files At Once with Wildcards

rm *

Wildcards such as * help to delete several files with one keystroke.

```
$ pwd
/home/scott/libby/by_pool/lieberman_pool
$ ls
pool_01.jpg        pool_03.jpg
pool_01.jpg_bak    pool_03.jpg_bak
$ rm *_bak
$ ls
pool_01.jpg    pool_03.jpg
```

CAUTION: Be very, very, very careful when removing files using wildcards, or you may delete far more than you intended! A classic example is typing **rm *txt** instead of typing **rm * txt** (see the errant space?). Instead of deleting all text files, the star means that all files were deleted, and then rm tries to delete a file named txt. Oops!

Stop Yourself from Deleting Key Files   57

Remove Files Verbosely

`rm -v`

If you want to see what rm is doing as it does it, use
the -v (or --verbose) option.

```
$ pwd
/home/scott/libby/by_pool/lieberman_pool
$ ls
pool_01.jpg        pool_03.jpg
pool_01.jpg_bak    pool_03.jpg_bak
$ rm -v *_bak
removed 'pool_01.jpg_bak'
removed 'pool_03.jpg_bak'
$ ls
pool_01.jpg   pool_03.jpg
```

Stop Yourself from Deleting Key Files

`rm -i`

The -i option (or --interactive) provides a kind of
safety net. It asks you before deleting every file. This is
a good thing to use while you're running as root!

```
$ pwd
/home/scott/libby/by_pool/lieberman_pool
$ ls
pool_01.jpg        pool_03.jpg
pool_01.jpg_bak    pool_03.jpg_bak
$ rm -i *_bak
rm: remove regular file 'pool_01.jpg_bak'?
➥y
```

```
rm: remove regular file 'pool_03.jpg_bak'?
➡y
$ ls
pool_01.jpg   pool_03.jpg
```

When rm asks you what to do, a y is an agreement to
nuke the file, and an n is an order to spare the file and
continue onward to the next file.

Delete an Empty Directory

rmdir

Removing files isn't hard at all, but what about directories?

```
$ pwd
/home/scott/libby/by_pool
$ ls
pool_02.jpg   lieberman_pool   lieberman_pool_bak
$ ls lieberman_pool_bak
pool_01.jpg        pool_03.jpg
pool_01.jpg_bak    pool_03.jpg_bak
$ rm lieberman_pool_bak
rm: cannot remove 'lieberman_pool_bak/':
➡Is a directory
```

After a few moments of looking around, you might
find the rmdir command, which is specifically designed
for deleting directories. So you try it.

```
$ rmdir lieberman_pool_bak
rmdir: 'lieberman_pool_bak/': Directory not empty
```

Dang it! That doesn't work either. The rmdir command
only deletes empty directories. In this case, the

lieberman_pool_bak folder only contains four items, so it wouldn't be too hard to empty it and then use rmdir. But what if you want to delete a directory that contains 10 subdirectories that each contains 10 more subdirectories and every single subdirectory contains 25 files? You're going to be deleting forever. There has to be an easier way! For that, see the next section.

Remove Files and Directories That Aren't Empty

rm -Rf

There is an easier way to remove directories with files. Use the combination of the -R (or --recursive) and -f (or --force) options. The -r tells rm to go down into every subdirectory it finds and delete everything, while the -f tells rm to just do it without bothering you with the niceties, such as folders that aren't empty.

```
$ pwd
/home/scott/libby/by_pool
$ ls
pool_02.jpg   lieberman_pool   lieberman_pool_bak
$ ls lieberman_pool_bak
pool_01.jpg        pool_03.jpg
pool_01.jpg_bak    pool_03.jpg_bak
$ rm -Rf lieberman_pool_bak
$ ls
pool_02.jpg   lieberman_pool
```

Pow! That's a sure-fire way to get rid of a directory and all the files and subdirectories inside it.

CAUTION: The `rm -Rf` command can destroy your important files and your system.

The classic Linux warning is not to type **rm -Rf /*** as root. Yes, you will erase your system. No, it will not be pretty. Yes, you will feel stupid.

In general, be careful when using wildcards with `rm -Rf`. There's a huge difference between `rm -Rf libby*` and `rm -Rf libby *`. The former deletes everything in the working directory that begins with `libby`; the latter deletes any file or folder named exactly `libby`, and then deletes everything else in the directory.

You can also inadvertently create a disaster if you mean to enter **rm -Rf ~/libby/*** and instead fat finger your command and tell the shell **rm -Rf ~/libby /***. First the ~/libby directory leaves, and then your file system begins its rapid journey toward nonexistence.

Here's one that's bitten a few folks trying to be clever: Never type **rm -Rf .*/*** to delete a directory that begins with . because you'll also match .. and end up deleting everything above your current working folder as well. Oops!

Once again: Be careful using `rm -Rf` when you're a normal user. Be hyper vigilant and paranoid when using `rm -Rf` as root!

Delete Troublesome Files

Before leaving `rm`, you should know a couple of things about its relationship to certain files on your system. First, no matter how hard you try, you will not be able to remove the . or .. directories because they are required to keep your file system hierarchy in place. Besides, why would you want to remove them? Leave 'em alone!

How do you remove a file with a space in it? The normal way of invoking rm—the command, followed by the filename—won't work because rm thinks you're talking about two different files. Actually, removing Cousin Harold's picture isn't too hard. Just put the name of the file in quotation marks.

```
$ ls
cousin harold.jpg  -cousin_roy.jpg  cousin_beth.jpg
$ rm cousin harold.jpg
rm: cannot remove 'cousin': No such file or
➥directory
rm: cannot remove 'harold.jpg': No such file or
➥directory
$ rm "cousin harold.jpg"
$ ls
-cousin_roy.jpg  cousin_beth.jpg
```

Here's more of a head-scratcher: How do you remove a file whose name starts with -?

```
$ ls
-cousin_roy.jpg  cousin_beth.jpg
$ rm -cousin_roy.jpg
rm: invalid option -- c
Try 'rm --help' for more information.
```

D'oh! The rm command sees the - and thinks it's the start of an option, but it doesn't recognize an option that starts with c. It continues with ousin_roy.jpg and doesn't know what to do.

You have two solutions. You can preface the problematic filename with --, which indicates to the command that anything coming afterward should not be taken as an option, and is instead a file or folder.

```
$ ls
-cousin_roy.jpg  cousin_beth.jpg
$ rm -- -cousin_roy.jpg
$ ls
cousin_beth.jpg
```

Otherwise, you can use the . as part of your pathname, thus bypassing the space before the - that confuses the rm command and leads it into thinking the filename is actually an option.

```
$ ls
-cousin_roy.jpg  cousin_beth.jpg
$ rm ./-cousin_roy.jpg
$ ls
cousin_beth.jpg
```

It just goes to show that the ingenuity of Linux users runs deep. That, and try not to put a hyphen at the beginning of your filename!

Become Another User

`su username`

The su command (which stands for *switch user*, not, as is popularly imagined, *super user*) can allow one user to temporarily act as another, but it is most often used when you want to quickly become root in your shell, run a command or two, and then go back to being your normal, non-root user. Think of it as Clark Kent changing into his Superman duds, righting a few wrongs, and then going back to his non-super self.

Invoking su isn't difficult. Just enter **su**, followed by the user whose identity you want to assume.

```
$ ls
/home/scott/libby
$ whoami
scott
$ su gromit
Password:
$ whoami
gromit
$ ls
/home/scott/libby
```

There's a new command in that example, one that's
not exactly the most widely used: whoami. It just tells
you who you are, as far as the shell is concerned. Here,
you're using it to verify that su is working as you'd
expected.

Become Another User, with His Environment Variables

```
su -l
```

The su command only works if you know the password of the user. No password, no transformation. If it
does work, you switch to the shell that the user has
specified in the /etc/passwd file: sh, tcsh, or bash, for
instance. Most Linux users just use the default bash
shell, so you probably won't see any differences there.
Notice also in the previous example that you didn't
change directories when you changed users. In
essence, you've become gromit, but you're still using
scott's environment variables. It's as if you found
Superman's suit and put it on. You might look like
Superman (yeah, right!), but you wouldn't have any of
his powers.

The way to fix that is to use the -1 option (or --login).

```
$ ls
/home/scott/libby
$ whoami
scott
$ su -l gromit
Password:
$ whoami
gromit
$ ls
/home/gromit
```

Things look mostly the same as the "Become Another User" example, but things are very different behind the scenes. The fact that you're now in gromit's home directory should demonstrate that something has changed. The -1 option tells su to use a login shell, as though gromit actually logged in to the machine. You're now gromit in name, but you're using gromit's environment variables, and you're in gromit's home directory (where gromit would find himself when he first logged in to this machine). It's as though putting on Superman's skivvies also gave you the ability to actually leap tall buildings in a single bound!

Become root

su

At the beginning of this chapter, the point was made that most times su is used to become root. You could use su root, or better still, su -1 root, but there is a quicker way.

```
$ whoami
scott
$ su
Password:
$ whoami
root
```

Become root, with Its Environment Variables

```
su -
```

Entering **su** all by its lonesome is equivalent to typing in **su root**—you're root in name and power, but that's all. Behind the scenes, your non-root environment variables are still in place, as shown here:

```
$ ls
/home/scott/libby
$ whoami
scott
$ su
Password:
$ whoami
root
$ ls
/home/scott/libby
```

When you use su -, you not only become root, you also use root's environment variables.

```
$ ls
/home/scott/libby
$ whoami
scott
```

```
$ su -
Password:
$ whoami
root
$ ls
/root
```

Now that's better! Appending - after su is the same as su -l root, but requires less typing. You're root in name, power, and environment, which means you're fully root. To the computer, anything that root can do, you can do. Have fun with your superpowers, but remember that with great power comes great…aw, you know how it ends.

Conclusion

If this was law school, you would have learned in this chapter what misdemeanors, torts, and felonies are. If this was a hardware repair class, it would have been RAM, hard drives, and motherboards. Since this is a book about the Linux shell, you've examined the most basic commands that a Linux user needs to know to effectively use the command line: ls, pwd, cd, touch, mkdir, cp, mv, rm, and su. rmdir and whoami were thrown in as extra goodies. With these vital commands under your belt, you're ready to move ahead to learning about how to learn about commands. Twisty? You ain't seen nothin' yet.

3

Learning About Commands

In Chapter 2, "The Basics," you started learning about some basic system commands. You covered a lot, but even so, much was left out. The ls command is an incredibly rich, powerful tool, with far more options than were provided in Chapter 2. So how can you learn more about that command or others that pique your interest? And how can you discover commands if you don't even know their names? That's where this chapter comes in. Here you will find out how to learn more about the commands you already know, those you know you don't know, and even those that you don't know that you don't know!

Let's start with the two 800-pound gorillas—man and info—and move from there to some smaller, more precise commands that actually use much of the data collected by man. By the time you're finished, you'll be ready to start learning about the huge variety of tools available to you in your shell environment.

Find Out About Commands with man

`man 1s`

Want to find out about a Linux command? Why, it's easy! Let's say you want to find out more about the `1s` command. Enter **man 1s**, and the man (short for *manual*) page appears, chock full of info about the various facets of `1s`. Try the same thing for some of the other commands you've examined in this book. You'll find man pages for (almost) all of them.

Still, as useful as man pages are, they still have problems. You have to know the name of a command to really use them (although there are ways around that particular issue), and they're sometimes out of date and missing the latest features of a command. They don't always exist for every command, which can be annoying. But worst of all, even if you find one that describes a command in which you're interested and it's up to date, you might still have a big problem: It might be next to useless.

The same developers who write the programs usually (but not always) write the man pages. Most of the developers who write applications included with a Linux distribution are excellent programmers, but not always effective writers or explainers of their own work. They know how things work, but they too often forget that users don't know the things that the developers find obvious and intuitive.

With all of those problems, however, man pages are still a good resource for Linux users at all levels of experience. If you're going to use Linux on the command line, you need to learn how to use and read man pages.

As stated before, using this command isn't hard. Just enter **man**, followed by the command about which you want to learn more.

```
$ man ls
LS(1)                 User Commands                 LS(1)
NAME
  ls - list directory contents
SYNOPSIS
  ls [OPTION]... [FILE]...
DESCRIPTION
  List  information  about  the FILEs (the current
  directory by default).
  Sort entries alphabetically if none of -cftuSUX
  nor --sort.
  Mandatory arguments to long options are mandatory
  for short options too.
  -a, --all
    do not hide entries starting with .
  -A, --almost-all
    do not list implied . and ..
[Listing condensed due to length]
```

The list of data man provides in this case is quite extensive—over 200 lines worth, in fact. Of course, not all commands provide that much, and some provide far more. Your job is to read the various sections provided in a man page, which usually (but not always) consist of the following:

- NAME—The name of the command and a brief description

- SYNOPSIS—The basic format of the command

- DESCRIPTION—A longer overview of the command's purpose

- OPTIONS—The real meat and potatoes of man: The various options for the command, along with short explanations of each one

- FILES—Other files used by the command

- AUTHOR—Who wrote the command, along with contact information

- BUGS—Known bugs and how to report new ones

- COPYRIGHT—This one's obvious: Information about copyright

- SEE ALSO—Other, related commands

Moving around in a man page isn't that hard. To move down a line at a time, use the down arrow; to move up a line at a time, use the up arrow. To jump down a page, press the spacebar or f (for *forward*); to jump up a page, press b (for *backward*). When you reach the end of a man page, man might quit itself, depositing you back on the shell; it might, however, simply stop at the end without quitting, in which case you should press q to quit the program. In fact, you can press q at any time to exit man if you're not finding the information you want.

It can be hard to find a particular item in a man page, so sometimes you need to do a little searching. To search on a man page after it's open, type /, followed by your search term, and then press Enter. If your term exists, you'll jump to it; to jump to the next occurrence of the term, press Enter again (or n), and keep pressing Enter (or n) to jump down the screen to each occurrence; to go backward, press Shift+n.

Search for a Command Based on What It Does

`man -k`

With just a little training, you find that you can zoom around man pages and find exactly what you need...assuming you know which man page to read. What if you know a little about what a command does, but you don't know the actual name of the command? Try using the -k option (or --apropos) and search for a word or phrase that describes the kind of command you want to discover. You'll get back a list of all commands whose name or synopsis matches your search term.

```
$ man list
No manual entry for list
$ man -k list
last (1) - show listing of last logged in users
ls (1) - list directory contents
lshal (1) - List devices and their properties
lshw (1) - list hardware
lsof (8) - list open files
[Listing condensed due to length]
```

Be careful with the -k option, as it can produce a long list of results, and you might miss what you were looking for. Don't be afraid to try a different search term if you think it might help you find the command you need.

TIP: The -k option, also represented by --apropos, is exactly the same as the apropos command.

Quickly Find Out What a Command Does Based on Its Name

`man -f`

If you know a command's name but don't know what it does, there's a quick and dirty way to find out without requiring you to actually open the man page for that command. Use the -f option (or --whatis), and the command's synopsis appears.

```
$ man -f ls
ls (1)                  - list directory contents
```

TIP: Yes, the -f option, also known as --whatis, is the spitting image of the whatis command, which is examined in more detail later in this chapter.

Rebuild man's Database of Commands

`man -u`

Occasionally you'll try to use man to find out information about a command and man reports that there is no page for that command. Before giving up, try again with the -u option (or --update), which forces man to rebuild the database of commands and man pages it uses. It's often a good first step if you think things aren't quite as they should be.

```
$ man ls
No manual entry for ls
$ man -u ls
LS(1)              User Commands              LS(1)
NAME
  ls - list directory contents
SYNOPSIS
  ls [OPTION]... [FILE]...
[Listing condensed due to length]
```

Read a Command's Specific Man Page

`man [1-8]`

You might notice in the previous listing that the first line of man's page on ls references LS(1), while earlier, when you used the -k option, all the names of commands were also followed by numbers in parentheses. Most of them are 1, but one, lsof, is 8. So what's up with all of these numbers?

The answer is that man pages are categorized into various sections, numbered from 1 to 8, which break down as follows (and don't worry if you don't recognize some of the example, as many of them are pretty arcane and specialized):

1. General commands. Examples are cd, chmod, lp, mkdir, and passwd.

2. Low-level system calls provided by the kernel. Examples are intro and chmod.

3. C library functions. Examples are beep, HTML::Parser, and Mail::Internet.

4. Special files, such as devices found in /dev. Examples are `console`, `lp`, and `mouse`.

5. File formats and conventions. Examples are `apt.conf`, `dpkg.cfg`, `hosts`, and `passwd`.

6. Games. Examples are `atlantik`, `bouncingcow`, `kmahjongg`, and `rubik`.

7. Miscellanea, including macro packages. Examples are `ascii`, `samba`, and `utf-8`.

8. System administration commands used by `root`. Examples are `mount` and `shutdown`.

Almost every command we've looked at so far in this book falls into section 1, which isn't surprising because we're focused on general use of your Linux system. But notice how some commands fall into more than one section: `chmod`, for instance, is in both 1 and 2, while `passwd` can be found in 1 and 5. By default, if you enter **man passwd** in your shell, `man` defaults to the lower number, so you'll get the section 1 man page for `passwd`, which isn't very helpful if you want to learn about the file `passwd`. To see the man page for the file `passwd`, follow `man` with the section number for the data you want to examine.

```
$ man passwd
PASSWD(1)                                           PASSWD(1)
NAME
  passwd - change user password
SYNOPSIS
  passwd [-f|-s] [name]
  passwd [-g] [-r|-R] group
  passwd [-x max] [-n min] [-w warn] [-i inact]
login
  passwd {-l|-u|-d|-S|-e} login
```

```
DESCRIPTION
  passwd changes passwords for user and group
➥accounts. A normal user...
[Listing condensed due to length]
$ man 5 passwd
PASSWD(5)                                    PASSWD(5)
NAME
  passwd - The password file
DESCRIPTION
  passwd contains various pieces of information for
➥each user account.
[Listing condensed due to length]
```

Print Man Pages

`man -t`

As easy as it is to view man pages using a terminal program, sometimes it's necessary to print out a man page for easier reading and cogitation. Printing a man page isn't a one-step process, however, and the commands that round out this particular section are actually using principles that will be covered extensively later. But if you want to print out a man page, this is the way to do it. Just have faith that you'll understand what these commands mean more fully after reading upcoming chapters.

Let's say you have a printer that you have identified with the name hp_laserjet connected to your system. You want to print a man page about the ls command directly to that printer, so use the -t option (or --troff) and then pipe the output to the lpr command, identifying your printer with the -P option.

```
$ man -t ls | lpr -P hp_laserjet
```

NOTE: You'll learn about the pipe symbol (|) in Chapter 4, "Building Blocks," and 1pr in Chapter 6, "Printing and Managing Print Jobs."

In just a moment or two, depending upon the speed of your computer and your printer, hp_laserjet should begin spitting out the man pages for 1s. Maybe you don't want to actually print the pages, however. Maybe just creating PDFs of the man page for the 1s command would be enough. Once again, the commands to do so might seem a bit arcane now, but they will be far more comprehensible very soon.

Again, you use the -t option, but this time you send the output to a PostScript file named for the 1s command. If that process completes successfully, you convert the PostScript file to a PDF using the ps2pdf command, and then after that finishes correctly, you delete the original PostScript file because it's no longer needed.

```
$ man -t 1s > 1s.ps && ps2pdf 1s.ps && rm 1s.ps
```

NOTE: You'll learn about the > and && symbols in Chapter 4 and ps2pdf in Chapter 6.

If you want to make a printed library of man pages covering your favorite commands, or if you want that library in PDF format (which can then be printed to hard copies, if necessary), now you know how to do it. For something so simple, man is powerful and flexible, which makes it even more useful than it already is.

Learn About Commands with `info`

info

The `man` command, and the resulting man pages, are simple to work with, even if the content isn't always as user friendly as you might like. In response to that and other perceived shortcomings with man pages, the GNU Project, which is responsible in many ways for many of the commands you're reading about in this book, created its own format: Info pages, which use the `info` command for viewing.

Info pages tend to be better written, more comprehensive, and more user friendly in terms of content than man pages, but man pages are far easier to use. A man page is just one page, while Info pages almost always organize their contents into multiple sections, called *nodes*, which might also contain subsections, called *subnodes*. The trick is learning how to navigate not just around an individual page, but also between nodes and subnodes. It can be a bit overwhelming at first to just move around and find what you're seeking in Info pages, which is rather ironic: Something that was supposed to be nicer for newbies than `man` is actually far harder for the novice to learn and use.

There are many facets to `info`, and one of the best commands to use `info` against is, in fact, `info`. To learn how to use `info`, as well as read about `info`, enter the following command:

```
$ info info
```

This opens the Info page for the `info` command. Now you need to learn how to get around in this new Info world.

Navigate Within `info`

Within a particular section's screen, to move down, or forward, one line at a time, use the down arrow; to move up, or back, one line at a time, use the up arrow. When you reach the bottom, or end, of a particular section, your cursor stops and you are not able to proceed.

If you instead want to jump down a screen at a time, use your keyboard's PageDown button; to jump up a screen at a time, use the PageUp key instead. You are not able to leave the particular section you're in, however.

If you reach the end of the section and you want to jump back to the top, just press b, which stands for *beginning*. Likewise, e takes you to the "end."

If, at any time, as you're jumping around from place to place, you notice that things look a little strange, such as the letters or words being distorted, press Ctrl+l to redraw the screen, and all should be well.

Now that you know how to navigate within a particular section or node, let's move on to navigating between nodes. If you don't want to use PageDown and PageUp to move forward and backward within a section, you can instead use the spacebar to move down and the Backspace or Delete keys to move up. These keys offer one big advantage over PageDown and PageUp, besides being easier to reach: When you hit the end of a node, you automatically proceed onward to the next node, through subnodes if they exist. Likewise, going up moves you back to the previous node, through any

subnodes. Using the spacebar, or the Backspace or
Delete buttons, you can quickly run through an entire
set of Info pages about a particular command.

If you want to engage in fewer key presses, you can use
n (for *next*) to move on to the next node at the same
level. If you are reading a node that had subnodes and
you press n, you skip those subnodes and move to the
next node that's a peer of the one you're currently reading. If you reading a subnode and press n, however, you
jump to the next subnode. If n moves you to the next
node at the current level, then p moves you to the previous one (p for *previous*, get it?), again at the same level.

If you instead want to move forward to a node or
subnode, use the], or right square brace, key. If you're
reading a node and you press], you'll jump to that
node's first subnode, if one exists. Otherwise, you'll
move to that node's next peer node. To move backward
in the same fashion, use the [, or left square brace, key.

If you want to move up a node, to the parent of the
node you're currently reading, use the u (for *up*) key.
Be careful, though—it's easy to jump up past the home
page of the command you're reading about in Info to
what is termed the Directory node, the root node that
leads to all other Info nodes (another way to reach the
Directory node is to type **d**, for *directory*, at any time).

The Directory node is a particularly large example of a
type of page you find all throughout Info: a Menu
page, which lists all subnodes or nodes. If you ever find
yourself on a Menu page, you can quickly navigate to
one of the subnodes listed in that menu in one of two
ways. First, type an **m** (for *menu*) and then start typing
the name of the subnode to which you want to jump.
For instance, here's the first page you see when you
enter **info info** on the command line:

```
File: info.info,  Node: Top,  Next: Getting Started,
➡Up: (dir)

Info: An Introduction
*********************
The GNU Project distributes most of its on-line
manuals in the "Info format", which you read using
an "Info reader". You are probably using an Info
reader to read this now.
[content condensed due to length]


* Menu:
* Getting Started:: Getting started using an Info
➡reader.
* Expert Info:: Info commands for experts.
* Creating an Info File:: How to make your own Info
➡file.
* Index:: An index of topics, commands, and
➡variables.
```

To jump to Expert Info, you could type m, followed by
Exp. At this point, you could finish typing **ert Info**, or
you could just press the Tab key and Info fills in the rest
of the menu name that matches the characters you've
already entered. If Info complains, you have entered a
typo, or more than one menu choice matches the characters you've typed. Fix your typo, or enter more characters until it is obvious to Info which menu choice is
the one in which you're interested. If you realize that
you don't want to go to a Menu choice at this time,
press Ctrl+g to cancel your command, and go back to
reading the node on which you find yourself.

Alternatively, you could just use your up or down
arrow key to position the cursor over the menu choice
you want, and then press Enter. Either method works.

If you don't want to navigate Info pages and instead want to search, you can do that as well, in two ways: By searching just the titles of all nodes for the Info pages about a particular command, or by searching in the actual text of all nodes associated with a particular command. To search the titles, enter i (for *index* because this search uses the node index created by Info), followed by your search term, and press Enter. If your term exists somewhere in a node's title, you'll jump to it. If you want to repeat your search and go to the next result, press the comma key.

If you want to search text instead of titles, enter s (for *search*), followed by your search term or phrase, and then press Enter. To repeat that search, enter s, followed immediately by Enter. That's not as easy as just pressing the comma key like you do when you're searching titles, but it does work.

If at any time you get lost inside Info and need help, just press the ? key and the bottom half of your window displays all of the various options for Info. Move up and down in that section using the keys you've already learned. When you want to get out of help, press l.

Finally, and perhaps most importantly, to get out of Info altogether, just press q, for *quit*, which dumps you back in your shell. Whew!

Locate the Paths for a Command's Executable, Source Files, and Man Pages

whereis

The whereis command performs an incredibly useful function: It tells you the paths for a command's executable program, its source files (if they exist), and its man pages. For instance, here's what you might get for KWord, the word processor in the KOffice set of programs (assuming, of course, that the binary, source, and man files are all installed):

```
$ whereis kword
kword: /usr/src/koffice-1.4.1/kword /usr/bin/kword
➥/usr/bin/X11/kword usr/share/man/man1/kword.1.gz
```

The whereis command first reports where the source files are: /usr/src/koffice-1.4.1/kword. Then it informs you as to the location of any binary executables: /usr/bin/kword and /usr/bin/X11/kword. KWord is found in two places on this machine, which is a bit unusual but not bizarre. Finally, you find out where the man pages are: /usr/share/man/man1/kword.1.gz. Armed with this information, you can now verify that the program is in fact installed on this computer, and you know now how to run it.

If you want to search only for binaries, use the -b option.

```
$ whereis -b kword
kword: /usr/bin/kword /usr/bin/X11/kword
```

If you want to search only for man pages, the -m option is your ticket.

```
$ whereis -m kword
kword: /usr/share/man/man1/kword.1.gz
```

Finally, if you want to limit your search only to sources, try the -s option.

```
$ whereis -s kword
kword: /usr/src/koffice-1.4.1/kword
```

The whereis command is a good, quick way to find vital information about programs on the computer you're using. You'll find yourself using it more than you think.

Read Descriptions of Commands

`whatis`

Earlier in this chapter you found out about the -f option for man, which prints onscreen the description of a command found in a man page. If you can remember that man -f presents that information, bully for you. It might be easier, however, to remember the whatis command, which does exactly the same thing: Displays the man page description for a command.

```
$ man -f ls
ls (1)   - list directory contents
$ whatis ls
ls (1)   - list directory contents
```

The whatis command also supports regular expressions and wildcards. To search the man database using wildcards, use the -w option (or --wildcard).

```
$ whatis -w ls*
ls (1) - list directory contents
lsb (8) - Linux Standard Base support for Debian
lshal (1) - List devices and their properties
lshw (1) - list hardware
lskat (6) - Lieutnant Skat card game for KDE
[Listing condensed due to length]
```

Using wildcards might result in a slightly slower search than whatis without options, but it's pretty negligible on today's fast machines, so you probably don't have to worry about it.

Regular expressions can be used with the -r (or --regex) option.

```
$ whatis -r ^rm.*
rm (1) - remove files or directories
rmail (8) - handle remote mail received via uucp
rmdir (1) - remove empty directories
rmt (8) - remote magtape protocol module
```

TIP: There's not enough room in this book to cover regular expressions, but you can read more in *Sams Teach Yourself Regular Expressions in 10 Minutes* (ISBN: 0672325667) by Ben Forta.

Again, regular expressions are supposed to slow down the response you get with whatis, but you'll probably never notice it.

The whatis command is easy to remember (easier than man -f, some would say) and it quickly returns some important information, so memorize it.

Find a Command Based on What It Does

apropos

The whatis command is similar to man -f, and the apropos command is likewise similar to man -k. Both commands search man pages for the names and descriptions of commands, helping you if you know what a command does but can't remember its name.

NOTE: The word *apropos* isn't exactly in common usage, but it is a real word, and it means, essentially, "relevant" or "pertinent." The word *appropriate* has a somewhat similar meaning, but it's based on a different Latin root than *apropos*. Check the words out at www.answers.com for yourself if you're a fellow linguaphile.

Using `apropos` is easy: Just follow the command with a word or phrase describing the feature of the command in which you're interested.

```
$ man list
No manual entry for list
$ man -k list
last (1) - show listing of last logged in users
ls (1) - list directory contents
lshw (1) - list hardware
lsof (8) - list open files
[Listing condensed due to length]
$ apropos list
last (1) - show listing of last logged in users
ls (1) - list directory contents
lshw (1) - list hardware
lsof (8) - list open files
[Listing condensed due to length]
```

Just like `whatis`, you can use the `-w` (or `--wildcard`) or the `-r` (or `--regex`) options for searches. More interestingly, though, you can use the `-e` option (or `--exact`) when you want to tightly focus on a word or phrase, without any exception. For instance, in the previous listing, searching for *list* turned up the `last` command because it had the word *listing* in its description. Let's try that same search, but with the `-e` option.

```
$ apropos -e list
ls (1) - list directory contents
lshw (1) - list hardware
lsof (8) - list open files
[Listing condensed due to length]
```

This time, last doesn't show up because you wanted only results with the exact word *list*, not *listing*. In fact, the list of results for *list* went from 80 results without the -e option to 55 results with the -e option, which makes it far easier to precisely target your command searches and find exactly the command you want.

Find Out Which Version of a Command Will Run

which

Think back to the whereis command and what happened when you ran it against KWord using the -b option, for *show binaries only*.

```
$ whereis -b kword
kword: /usr/bin/kword /usr/bin/X11/kword
```

The executable for KWord is in two places. But which one will run first? You can tell that by running the which command.

```
$ which kword
/usr/bin/kword
```

The which command tells you which version of a command will run if you just type its name. In other words, if you type in **kword** and then press Enter, your shell executes the one found inside /usr/bin. If you want to run the version found in /usr/bin/X11, you have to change directories using the cd command and then enter ./kword, or use the absolute path for the command and type out **/usr/bin/X11/kword**.

The which command is also a speedy way to tell if a command is on your system. If the command is on your system and in your PATH, you'll be told where to find it; if the command doesn't exist, you're back on the command line with nothing.

```
$ which arglebargle
$
```

If you want to find all the locations of a command (just like you would if you used whereis -b), try the -a (for *all*) option.

```
$ which -a kword
/usr/bin/kword
/usr/bin/X11/kword
```

Conclusion

The title of this chapter is "Learning About Commands," and that's what we've covered. By now, you've seen that there are a variety of ways to find out more about your options on the command line. The two big dogs are man and info, with their volumes of data and descriptions about virtually all the commands found on your Linux computer. Remember that whereis, whatis, apropos, and which all have their places as well, especially if your goal is to avoid having to wade through the sometimes overwhelming verbiage of man and info, an understandable but often impossible goal. Sometimes you just have to roll up your sleeves and start reading a man page. Think of it like broccoli: You might not enjoy it, but it's good for you.

It's true that many of the commands in this chapter overlap to a degree. For instance, man -k is the same as apropos and man -f is just like whatis, while whereis -b is functionally equivalent to which -a. The choice of which one to use in a given situation is up to you. It's still a good idea, however, to know the various similarities, so you'll be able to read shell scripts or instructions given by others and understand exactly what's happening. Linux is all about variety and choice, even in such seemingly small matters as commands run in the shell.

## 4

Building Blocks

When you're young, you learn numbers, and then later you learn how to combine and work with those numbers using symbols such as +, −, ×, and =. So far in this book, you've learned several commands, but each one has been run one at a time. Commands can actually be combined in more complex and more interesting ways, however, using various symbols such as |, >, >>, and <. This chapter takes a look at those building blocks that enable you to do some useful things with the commands you've learned and the commands you'll be examining in greater detail in subsequent chapters.

Run Several Commands Sequentially

What if you have several commands you need to run consecutively, but some of them are going to take a long time, and you don't feel like babysitting your computer? For instance, what if you have a huge number of John Coltrane MP3s in a zipped archive file, and you want to unzip them, place them in a new subdirectory, and then delete the archive file? Normally you'd have to run those commands one at a time, like this:

NOTE: In order to save space, I removed the owner and group from the long listing.

```
$ ls -l /home/scott/music
-rw-r--r-- 1437931 2005-11-07 17:19 JohnColtrane.zip
$ unzip /home/scott/music/JohnColtrane.zip
$ mkdir -p /home/scott/music/coltrane
$ mv /home/scott/music/JohnColtrane*.mp3
➥/home/scott/music/coltrane/
$ rm /home/scott/music/JohnColtrane.zip
```

JohnColtrane.zip is a 1.4GB file, and even on a fast machine, unzipping that monster is going to take some time, and you probably have better things to do than sit there and wait. Command stacking to the rescue!

Command stacking puts all the commands you want to run on one line in your shell, with each specific command separated by a semicolon (;). Each command is then executed in sequential order and each must terminate— successfully or unsuccessfully—before the next one runs. It's easy to do, and it can really save you some time.

With command stacking, the previous series of commands now looks like this:

```
$ ls -l /home/scott/music
-rw-r--r-- 1437931 2005-11-07 17:19 JohnColtrane.zip
$ unzip /home/scott/music/JohnColtrane.zip ;
➥mkdir -p /home/scott/music/coltrane ;
➥mv /home/scott/music/JohnColtrane*.mp3
➥/home/scott/music/coltrane/ ;
➥rm /home/scott/music/JohnColtrane.zip
```

Of course, you can also use this method to introduce short delays as commands run. If you want to take a screenshot of everything you see in your monitor, just run the following command (this assumes you have the ImageMagick package installed, which virtually all Linux distributions do):

```
$ sleep 3 ; import -frame window.tif
```

The sleep command in this case waits three seconds, and then the screenshot is taken using import. The delay gives you time to minimize your terminal application and bring to the foreground any windows you want to appear in the screenshot. The ; makes it easy to separate the commands logically so you get maximum use out of them.

CAUTION: Be very careful when command stacking, especially when deleting or moving files! Make sure what you typed is what you want because the commands will run, one right after another, and you might end up with unexpected surprises.

Run Commands Only If the Previous Ones Succeed

`&&`

In the previous section, you saw that ; separates commands, as in this example:

```
$ unzip /home/scott/music/JohnColtrane.zip ;
➥mkdir -p /home/scott/music/coltrane ;
➥mv /home/scott/music/JohnColtrane*.*mp3
➥/home/scott/music/coltrane/ ;
➥rm /home/scott/music/JohnColtrane.zip
```

What if you fat finger your command, and instead type this:

```
$ unzip /home/scott/JohnColtrane.zip ;
➥mkdir -p /home/scott/music/coltrane ;
➥mv /home/scott/music/JohnColtrane*.*mp3
➥/home/scott/music/coltrane/ ;
➥rm /home/scott/music/JohnColtrane.zip
```

Instead of `unzip /home/scott/music/JohnColtrane.zip`, you accidentally enter **unzip /home/scott/JohnColtrane. zip**. You fail to notice this, so you go ahead and press Enter, and then get up and walk away. Your computer can't unzip `/home/scott/JohnColtrane.zip` because that file doesn't exist, so it blithely continues onward to the next command (`mkdir`), which it performs without a problem. However, the third command can't be performed (`mv`) because there aren't any MP3 files to move because `unzip` didn't work. Finally, the fourth command runs, deleting the zip file (notice that you provided the correct path this time) and leaving you with no way to recover and start over. Oops!

NOTE: Don't believe that this chain of events can happen? I did something very similar to it just a few days ago. Yes, I felt like an idiot.

That's the problem with using ;—commands run in sequence, regardless of their successful completion. A better method is to separate the commands with &&, which also runs each command one after the other, but only if the previous one completes successfully (technically, each command must return an exit status of 0 for the next one to run). If a command fails, the entire chain of commands stops.

If you'd used && instead of ; in the sequence of previous commands, it would have looked like this:

```
$ unzip /home/scott/JohnColtrane.zip &&
➥mkdir -p /home/scott/music/coltrane &&
➥mv /home/scott/music/JohnColtrane.*mp3
➥/home/scott/music/coltrane/ &&
➥rm /home/scott/music/JohnColtrane.zip
```

Because the first unzip command couldn't complete successfully, the entire process stops. You walk back later to find that your series of commands failed, but JohnColtrane.zip still exists, so you can try once again. Much better!

Here are two more examples that show you just how useful && can be. In Chapter 13, "Installing Software," you're going to learn about apt, a fantastic way to upgrade your Debian-based Linux box. When you use apt, you first update the list of available software, and then find out if there are any upgrades available. If the list of software can't be updated, you obviously don't want to bother looking for upgrades. To make sure the second process doesn't (uselessly) occur, separate the commands with &&:

```
# apt-get update && apt-get upgrade
```

Example two: You want to convert a PostScript file to a PDF using the ps2pdf command, print the PDF, and then delete the PostScript file. The best way to set up these commands is with &&:

```
$ ps2pdf foobar.ps && lpr foobar.pdf && rm foobar.ps
```

If you had instead used ; and ps2pdf failed, the PostScript file would still end up in nowheresville, leaving you without a way to start over.

Now are you convinced that && is often the better way to go? If there's no danger that you might delete a file, ; might be just fine, but if one of your commands involves rm or something else from where there is no recovery, you'd better use && and be safe.

Run a Command Only If the Previous One Fails

```
||
```

The && runs each command in sequence only if the previous one completes successfully. The || does the opposite: If the first command fails (technically, it returns an exit status that is not 0), only then does the second one run. Think of it like the words *either/or*— either run the first command or the second one.

The || is often used to send an alert to an administrator when a process stops. For instance, to ensure that a particular computer is up and running, an administrator might constantly query it with the ping command (you'll find out more about ping in Chapter 14, "Connectivity"); if ping fails, an email is sent to the administrator to let him know.

```
ping -c 1 -w 15 -n 72.14.203.104 ||
{
  echo "Server down" | mail -s 'Server down'
➥admin@google.com
}
```

NOTE: Wondering what the | is? Look ahead in this chapter to the "Use the Output of One Command As Input for Another" section to find out what it is and how to use it.

With just a bit of thought, you'll start to find many places where || can help you. It's a powerful tool that can really prove useful.

Plug the Output of a Command into Another Command

$()

Command substitution takes the output of a command and plugs it in to another command as though you had typed that output in directly. Surround the initial command that's run—the one that's going to produce the output that's plugged in—with $(). An example makes this much clearer.

Let's say you just arrived home from a family dinner, connected your digital camera to your Linux box, pulled the new photos off of it, and now you want to put them in a folder named today's date.

```
$ pwd
/home/scott/photos/family
$ ls -1F
2005-11-01/
2005-11-09/
2005-11-15/
$ date "+%Y-%m-%d"
2005-11-24
$ mkdir $(date "+%Y-%m-%d")
$ ls -1F
2005-11-01/
2005-11-09/
2005-11-15/
2005-11-24/
```

In this example, `date "+%Y-%m-%d"` is run first, and then the output of that command, 2005-11-24, is used by `mkdir` as the name of the new directory. This is powerful stuff, and as you look at the shell scripts written by others (which you can easily find all over the Web) you'll find that command substitution is used all over the place.

NOTE: In the past, you were supposed to surround the initial command with backticks, the ` character at the upper left of your keyboard. Now, however, you're better advised to use the characters used in this section: $().

Understand Input/Output Streams

To take advantage of the information in this chapter, you need to understand that there are three input/output streams for a Linux shell: standard input, standard output, and standard error. Each of these streams has a file descriptor (or numeric identifier), a common abbreviation, and a usual default.

For instance, when you're typing on your keyboard, you're sending input to standard input, abbreviated as stdin and identified as 0. When your computer presents output on the terminal, that's standard output, abbreviated as stdout and identified as 1. Finally, if your machine needs to let you know about an error and displays that error on the terminal, that's standard error, abbreviated as stderr and identified as 2.

Let's look at these three streams using a common command, `ls`. When you enter `ls` on your keyboard, that's using stdin. After typing `ls` and pressing Enter, the list of files and folders in a directory appears as stdout. If you try to run ls against a folder that doesn't exist, the error message that appears on your terminal is courtesy of stderr.

Table 4.1 can help you keep these three streams straight.

Table 4.1   The Three Input/Output Streams

File Descriptor (Identifier)	Name	Common Abbreviation	Typical Default
0	Standard input	stdin	Keyboard
1	Standard output	stdout	Terminal
2	Standard error	stderr	Terminal

In this chapter, we're going to learn how to redirect input and output. Instead of having output appear on the terminal, for instance, you can redirect it to another program. Or instead of acquiring input from your typing, a program can get it from a file. After you understand the tricks you can play with stdin and stdout, there are many powerful things you can do.

Use the Output of One Command As Input for Another

It's a maxim that Unix is made up of small pieces, loosely joined. Nothing embodies that principle more than the concept of pipes. A pipe is the | symbol on your keyboard, and when placed between two commands, it takes the output from the first and uses it as input for the second. In other words, | redirects stdout so it is sent to be stdin for the next command.

Here's a simple example that helps to make this concept clear. You already know about ls, and you're going to find out about the less command in Chapter 5, "Viewing Files." For now, know that less allows you to page through text files one screen at a time. If you run ls on a directory that has many files, such as /usr/bin, things just zoom by too fast to read. If you pipe the output of ls to less, however, you can page through the output one screen at a time.

```
$ pwd
/usr/bin
$ ls -1

zipinfo
zipnote
zipsplit
zsoelim
zxpdf
[Listing truncated due to length - 2318 lines!]
$ ls -1 | less
411toppm
7z
7za
822-date
a2p
```

You see one screen of results at a time when you pipe the results of ls -1 through to less, which makes it much easier to work with.

Here's a more advanced example that uses two commands discussed later: ps and grep. You'll learn in Chapter 9, "Finding Stuff: Easy," that ps lists running processes and in Chapter 12, "Monitoring System Resources," that grep helps find lines in files that match a pattern. Let's say that Firefox is acting strange, and you suspect that multiple copies are still running in the background. The ps command lists every process running on your computer, but the output tends to be lengthy and flashes by in an instant. If you pipe the output of ps to grep and search for *firefox*, you'll be able to tell immediately if Firefox in fact is still running.

NOTE: In order to save space in this listing, I removed the owner, which in every instance was the same person.

```
$ ps ux
1504   0.8   4.4   75164 46124 ? S Nov20 1:19 kontact
19003  0.0   0.1   3376  1812 pts/4 S+ 00:02 0:00 ssh
➥admin@david.hartley.com
21176  0.0   0.0      0     0 ? Z 00:14 0:00
➥[wine-preloader] <defunct>
24953  0.4   3.3   51856 34140 ? S 00:33 0:08 kdeinit:
➥kword /home/scott/documents/clientele/current
[Listing truncated for length]
$ ps ux | grep firefox
scott  8272   4.7  10.9 184072 112704 ? Sl Nov19 76:45
➥/opt/firefox/firefox-bin
```

From 58 lines of output to one—now that's much easier to read!

NOTE: Keep in mind that many programs can work with pipes, but not all. The text editor vim (or pico, nano, or emacs), for instance, takes over the entire shell so that all input from the keyboard is assumed to be directed at vim, while all output is displayed somewhere in the program. Because vim has total control of the shell, you can't pipe output using the program. You'll learn to recognize non-pipable programs as you use the shell over time.

Redirect a Command's Output to a File

>

Normally, output goes to your screen, otherwise known as stdout. If you don't want output to go to the screen and instead want it to be placed into a file, use the > (greater than) character.

```
$ pwd
/home/scott/music
$ ls -1F
Hank_Mobley/
Horace_Silver/
John_Coltrane/
$ ls -1F Hank_Mobley/* > hank_mobley.txt
$ cat hank_mobley.txt
1958_Peckin'_Time/
1960_Roll_Call/
1960_Soul_Station/
1961_Workout/
1963_No_Room_For_Squares/

$ ls -1F
Hank_Mobley/
hank_mobley.txt
Horace_Silver/
John_Coltrane/
```

Notice that before you used the >, the file hank_mobley.txt didn't exist. When you use > and redirect to a file that doesn't already exist, that file is created. Here's the big warning: If hank_mobley.txt had already existed, it would have been completely overwritten.

CAUTION: Once again: Be careful when using redirection, as you could potentially destroy the contents of a file that contains important stuff!

Prevent Overwriting Files When Using Redirection

There's a way to prevent overwriting files when redirecting, however—the noclobber option. If you set noclobber to on, bash won't allow redirection to overwrite existing files without your explicit permission. To turn on noclobber, use this command:

```
$ set -o noclobber
```

At that point, if you want to use redirection and overwrite a file, use >| instead of just >, like this:

```
$ pwd
/home/scott/music
$ ls -1F
Hank_Mobley/
hank_mobley.txt
Horace_Silver/
John_Coltrane/
$ ls -1F Hank_Mobley/* > hank_mobley.txt
ERROR
$ ls -1F Hank_Mobley/* >| hank_mobley.txt
$ cat hank_mobley.txt
1958_Peckin'_Time/
1960_Roll_Call/
1960_Soul_Station/
1961_Workout/
1963_No_Room_For_Squares/
```

If you decide you don't like or need noclobber, you can turn it off again:

```
$ set +o noclobber
```

To permanently turn on noclobber, you need to add set -o noclobber to your .bashrc file.

Append a Command's Output to a File

>>

As you learned previously, the > character redirects output from stdout to a file. For instance, you can redirect the output of the date command to a file easily enough:

```
$ date
Mon Nov 21 21:33:58 CST 2005
$ date > hank_mobley.txt
$ cat hank_mobley.txt
Mon Nov 21 21:33:58 CST 2005
```

Remember that > creates a new file if it doesn't already exist and overwrites a file that already exists. If you use >> instead of >, however, your output is appended to the bottom of the named file (and yes, if the file doesn't exist, it's created).

```
$ cat hank_mobley.txt
Mon Nov 21 21:33:58 CST 2005
$ ls -1F Hank_Mobley/* >> hank_mobley.txt
$ cat hank_mobley.txt
Mon Nov 21 21:33:58 CST 2005
1958_Peckin'_Time/
```

```
1960_Roll_Call/
1960_Soul_Station/
1961_Workout/
1963_No_Room_For_Squares/
```

CAUTION: Be careful with >>. If you accidentally type >
instead, you won't append, you'll overwrite!

Use a File As Input for a Command

<

Normally your keyboard provides input to commands,
so it is termed stdin. In the same way that you can
redirect stdout to a file, you can redirect stdin so it
comes from a file instead of a keyboard. Why is this
handy? Some commands can't open files directly, and
in those cases, the < (lesser than) is just what you need.

For instance, normally the echo command repeats what
you type on stdin, as shown here:

```
$ echo "This will be repeated"
This will be repeated.
```

However, you can use the < to redirect input, and the
echo command uses the contents of a file instead of
stdin. In this case, let's use the hank_mobley.txt file created in the previous section.

```
$ echo < hank_mobley.txt
Mon Nov 21 21:33:58 CST 2005
1958_Peckin'_Time/
1960_Roll_Call/
1960_Soul_Station/
1961_Workout/
1963_No_Room_For_Squares/
```

You're not going to use the < all the time, but it will be exactly what you need in a number of situations, so keep it in mind.

Conclusion

This book started with some simple commands, but now you've learned the building blocks that allow you to combine those commands in new and interesting ways. Going forward, it's going to get more complicated, but it's going to get more powerful as well. The things covered in this chapter are a key factor in gaining that power. Now, onward!

## 5

Viewing Files

One of the great things about most Linux boxes is that virtually all important system configurations, logs, and information files are in ASCII text format. Because ASCII is a well-supported, ancient (in computer terms) standard, there's a wealth of software commands you can use to view the contents of those text files. This chapter looks at four commands you'll use constantly when reading ASCII text files.

View Files on stdout

cat

DOS users have the type command that displays the contents of text files on a screen. Linux users can use cat, which does the same thing. Want to view a file in the shell? Try cat.

```
$ cat Hopkins_-_The_Windhover.txt
I caught this morning morning's minion, kingdom
of daylight's dauphin, dapple-dawn-drawn Falcon,
➥in his riding
  Of the rolling level underneath him steady air,
```

```
➥and striding
High there, how he rung upon the rein of a wimpling
➥wing
In his ecstasy! then off, off forth on swing,
  As a skate's heel sweeps smooth on a bow-bend:
➥the hurl and gliding
  Rebuffed the big wind. My heart in hiding
Stirred for a bird, -- the achieve of, the mastery
➥of the thing!

Brute beauty and valour and act, oh, air, pride,
➥plume, here
  Buckle! AND the fire that breaks from thee then,
➥a billion

Times told lovelier, more dangerous, o my chevalier!
  No wonder of it: sheer plod makes plough down
sillion
Shine, and blue-bleak embers, ah my dear,
  Fall, gall themselves, and gash gold-vermilion.
$
```

The cat command prints the file to the screen, and then deposits you back at the command prompt. If the file is longer than your screen, you need to scroll up to see what flashed by.

That's the big problem with cat: If the document you're viewing is long, it zooms by, maybe for quite a while, making it hard to read (can you imagine what this would produce: cat Melville_-_Moby_Dick.txt?). The solution to that is the less command, discussed in "View Text Files a Screen at a Time" later in this chapter.

Concatenate Files to stdout

```
cat file1 file2
```

cat is short for *concatenate*, which means "to join together." The original purpose of cat is to take two or more files and concatenate them into one file (the fact that you can use the cat command on just one file and print it on the screen is a bonus). For instance, let's say you have a short poem by A. E. Housman and one by Francis Quarles, and you want to view them at the same time.

```
$ cat housman_-_rue.txt quarles_-_the_world.txt
WITH rue my heart is laden
  For golden friends I had,
For many a rose-lipt maiden
  And many a lightfoot lad.
By brooks too broad for leaping
  The lightfoot boys are laid;
The rose-lipt girls are sleeping
  In fields where roses fade.
The world's an Inn; and I her guest.
I eat; I drink; I take my rest.
My hostess, nature, does deny me
Nothing, wherewith she can supply me;
Where, having stayed a while, I pay
Her lavish bills, and go my way.
```

Notice that cat doesn't separate the two files with a horizontal rule, a dash, or so forth. Instead, cat mashes the two files together and spits them out. If you want more of a separation—having the last line of "With rue my heart is laden" jammed up right next to the first line of "On the world" makes them hard to read, for instance—make sure there's a blank line at the end of each file you're going to concatenate together.

Concatenate Files to Another File

```
cat file1 file2 > file3
```

In the previous example, you concatenated two files and printed them on the screen to stdout. This might not be what you want, though. If you're concatenating two files, it might be nice to save the newly joined creation as another file you can use. To do this, redirect your output from stdout to a file, as you learned in Chapter 4, "Building Blocks."

```
$ ls
housman_-_rue.txt quarles_-_the_world.txt
$ cat housman_-_rue.txt quarles_-_the_world.txt >
➥poems.txt$ ls
housman_-_rue.txt poems.txt quarles_-_the_world.txt
```

Now you can do whatever you want with poems.txt. If you want to add more poems to it, that's easy enough to do:

```
$ cat housman_-_one-and-twenty.txt >> poems.txt
```

Notice that the >> was used to append the new poem to poems.txt this time. The following command would *not* have worked:

```
$ cat housman_-_one-and-twenty.txt poems.txt >
➥poems.txt
```

If you tried concatenating a file to itself, you'd see this error message, helpfully explaining that it is impossible to fulfill your request:

```
cat: poems.txt: input file is output file
```

Concatenate Files and Number the Lines

```
cat -n file1 file2
```

When working with poems and source code, it's really nice to have numbered lines so that references are clear. If you want to generate line numbers when you use cat, add the -n option (or --number).

```
$ cat -n housman_-_rue.txt quarles_-_the_world.txt
     1   WITH rue my heart is laden
     2     For golden friends I had,
     3   For many a rose-lipt maiden
     4     And many a lightfoot lad.
     5   By brooks too broad for leaping
     6     The lightfoot boys are laid;
     7   The rose-lipt girls are sleeping
     8     In fields where roses fade.
     9   The world's an Inn; and I her guest.
    10   I eat; I drink; I take my rest.
    11   My hostess, nature, does deny me
    12   Nothing, wherewith she can supply me;
    13   Where, having stayed a while, I pay
    14   Her lavish bills, and go my way.
```

Line numbers can be incredibly useful, and cat provides a quick and dirty way to add them to a file.

NOTE: For a vastly better cat, check out dog (more information is available at http://opensource.weblogsinc.com/2005/02/17/why-dogs-are-betters-than-cats). Instead of local files, you can use dog to view the HTML source of web pages on stdout, or just a list of images or links on the specified web pages. The dog command converts all characters to lowercase or vice versa; converts line endings to Mac OS, DOS, or Unix; and even allows you to specify a range of characters to output (lines 5–25, for instance). Not to mention, the man page for dog is one of the funniest ever. This is one dog that knows a lot of new tricks!

And here's another program that was created in response to cat: tac. Yes, that's cat backward. And that's what tac does: It concatenates files backward. That's not something you'll use all the time, but when you do need that functionality, it's nice to know that it's easily available.

View Text Files a Screen at a Time

```
less file1
```

The cat command is useful, but if you're trying to read a long file, it's not useful at all because text just flows past in an unending, unreadable stream. If you're interested in viewing a long file on the command line (and by "long," think more than a page or two), you don't want cat; you want less.

The less command is an example of a *pager*, a program that displays text files one page at a time. Others are more, pg, and most; in fact, less was released back in 1985 as an improved more, proving once again that less is more!

Opening a file with less—even an enormous one like Milton's *Paradise Lost*—couldn't be easier:

```
$ less Paradise_Lost.txt
```

The less command takes over your entire screen, so you have to navigate within less using your keyboard, and you have to quit less to get back to the command line. To navigate inside less, use the keys in Table 5.1:

Table 5.1   **Key Commands for** `less`

Key Command	Action
PageDn, e, or spacebar	Forward one page
PageUp or b	Back one page
Return, e, j, or down arrow	Forward one line
y, k, or up arrow	Back one line
G or p	Forward to end of file
1G	Back to beginning of file
Esc-), or right arrow	Scroll right
Esc-(, or left arrow	Scroll left
Q	Quit less

As you can see, you have many options for most commands. Probably the two you'll use most often are those used to move down a page at a time and quit the program.

To view information about the file while you're in `less`, press =, which displays some data at the very bottom of your screen similar to the following:

```
Paradise_Lost.txt lines 7521-7560/10762 byte 166743
➡/237306 70%  (press RETURN)
```

As you can see, you're helpfully told to press Enter to get rid of the data and go back to using `less`.

In the same way that you could tell `cat` to stick in line numbers for a file, you can also order `less` to display line numbers. Those numbers only appear, of course, while you're using `less`. After you press q, the numbers are gone. To view the file, but with numbers at the start of each line, start `less` with the -N (or --LINE-NUMBERS) option, and yes, you must use all caps:

```
$ less -N Paradise_Lost.txt
```

Search Within Your Pager

If you're using less to view a large file or an especially dense one, it can be difficult to find the text in which you're particularly interested. For instance, what if you want to know if Milton uses the word *apple* in *Paradise Lost* to describe the fruit that Adam and Eve ate? While in less, press / and then type in the pattern for which you'd like to search—and you can even use regular expressions if you'd like. After your pattern is in place, press Enter and less jumps to the first instance of your search pattern, if it exists. If your pattern isn't in the file, less tells you that:

```
Pattern not found  (press RETURN)
```

Repeating your search is also easy and can be done either forward or backward in your file. Table 5.2 covers the main commands you need for searching within less.

Table 5.2   Search Commands for less

Key Command	Action
/pattern	Search forward for pattern using regex
n	Repeat search forward
N	Repeat search backward

NOTE: No, Milton never explicitly refers to the fruit as an apple; instead, it's just a "fruit." Yes, I worked on a doctorate in Seventeenth Century British Literature for a number of years. No, I didn't finish it, which explains why I'm writing this book and not one solely devoted to John Milton and Restoration literature.

Edit Files Viewed with a Pager

It's true that less itself is not an editor, just a viewer, but you can pass the file you're viewing with less to a text editor such as vim or nano for editing by pressing v. Try it. View a file with less, and then press v. Within a second or two, less disappears and a full-screen text editor takes its place. Make your edits, quit your editor, and you're back in less with your new changes in place.

If you aren't happy with the editor that you find yourself in when you press v, you can change it to one of your choice. For instance, if you want to use vim, run the following command before using less:

```
$ export EDITOR=vim
```

You only need to run that command once per session, and every time you open less after that, vim will be your editor. If you end the session, however, you'll need to enter the export command again, which can quickly grow tedious. Better to add the following line to your .bashrc file, so that it's automatically applied:

```
export EDITOR=vim
```

View the First 10 Lines of a File

head

If you just need to see the first 10 lines of a file, such as Chaucer's *Canterbury Tales*, there's no need to use either cat or less. Instead, use the head command, which prints out exactly the first 10 lines of a file and then deposits you back on the command line.

```
$ head Canterbury_Tales.txt
Here bygynneth the Book of the Tales of Caunterbury

General Prologue

Whan that Aprill, with his shoures soote
The droghte of March hath perced to the roote
And bathed every veyne in swich licour,
Of which vertu engendred is the flour;
Whan Zephirus eek with his sweete breeth
Inspired hath in every holt and heeth
$
```

The head command is great for quick glances at a text file, even if that file is enormous. In just a second, you see enough to know if it's the file you need or not.

View the First 10 Lines of Several Files

```
head file1 file2
```

You can use head to view the first 10 lines of several files at one time. This sounds a bit similar to cat, and it is, except that head helpfully provides a header that separates the files so it's clear which one is which. Here's the first ten lines of Chaucer's *Canterbury Tales* and Milton's *Paradise Lost*.

```
$ head Canterbury_Tales.txt Paradise_Lost.txt
==> Canterbury_Tales.txt <==
Here bygynneth the Book of the Tales of Caunterbury

General Prologue

Whan that Aprill, with his shoures soote
```

```
The droghte of March hath perced to the roote
And bathed every veyne in swich licour,
Of which vertu engendred is the flour;
Whan Zephirus eek with his sweete breeth
Inspired hath in every holt and heeth

==> Paradise_Lost.txt <==
Book I

Of Man's first disobedience, and the fruit
Of that forbidden tree whose mortal taste
Brought death into the World, and all our woe,
With loss of Eden, till one greater Man
Restore us, and regain the blissful seat,
Sing, Heavenly Muse, that, on the secret top
Of Oreb, or of Sinai, didst inspire
That shepherd who first taught the chosen seed
```

The head command automatically separates the two excerpts with a space and then a header, which really makes it easy to see the different files clearly.

View the First Several Lines of a File or Files

If you don't want to see the first 10 lines of a file, you can tell head to show you a different number of lines by using the -n option followed by a number such as 5 (or --lines=5). If you specify two or more files, such as Chaucer's *Canterbury Tales* and Milton's *Paradise Lost*, the results show all the files.

```
$ head -n 5 Canterbury_Tales.txt Paradise_Lost.txt
==> Canterbury_Tales.txt <==
```

```
Here bygynneth the Book of the Tales of Caunterbury

General Prologue

Whan that Aprill, with his shoures soote

==> Paradise_Lost.txt <==
Book I

Of Man's first disobedience, and the fruit
Of that forbidden tree whose mortal taste
Brought death into the World, and all our woe,
```

Notice that the five lines include blank lines as well as those with text. Five lines are five lines, no matter what those lines contain.

View the First Several Bytes, Kilobytes, or Megabytes of a File

The -n option allows you to specify the number of lines you view at the top of a file, but what if you what to see a certain number of bytes? Or kilobytes? Or even (and this is a bit silly because it would scroll on forever) megabytes? Then use the -c (or --bytes=) option.

To see the first 100 bytes of Chaucer's *Canterbury Tales*, you'd use this:

```
$ head -c 100 Canterbury_Tales.txt
Here bygynneth the Book of the Tales of Caunterbury
```

General Prologue

Whan that Aprill, with his sh

100 bytes means 100 bytes, and if that means the display is cut off in the middle of a word, so be it.

To view the first 100KB of Chaucer's *Canterbury Tales*, you'd use this:

```
$ head -c 100k Canterbury_Tales.txt
Here bygynneth the Book of the Tales of Caunterbury

General Prologue

Whan that Aprill, with his shoures soote
The droghte of March hath perced to the roote
And bathed every veyne in swich licour,
Of which vertu engendred is the flour;
Whan Zephirus eek with his sweete breeth
Inspired hath in every holt and heeth
```

And to view the first 100MB of Chaucer's *Canterbury Tales*, you'd use...no, that would take up the rest of the book! But if you wanted to do it, try this:

```
$ head -c 100m Canterbury_Tales.txt
```

The *m* here means 1048576 bytes, or 1024 × 1024.

View the Last 10 Lines of a File

```
tail
```

The head command allows you to view the first 10 lines of a file, and in typical whimsical Unix fashion, the tail command allows you to view the last 10 lines of a file. From head to tail, get it?

```
$ tail Paradise_Lost.txt
To the subjected plain - then disappeared
They, looking back, all the eastern side beheld
Of Paradise, so late their happy seat,
Waved over by that flaming brand; the gate
With dreadful faces thronged and fiery arms.
Some natural tears they dropped, but wiped them
➥soon;
The world was all before them, where to choose
Their place of rest, and Providence their guide.
They, hand in hand, with wandering steps and slow,
Through Eden took their solitary way.
```

Why use tail? Most often, to view the end of a log file to see what's going on with an application or your system. Of course, there's an important option you want to use in that case, as you'll learn in the upcoming "View the Constantly Updated Last Lines of a File or Files" section.

View the Last 10 Lines of Several Files

```
tail file1 file2
```

You can view the first 10 lines of several files at one time using head; unsurprisingly, you can do the same thing with tail.

```
$ tail Paradise_Lost.txt Miller's_Tale.txt
==> Paradise_Lost.txt <==
To the subjected plain - then disappeared
They, looking back, all the eastern side beheld
Of Paradise, so late their happy seat,
Waved over by that flaming brand; the gate
```

```
With dreadful faces thronged and fiery arms.
Some natural tears they dropped, but wiped them
➥soon;
The world was all before them, where to choose
Their place of rest, and Providence their guide.
They, hand in hand, with wandering steps and slow,
Through Eden took their solitary way.
==> Miller's_Tale.txt <==
With othes grete he was so sworn adoun
That he was holde wood in al the toun;
For every clerk anonright heeld with oother.
They seyde, "The man is wood, my leeve brother";
And every wight gan laughen at this stryf.
Thus swyved was this carpenteris wyf,
For al his kepyng and his jalousye;
And Absolon hath kist hir nether ye;
And Nicholas is scalded in the towte.
This tale is doon, and God save al the rowte!
```

Also like head, tail includes a header/separator between the entries, which is helpful.

View the Last Several Lines of a File or Files

tail -n

Continuing the similarities between head and tail, you can specify the number of a file's lines you want to see instead of accepting the default of 10 by utilizing the -n (or --lines=) option. Want to see more than one file? Just add it to your command.

```
$ tail -n 4 Paradise_Lost.txt Miller's_Tale.txt
==> Paradise_Lost.txt <==
```

```
The world was all before them, where to choose
Their place of rest, and Providence their guide.
They, hand in hand, with wandering steps and slow,
Through Eden took their solitary way.
==> Miller's_Tale.txt <==
For al his kepyng and his jalousye;
And Absolon hath kist hir nether ye;
And Nicholas is scalded in the towte.
This tale is doon, and God save al the rowte!
```

Do you have more than one log file that you want to view? Then this is a useful command. But it's still not perfect. For the perfect command, read the next section.

View the Constantly Updated Last Lines of a File or Files

```
tail -f
tail -f --pid=PID# terminates after PID dies.
```

The great thing about log files is that they constantly change as things happen on your system. The tail command shows you a snapshot of a file, and then deposits you back on the command line. Want to see the log file again? Then run tail again…and again…and again. Blech!

With the -f (or --follow) option, tail doesn't close. Instead, it shows you the last 10 lines of the file (or a different number if you add -n to the mix) as the file changes, giving you a way to watch all the changes to a log file as they happen. This is wonderfully useful if you're trying to figure out just what is happening to a system or program.

For instance, a web server's logs might look like this:

NOTE: In order to save space, I've removed the IP address, date, and time of the access.

```
$ tail -f /var/log/httpd/d20srd_org_log_20051201
"GET /srd/skills/bluff.htm HTTP/1.1"...
"GET /srd/skills/senseMotive.htm HTTP/1.1"...
"GET /srd/skills/concentration.htm HTTP/1.1"...
"GET /srd/classes/monk.htm HTTP/1.1"...
"GET /srd/skills/escapeArtist.htm HTTP/1.1"...
```

It's hard to represent in a book, but this file doesn't close. Instead, tail keeps it open, and makes sure that any new changes are shown. The file continues to scroll up, apparently forever or until you press Ctrl+c, which cancels the command and deposits you back on the command line.

Try it with one of your log files, such as /var/log/syslog. Add in the q option to see only a certain number of lines to begin with, and then try it with two files, such as /var/log/syslog and /var/log/daemon.log, and see what happens (hint: It's remarkably similar to what you saw in "View the First 10 Lines of Several Files," but with constant updates).

Conclusion

You've looked at four commands in this chapter: cat, less, head, and tail. They all show you text files in read-only mode, but they do so in different ways. The cat command shows you the whole file all at once, while less allows you to page through a file one screen at a time. The head and tail commands are two sides of the same coin—or, rather, the same file—as the former enables you to view the beginning of a file and the latter displays the end. Together, these four commands make it easy to view just about any part of a text file that you might need to see.

6

Printing and Managing Print Jobs

Over the years, Linux has had several printing systems, including the venerable Line Printer Daemon (LPD) and LPR Next Generation (LPRng) that are still found in vestigial form on modern Linux distributions. In the past few years, however, most distributions have settled on the Common Unix Printing System (CUPS) as their backend of choice. CUPS is well supported, easy to use, modern, and a perfect drop-in replacement for LPD and LPRng. The same commands used with LPD and LPRng still work, but now they call functions in CUPS.

This chapter focuses on CUPS because it is the printing system with which most Linux users work. This chapter does *not* cover how to set up and configure a printer. Most distributions now provide easy-to-use GUI configuration tools to do just that, so you're going to focus on actually querying and using the printer via the command line.

NOTE: Linux Journal's "Overview of Linux Printing Systems," available at www.linuxjournal.com/article/6729, provides an excellent look at the various options Linux users have today, with special focus on the current favorite, CUPS. For more on CUPS, see Linux Journal's "The CUPS Printing System" at www.linuxjournal.com/article/8618, a very good look at this essential technology. The best place to go for information about CUPS is, unsurprisingly, the CUPS Software Users Manual, which you can find at www.cups.org/doc-1.1/sum. html. It's long and sometimes obtuse, but full of valuable advice and help, and it's an essential resource.

List All Available Printers

```
lpstat -p
```

Before you can begin working with your printers, you need to know what makes up "your printers." To find the printers configured on your system, use the lpstat command (short for *line printer status*) along with the -p option.

```
$ lpstat -p
printer bro is idle. enabled since Jan 01 00:00
printer bro_wk is idle. enabled since Jan 01 00:00
printer wu is idle. enabled since Jan 01 00:00
```

As you can see, this system has three printers—bro, bro_websanity, and wu_eads14—and none of them are printing anything at the moment.

Determine Your Default Printer

```
lpstat -d
```

You know all of your printers, thanks to running lpstat -p, but which one is the default? As you're going to see soon, you can send a print job to a specific printer, or you can quickly send it to your default printer. To find out which printer is the default, use the lpstat command with the -d (for *default*) option.

```
$ lpstat -d
system default destination: bro
```

Of course, if you only have one printer connected to your computer, you probably don't need to run this command. But for laptop users who move around to different locations and who print to different printers, this command is essential.

Find Out How Your Printers Are Connected

```
lpstat -s
```

Laptop users find this next command particularly helpful, as it tells them how they access the printers available to them. When you first set up a printer, you must specify how you connect to it. You have several choices:

- Local (parallel, serial, or USB)
- Remote LPD queue
- SMB shared printer (Windows)
- Network printer (TCP)
- Remote CUPS server (IPP/HTTP)
- Network printer with IPP (IPP/HTTP)

To find out what printers are configured for your computer and how you connect to those printers, use lpstat with the -s option.

```
$ lpstat -s
system default destination: bro
device for bro: socket://192.168.0.160:9100
device for bro_wk: socket://192.168.1.10:9100
device for wu: socket://128.252.93.10:9100
```

In this case, every printer is a network printer, so it uses socket://, followed by the printer's IP address and its port (9100 is standard for most networked printers, although you might see port 35 used as well). That's pretty easy, but it can quickly get much more complicated.

Although CUPS is user-friendly in many areas, it's famously obtuse when it comes to the Uniform Resource Indicators (URIs) used to indicate the locations of printers vis-à-vis your Linux box. Table 6.1 lists each connection method and the type of URI you might see, which should help you understand the list of printers and URIs you see when you run lpstat -s.

NOTE: Assume that the printer in the following examples is named bro and located on the network at 192.168.0.160. That isn't relevant in every situation, of course. If the printer is connected via a parallel cable, its IP address doesn't matter.

Table 6.1   Printer Connections and CUPS URIs

Connection Method	Sample URI (Printer bro at 192.168.0.160)
Parallel	parallel:/dev/lp0
Serial	serial:/dev/ttyS1?baud=115200
USB	usb:/dev/usb/lp0
Remote LPD queue	lpd://192.168.0.160/LPT1

Table 6.1   continued

Connection Method	Sample URI (Printer bro at 192.168.0.160)
SMB shared printer (Windows)	smb://username:password@ 192.168.0.160/bro
Network printer (TCP)	socket://192.168.0.160:9100
Remote CUPS server (IPP/HTTP)	ipp://192.168.0.160:631/ printers/bro, http:// 192.168.0.160/printers/bro
Network printer with IPP (IPP/HTTP)	ipp://192.168.0.160:631/ printers/bro, http:// 192.168.0.160/printers/bro

Thanks to the rise of network printing in the past several years, it's getting simpler to connect to printers via socket, ipp, or http. Even so, you're still going to run into legacy printers that require the older, more complicated connection methods, so it's good to familiarize yourself with them.

TIP: A bonus is that lpstat -s in essence duplicates the functionality of lpstat -p -d, as it lists all printers known by your system, as well as the default printer. If you want to know all that information quickly, this is a good command to use.

Get All the Information About Your Printers at Once

`lpstat -t`

Now for the mighty command. The nice thing about using lpstat -p, lpstat -d, or lpstat -s is that you only get the precise bit of information you want. If you want everything all at once, however, use lpstat with the -t option, which dumps everything lpstat knows about your printers onto your shell.

```
$ lpstat -t
scheduler is running
system default destination: bro
device for bro: socket://192.168.0.160:9100
device for bro_wk: socket://192.168.1.10:9100
device for wu: socket://128.252.93.10:9100
bro accepting requests since Jan 01 00:00
bro_wk accepting requests since Jan 01 00:00
wu accepting requests since Jan 01 00:00
printer bro is idle. enabled since Jan 01 00:00
printer bro_wk is idle. enabled since Jan 01 00:00
printer wu is idle. enabled since Jan 01 00:00
```

You get it all: your default printer, a list of all printers known to your system, the connection methods and locations of those printers, and the status of all printers. The more printers you have configured on your computer, the longer this listing. For some of you, it will be overwhelming, so you might find that lpstat with one of the other options you've examined is a better choice.

Print Files to the Default Printer

```
lpr
```

Now that you know what printers are on your system, it's time to actually use them to print something. Printing to your default printer (determined with lpstat -d) is easy.

```
$ lpr Lovecraft_-_Call_of_Cthulhu.txt
```

That's it: Just `lpr` and the name of the text file. Pretty simple.

NOTE: You probably expect that you can print ASCII text files on the command line using CUPS, but it might surprise you to learn that you can also print PDFs or PostScript files. But that's it; don't try to print Word, OpenOffice.org, or any other kind of non-text-based or non-PostScript-based documents, or your printer will spew out pages of garbage!

Print Files to Any Printer

```
lpr -P
```

Printing to the default printer, as shown in the previous section, is pretty easy. If you have more than one printer, however, and you want to print to one that is not the default, simply use the -P option, followed by the name of the printer.

```
$ lpr -P bro_wk Lovecraft_-_Call_of_Cthulhu.txt
```

If you don't know the names of your printers, use `lpstat -p`, as discussed previously in the "List All Available Printers" section.

NOTE: You'll notice that the filename has underscores instead of spaces, which makes it much easier to deal with on the command line. If the filename has spaces in it, you have to use one of the following methods for referencing it:

```
$ lpr -P bro_wk "Lovecraft - Call of Cthulhu.txt"
```

or

```
$ lpr -P bro_wk Lovecraft\ -\ Call\ of\ Cthulhu.txt
```

If the filename does have spaces, it's probably easiest to use tab completion so you don't have to type out the name yourself. For instance, you'd enter **lpr -P bro_wk Love** and then press the Tab key, allowing bash to finish the filename. For more on tab completion, see www.slackbook. org/html/shell-bash.html#SHELL-BASH-TAB.

Print More Than One Copy of a File

`lpr -#`

If you want to print more than one copy of document, use the -# (the pound sign) option, followed by the number of copies you want:

```
$ lpr -# 2 -P bro Lovecraft_-_Call_of_Cthulhu.txt
```

The number can range from 1 to 100. Want more than 100? Repeat the command. Or write a script. Or hire a professional printer!

List Print Jobs

`lpq`

If you have several jobs queued up to print, you might want to see that list. Perhaps you want to cancel one or more of the jobs (more on how to do that ahead, in the next few sections), you want to find out why a job is taking so long to print, or maybe you just want to know how many print jobs are in line. The lpq command (as in "lp queue") lists all jobs currently printing on the default printer.

```
$ lpq
bro is ready and printing
Rank   Owner Job File(s)                 Total Size
active scott 489 Lovecraft_-_Call_of_C 108544 bytes
```

If you want to find out the status of print queues for all your printers, not just your default, simply append -a (as in *all*) after lpq:

```
$ lpq -a
Rank   Owner Job File(s)                 Total Size
active scott 489 Lovecraft_-_Call_of_C 108544 bytes
1st    scott 490 ERB_-_A Princess_of_M 524288 bytes
```

Keep in mind two things. First, the listing provided by lpq -a is cut off, so while the filenames are actually Lovecraft_-_Call_of_Cthulhu.txt and ERB_-_A Princess_of_Mars.txt, you don't see the entire name because lpq only shows a certain number of characters.

Second, and this is very important, lpq is not showing all the print jobs the printer knows about, only those that your machine knows about. From the printer's perspective, the print queue might actually look like this:

- Lovecraft_-_Call_of_Cthulhu.txt
- Doyle_-_The_Lost_World.txt
- ERB_-_A Princess_of_Mars.txt

To find out the actual queue on the printer, you have to use whatever management utilities come with that device, which is far beyond the scope of this book.

List Print Jobs by Printer

lpstat

The lpq command shows you the files that are queued to print, but it doesn't tell you to which printer the files are being sent. To learn that, you need to use the lpstat command, covered earlier in "List All Available Printers." This time, however, simply use lpstat without any options at all:

```
$lpstat
bro-489    rsgranne 108544 Tue 10 Dec 2005
bro_wk-490 rsgranne 524288 Tue 10 Dec 2005
```

The result is a list of print jobs, with the name of each printer handling the job at the beginning of each line. Did you accidentally send a job to a printer to which you're not currently connected? Find out with lpstat and then delete the job, which you'll learn in the next section.

Cancel the Current Print Job Sent to the Default Printer

lprm

Do you want to cancel the current print job being sent to your default printer? Just use lprm (as in "lp remove"):

```
$ lprm
```

Be sure to issue this command with haste. Many printers now are so fast and have so much memory that the job might have already left your machine and be running on the printer. In that case, find the Cancel button on your printer and press it quickly!

Cancel a Print Job Sent to Any Printer

```
lprm job ID
```

In the previous section, you learned how to cancel the current print job going to the default printer. But what if the job is queued and won't start for another few minutes? Or what if the job is heading for a printer that's not the default? In those cases, you want to still use lprm, but you want to tell the command which job to cancel by referencing the job's ID number.

Look back at the examples in "List Print Jobs." The third column is labeled "Job" and has a number in it. Now look back at "List Print Jobs by Printer." After the name of each printer is a hyphen and then a number—the same number seen in "List Print Jobs." That number is the job ID number. Specify that number to lprm, and that exact job will be removed.

```
$lpstat
bro-489      rsgranne 108544 Tue 10 Dec 2005
bro_wk-490 rsgranne 524288 Tue 10 Dec 2005
$ lprm 490
$lpstat
bro-489      rsgranne 108544 Tue 10 Dec 2005
```

You can really save yourself from a needless waste of paper, toner, and ink using this particular command. Next time you realize that you just sent a 500-page document full of large pictures to your printer and stop it using lprm and a job ID number, send an email my way and thank me.

Cancel All Print Jobs

```
lprm -
```

What if you have several print jobs you want to cancel? You could delete them all by specifying all of their job ID numbers, like this:

```
$ lprm 489 490 491 492 493
```

That's too much typing, however. If you want to get rid of all print jobs you've queued on every printer, just follow lprm with a hyphen:

```
$ lprm -
```

It's quick, it's painless, and it's lazy in the best Linux tradition. Nothing to be ashamed of there!

Conclusion

Printing is a central activity people perform on their computers, so it's important to learn how to print effectively. Part of printing is knowing how to query printers and jobs as well as send those jobs to printers in the first place. Of course, not all jobs need to be printed, so it's important to know how to cancel unnecessary jobs as well. This chapter covers the major tasks you'll need to work with your printers from within Linux, but let me leave you with a final bit of advice: Automatic duplex printers that work with Linux have now fallen in price drastically, and they'll help you save a small fortune in paper. Check one out when you're next in the market for a printer. You'll be glad you did.

## 7

Ownerships and Permissions

From the beginning, Linux was designed to be a multiuser system (unlike Windows, which was designed as a sole user OS, the source of much of its security problems even to this day). This meant that different users would be on the system, creating files, deleting directories, and reading various items. To keep everyone from stepping on each other's toes and damaging the underlying operating system itself, a system of permissions was created early on. Mastering the art of Linux permissions will aid you as you use your Linux box, whether it's a workstation used by one person or a server accessed by hundreds. The tools are simple, but the power they give you is complex. Time to jump in!

Change the Group Owning Files and Directories

chgrp

By default on virtually every Linux system, when you create a new file (or directory), you are that file's owner and group. For instance, let's say you're going to write a new script that can be run on your system.

NOTE: To save space, I've replaced information you'd normally see with `ls -l` by an ellipses.

```
$ touch new_script.sh
$ ls -l
-rw-r--r-- 1 scott scott ... script.sh
```

NOTE: The user name and group name happen to both be "scott" on this machine, but that's not necessarily the case on every machine. When a file is created, the user's UID (her User ID number) becomes the owner of the file, while the user's GID (her Group ID number) becomes the group for the file.

But what if you are part of an admins group on your machine and you want your script to be available to other members of your group so they can run it? In that case, you need to change your group from scott to admins using the chgrp command.

```
$ chgrp admins new_script.sh
$ ls -l
-rw-r--r-- 1 scott admins ... script.sh
```

> NOTE: Yes, the script still won't run because it's not exe-
> cutable. That process is covered later in this chapter with
> chmod.

You should know a couple of things about chgrp.
When you run chgrp, you can use a group's name or
the group's numeric ID. How do you find the number
associated with a group? The easiest way is just to use
cat on /etc/group, the file that keeps track of groups
on your machine, and then take a look at the results.

```
$ cat /etc/group
bind:x:118:
scott:x:1001:
admins:x:1002:scott,alice,bob
[list truncated for length]
```

The other point to make about chgrp involves security:
You can only change permissions for a group if you
are a member of that group. In other words, Scott,
Alice, or Bob can use chgrp to make admins a group
for a file or directory, but Carol cannot because she's
not a member of admins.

Recursively Change the Group Owning a Directory

chgrp -R

Of course, you might not want to change the group of
just one file or directory. If you want to change the
groups of several files in a directory, you can use a
wildcard. If you want to change the contents of a
directory and everything below it, use the -R (or
--recursive) option.

```
$ pwd
/home/scott/pictures/libby
$ ls -F
by_pool/  libby_arrowrock.jpg  libby.jpg  on_floor/
$ ls -1F *
-rw-r--r-- 1 scott scott ... libby_arrowrock.jpg
-rw-r--r-- 1 scott scott ... libby.jpg

by_pool/:
-rw-r--r-- 1 scott scott ... libby_by_pool_02.jpg
drwxr-xr-x 2 scott scott ... lieberman_pool

on_floor/:
-rw-r--r-- 1 scott scott ... libby_on_floor_01.jpg
-rw-r--r-- 1 scott scott ... libby_on_floor_02.jpg
$ chgrp -R family */*
$ ls -1 *
-rw-r--r-- 1 scott family ... libby_arrowrock.jpg
-rw-r--r-- 1 scott family ... libby.jpg

by_pool:
-rw-r--r-- 1 scott family ... libby_by_pool_02.jpg
drwxr-xr-x 2 scott family ... lieberman_pool

on_floor:
-rw-r--r-- 1 scott family ... libby_on_floor_01.jpg
-rw-r--r-- 1 scott family ... libby_on_floor_02.jpg
```

CAUTION: If you used chgrp -R family *, you wouldn't change any of the dot files in the /home/scott/ pictures/libby directory. However, chgrp -R family .* should not be used. It changes all the dot files in the current directory, but .* also matches .., so all the files in the parent directory are also changed, which is probably not what you want!

Keep Track of Changes Made to a File's Group with chgrp

```
chgrp -v
chgrp -c
```

You've probably noticed that chgrp, like all well-behaved Linux applications, only gives you feedback if there's a problem. If a program works and does its job correctly, it doesn't bother you with "Hey! I did it, and it worked!" Instead, Linux command–line applications are only noisy when an issue needs to be resolved.

If you want to know what chgrp is doing while it's doing it, first try the -v (or --verbose) option. This tells you, every step of the way, just what tasks chgrp performs.

```
$ ls -1F
drwxr-xr-x 4 scott scott ... by_pool/
-rw-r--r-- 1 scott scott ... libby_arrowrock.jpg
-rw-r--r-- 1 scott family ... libby.jpg
-rw-r--r-- 1 scott scott ... libby_on_couch.jpg
drwxr-xr-x 2 scott scott ... on_floor/
$ chgrp -v family *
changed group of 'by_pool' to family
changed group of 'libby_arrowrock.jpg' to family
group of 'libby.jpg' retained as family
changed group of 'libby_on_couch.jpg' to family
changed group of 'on_floor' to family
$ ls -1F
drwxr-xr-x 4 scott family ... by_pool/
-rw-r--r-- 1 scott family ... libby_arrowrock.jpg
-rw-r--r-- 1 scott family ... libby.jpg
-rw-r--r-- 1 scott family ... libby_on_couch.jpg
drwxr-xr-x 2 scott family ... on_floor/
```

Notice what happened in this example. The `libby.jpg` file was already a member of the `family` group, but `-v` went ahead and reported on it anyway, making sure that you knew that `libby.jpg`'s group was kept as `family`. If you're changing groups, you probably don't need to know about items that already belong to the new group. In cases like that, you want to use the `-c` (or `--changes`) option, which (unsurprisingly) only reports changes made.

```
$ ls -1F
drwxr-xr-x 4 scott scott ... by_pool/
-rw-r--r-- 1 scott scott ... libby_arrowrock.jpg
-rw-r--r-- 1 scott family ... libby.jpg
-rw-r--r-- 1 scott scott ... libby_on_couch.jpg
drwxr-xr-x 2 scott scott ... on_floor/
$ chgrp -c family *
changed group of 'by_pool' to family
changed group of 'libby_arrowrock.jpg' to family
changed group of 'libby_on_couch.jpg' to family
changed group of 'on_floor' to family
$ ls -1F
drwxr-xr-x 4 scott family ... by_pool/
-rw-r--r-- 1 scott family ... libby_arrowrock.jpg
-rw-r--r-- 1 scott family ... libby.jpg
-rw-r--r-- 1 scott family ... libby_on_couch.jpg
drwxr-xr-x 2 scott family ... on_floor/
```

This time, nothing was reported to you about `libby.jpg` because it was already in the `family` group. So if you want a full report, even for files that won't be changed, use `-v`; for a more concise listing, use `-c`.

Change the Owner of Files and Directories

chown

Changing a file's group is important, but it's far more likely that you'll change owners. To change groups, use chgrp; to change owners, use chown.

```
$ ls -l
-rw-r--r-- 1 scott scott ... libby_arrowrock.jpg
-rw-r--r-- 1 scott family ... libby.jpg
-rw-r--r-- 1 scott scott ... libby_on_couch.jpg
$ chown denise libby.jpg
$ ls -l
-rw-r--r-- 1 scott scott ... libby_arrowrock.jpg
-rw-r--r-- 1 denise family ... libby.jpg
-rw-r--r-- 1 scott scott ... libby_on_couch.jpg
```

Some of the points previously made about chgrp in "Change the Group Owning Files and Directories" apply to chown as well. The chgrp command uses either a user's name or her numeric ID. The numeric ID for users can be seen by running cat /etc/passwd, which gives you something like this:

```
bind:x:110:118::/var/cache/bind:/bin/false
scott:x:1001:1001:Scott,,,:/home/scott:/bin/bash
ntop:x:120:120::/var/lib/ntop:/bin/false
```

The first number you see is the numeric ID for that user (the second number is the numeric ID for the main group associated with the user).

Also, you can only change the owner of a file if you are the current owner (or root, of course). That shouldn't surprise you, but it's good to remember nonetheless.

> **CAUTION:** If you use chown -R scott *, you do not change any of the dot files in the directory. However, chown -R scott .* should not be used. It changes all the dot files in the current directory, but .* also matches .., so all the files in the parent directory are also changed, which is probably not what you want.

Change the Owner and Group of Files and Directories

`chown owner:group`

You've seen that you can use chgrp to change groups and chown to change owners, but it's possible to use chown to kill two birds with one stone. After chown, specify the user and then the group, separated by a colon, and finally the file or directory (this is one reason why you should avoid using colons in user or group names).

```
$ ls -l
-rw-r--r-- 1 scott scott ... libby.jpg
$ chown denise:family libby.jpg
$ ls -l
-rw-r--r-- 1 denise family ... libby.jpg
```

You can even use chown to change only a group by leaving off the user in front of the colon.

```
$ ls -l
-rw-r--r-- 1 scott scott ... libby.jpg
$ chown :family libby.jpg
$ ls -l
-rw-r--r-- 1 scott family ... libby.jpg
```

TIP: What if a user or group does have a colon in its name? Just type the backslash in front of that colon, which "escapes" the character and tells the system that it's just a colon, and not a separator between a user and group name:

$ chown denise:family\:parents libby.jpg

This works, but it's better to disallow colons in user and group names in the first place.

Because chown does everything chgrp does, there's very little reason to use chgrp, unless you feel like it.

NOTE: When you separate the user and group, you can actually use either a . or : character. New recommendations are to stick with the :, however, because the . is deprecated.

Understand the Basics of Permissions

Before moving on to the chmod command, which allows you to change the permissions associated with a file or directory, let's review how Linux understands those permissions.

NOTE: Linux systems are beginning to use a more granular and powerful permission system known as Access Control Lists (ACLs). At this time, however, ACLs are still not widely used, so they're not covered here. For more info about ACLs, see "Access Control Lists" at *Linux Magazine* (www.linux-mag.com/2004-11/guru_01.html) and "An ACL GUI for Linux" at The Open Source Weblog (http://opensource.weblogsinc.com/2005/12/06/an-acl-gui-for-linux/).

Linux understands that three sets of users can work with a file or directory: the actual owner (also known as the file's user), a group, and everyone else on the system. Each of these sets is represented by a different letter, as shown in Table 7.1.

Table 7.1   Users and Their Abbreviations

User Group	Abbreviation
User (owner)	u
Group	g
Others	o

In the "List Permissions, Ownership, and More" section in Chapter 2, "The Basics," you learned about long permissions, which indicate what users can do with files and directories. In that section, you looked at three attributes: read, write, and execute, represented by r, w, and x, respectively. Additional possibilities are suid, sgid, and the sticky bit, represented by s (or S on some systems), s (or S), and t (or T). Keep in mind, however, that all of these can have different meanings depending on whether the item with the attribute is a file or a directory. Table 7.2 summarizes each attribute, its abbreviation, and what it means.

Table 7.2   Permission Letters and Their Meanings

File Attribute	Abbreviation	Meaning for File	Meaning for Directory
Readable	r	Can view.	Can list with ls.
Writable	w	Can edit.	Can delete, rename, or add files.

Table 7.2   continued

File Attribute	Abbreviation	Meaning for File	Meaning for Directory
Executable	x	Can run as program.	Can access to read files and subdirectories or to run files.
suid	s	Any user can execute the file with owner's permissions.	Not applicable.
sgid	s	Any user can execute the file with group's permissions.	All newly created files in a directory belong to the group owning the directory.
Sticky bit	t	Tells OS that the file will be frequently executed, so it's constantly kept in swap space for fast access (only for older Unix systems; Linux ignores).	User cannot delete or rename files, unless he is the file's or containing directory's owner.

NOTE: The root user can always do anything to any file or directory, so the previous table doesn't apply to root.

Each of these file attributes is covered in more detail in the following sections. Now that you understand the basics, let's look at using the chmod command to change the permissions of files and directories.

Change Permissions on Files and Directories Using Alphabetic Notation

`chmod [ugo][+-=][rwx]`

You can use two notations with chmod: alphabetic or numeric. Both have their advantages, but it's sometimes easier for users to learn the alphabetic system first. Basically, the alphabetic method uses a simple formula: the user group you want to affect (u, g, o); followed by a plus sign (+) to grant permission, a minus sign (−) to remove permission, or an equal sign (=) to set exact permission; followed by the letters (r, w, x, s, t) representing the permission you want to alter. For instance, let's say you want to allow members of the family group to be able to change a picture.

```
$ ls -l
-rw-r--r-- 1 scott family ... libby.jpg
$ chmod g+w libby.jpg
$ ls -l
-rw-rw-r-- 1 scott family ... libby.jpg
```

Easy enough. But what if you had wanted to give both the family group and all other users write permission on the file?

```
$ ls -l
-rw-r--r-- 1 scott family ... libby.jpg
$ chmod go+w libby.jpg
$ ls -l
-rw-rw-rw- 1 scott family ... libby.jpg
```

Of course, because you're really giving all users—the owner, the group, and the world—read and write access, you could have just done it like this:

```
$ ls -l
-rw-r--r-- 1 scott family ... libby.jpg
$ chmod a=rw libby.jpg
$ ls -l
-rw-rw-rw- 1 scott family ... libby.jpg
```

You realize you made a mistake, and need to remove the capability of the family group and the world to alter that picture, and also ensure that the world can't even see the picture.

```
$ ls -l
-rw-rw-rw- 1 scott family ... libby.jpg
$ chmod go-w libby.jpg
$ ls -l
-rw-r--r-- 1 scott family ... libby.jpg
$ chmod o-r libby.jpg
$ ls -l
-rw-r----- 1 scott family ... libby.jpg
```

Instead of the -, you could have used the =:

```
$ ls -l
-rw-rw-rw- 1 scott family ... libby.jpg
$ chmod g=r libby.jpg
$ ls -l
```

```
-rw-r--rw- 1 scott family ... libby.jpg
$ chmod o= libby.jpg
$ ls -l
-rw-r----- 1 scott family ... libby.jpg
```

Notice on the last chmod that o equaled nothing, effectively removing all permissions for all other users on the system. Now that's fast and efficient!

The advantage to the alphabetic system is that it's often fast, but you can also see its main disadvantage in the last example: If you want to make changes to two or more user groups and those changes are different for each user group, you end up running chmod at least two times. The next section shows how numeric permissions get around that problem.

Change Permissions on Files and Directories Using Numeric Permissions

`chmod [0-7][0-7][0-7]`

Numeric permissions (also known as octal permissions) are built around the binary numeric system. We're going to skip the complicated reasons why the permissions have certain numbers and focus on the end meaning: read (r) has a value of 4, write (w) is 2, and execute (x) is 1. Remember that Linux permissions recognize three user groups—the owner, the group, and the world—and each user group can read, write, and execute. (See Table 7.3.)

Table 7.3   Permissions and Numeric Representations

	Owner	Group	World
Permissions	r; w; x	r; w; x	r; w; x
Numeric representation	4; 2; 1	4; 2; 1	4; 2; 1

Permissions under this schema become a matter of simple addition. Here are a few examples:

- A user has read and write permissions for a file or directory. Read is 4, write is 2, and execute is 0 (because it's not granted). 4 + 2 + 0 = 6.

- A user has read and execute permissions for a file. Read is 4, write is 0 (because that permission hasn't been granted), and execute is 1. 4 + 0 + 1 = 5.

- A user has read, write, and execute permissions for a directory. Read is 4, write is 2, and execute is 1. 4 + 2 + 1 = 7.

Under this method, the most a user group can have is 7 (read, write, and execute), and the least is 0 (cannot read, write, or execute). Because there are three user groups, you have three numbers, each between 0 and 7, and each representing what permissions that user group has associated with it. Table 7.4 shows the possible numbers and what they mean.

Table 7.4   Numeric Permissions Represented with `ls -l`

Number	`ls -l` Representation
0	`---`
1	`--x`
2	`-w-`
3	`-wx`
4	`r--`

Table 7.4 **continued**

Number	`ls -l` Representation
5	r-x
6	rw-
7	rwx

Although a wide variety of permissions can be set, a few tend to reappear constantly. Table 7.5 shows the common permissions and what they mean.

Table 7.5 **Common Permissions Represented with `ls -l`**

`chmod` Command	`ls -l` Representation	Meaning
chmod 400	-r--------	Owner can read; no one else can do anything.
chmod 644	-rw-r--r--	Everyone can read; only owner can edit.
chmod 660	-rw-rw----	Owner and group can read and edit; world can do nothing.
chmod 664	-rw-rw-r--	Everyone can read; owner and group can edit.
chmod 700	-rwx------	Owner can read, write, and execute; no one else can do anything.
chmod 744	-rwxr--r--	Everyone can read; only owner can edit and execute.
chmod 755	-rwxr-xr-x	Everyone can read and execute; only owner can edit.
chmod 777	-rwxrwxrwx	Everyone can read, edit, and execute (not usually a good idea).

> **CAUTION:** Yes, you can set chmod 000 on a file or directory, but now the only user who can do anything with it or use chmod to change permissions again is root.

Octal permissions should now make a bit of sense. They require a bit more cogitation to understand than alphabetic permissions, but they also allow you to set changes in one fell swoop. Let's revisit the examples from "Change Permissions on Files and Directories Using Alphabetic Notation" but with numbers instead.

Let's say you want to allow members of the family group to be able to change a picture.

```
$ ls -l
-rw-r--r-- 1 scott family ... libby.jpg
$ chmod 664 libby.jpg
$ ls -l
-rw-rw-r-- 1 scott family ... libby.jpg
```

What if you had wanted to give both the family group and all other users write permission on the file?

```
$ ls -l
-rw-r--r-- 1 scott family ... libby.jpg
$ chmod 666 libby.jpg
$ ls -l
-rw-rw-rw- 1 scott family ... libby.jpg
```

You realize you made a mistake, and you need to remove the capability of the family group and the world to alter that picture and also ensure that the world can't even see the picture.

```
$ ls -l
-rw-rw-rw- 1 scott family ... libby.jpg
```

```
$ chmod 640 libby.jpg
$ ls -l
-rw-r----- 1 scott family ... libby.jpg
```

This example shows the key advantage of this method. What took two steps with alphabetic notation—first chmod go-w and then chmod o-r (or chmod g=r and then chmod o=)—only takes a single command with numeric notation. For this reason, you often see advanced Linux gurus use octal notation because it's quicker and more seemingly precise.

Change Permissions Recursively

`chmod -R`

You've probably noticed by now that many Linux commands allow you to apply them recursively to files and directories, and chmod is no different. With the -R (or --recursive) option, you can change the permissions of hundreds of file system objects in seconds— just be sure that's what you want to do.

```
$ pwd
/home/scott/pictures/libby

$ ls -lF
drwxrw---- 2 scott scott ... by_pool/
-rw-r--r-- 1 scott scott ... libby_arrowrock.jpg
-rw-r--r-- 1 scott scott ... libby.jpg
drwxrw---- 2 scott scott ... on_floor/
$ ls -l *
-rw-r--r-- 1 scott scott ... libby_arrowrock.jpg
-rw-r--r-- 1 scott scott ... libby.jpg

by_pool:
```

```
-rw-r--r-- 1 scott scott ... libby_by_pool_02.jpg
-rwxr-xr-x 2 scott scott ... lieberman_pool.jpg

on_floor:
-rw-r--r-- 1 scott scott ... libby_on_floor_01.jpg
-rw-r--r-- 1 scott scott ... libby_on_floor_02.jpg
$ chgrp -R family *
$ chmod -R 660 *
chmod: 'by_pool': Permission denied
chmod: 'on_floor': Permission denied
```

"Permission denied?" What happened? Take a look at
Table 7.2. If a file is executable, it can be run as a program, but a directory must be executable to allow users
access inside it to read its files and subdirectories.
Running chmod -R 660 * removed the x permission
from everything—files and directories. When chmod
went to report what it had done, it couldn't because it
couldn't read inside those directories, since they were
no longer executable.

So what should you do? There really isn't a simple
answer. You could run chmod using a wildcard that only
affects files of a certain type, like this:

$ **chmod -R 660 *.jpg**

That would only affect images and not directories, so
you wouldn't have any issues. If you have files of more
than one type, however, it can quickly grow tedious, as
you'll have to run chmod once for every file type.

If you have many subdirectories within subdirectories,
or too many file types to deal with, you can be really
clever and use the find command to look for all files
that are not directories and then change their permissions. You'll learn more about that in Chapter 10, "The
find Command."

The big takeaway here: When changing permissions recursively, be careful. You might not get what you expected and end up preventing access to files and subdirectories accidentally.

Set and Then Clear suid

```
chmod u[+-]s
```

n the "Understand the Basics of Permissions" section, you looked at several possible permissions. You've focused on r, w, and x because those are the most common, but others can come in handy at times. Let's take a look at suid, which only applies to executable files, never directories.

After suid is set, suid means that a user can execute a file with the owner's permissions, as though it was the owner of the program running it. You can see a common example of suid in action by looking at the permissions for the passwd command, which allows users to set and change their passwords.

```
$ ls -l /usr/bin/passwd
-rwsr-xr-x 1 root root ... /usr/bin/passwd
```

You can see that passwd is set as suid because it has an s where the user's x should be. The root user owns passwd, but it's necessary that ordinary users be allowed to run the command, or they wouldn't be able to change their passwords on their own. To make the passwd command executable for everyone, x is set for the user, the group, and all users on the system. That's not enough, however. The answer is to set passwd as suid root, so anyone can run it with root's permissions for that command.

NOTE: You might see both an s and an S to indicate that
suid is set. You see an s if the owner already had execute
permissions (x) before you set suid, and an S if the owner
didn't have execute set before suid was put in place. The
end result is the same, but the capitalization tells you
what was in place originally.

You can set and unset suid in two ways: using the
alphabet or using numbers. The alphabet method
would look like this:

```
$ pwd
/home/scott/bin
$ ls -l
-rwxr-xr-- 1 scott admins ... backup_data
$ chmod u+s backup_data
$ ls -l
-rwsr-xr-- 1 scott admins ... backup_data
```

Now anyone in the admins group can run the
backup_data script as though they were the user scott.
But note that anyone not in the admins group is shut
out because it only has read permission for the program. If it was necessary for everyone on the system to
be able to run backup_data as scott, the permissions
would be -rwsr-xr-x.

Removing suid is a matter of using u- instead of u+.

```
$ ls -l
-rwsr-xr-- 1 scott admins ... backup_data
$ chmod u-s backup_data
$ ls -l
-rwxr-xr-- 1 scott admins ... backup_data
```

Setting suid via octal permissions is a bit more complicated, only because it introduces a new facet to the
numeric permissions you've been using. You'll recall
that numeric permissions use three digits, with the first
representing what is allowed for the owner, the second
for the group, and the third for all other users. It turns
out that there's actually a fourth digit that appears to
the left of the owner's number. That digit is a 0 the
vast majority of the time, however, so it's not necessary
to display or use it. In other words, chmod 644
libby.jpg and chmod 0644 libby.jpg are exactly the
same thing. You only need that fourth digit when you
want to change suid (or sgid or the sticky bit, as you'll
see in the following sections).

The number for setting suid is 4, so you'd change
backup_data using numbers like this:

```
$ pwd
/home/scott/bin
$ ls -l
-rwxr-xr-- 1 scott admins ... backup_data
$ chmod 4754 backup_data
$ ls -l
-rwsr-xr-- 1 scott admins ... backup_data
```

Removing suid is a matter of purposely invoking the
0 because that sets things back to the default state,
without suid in place.

```
$ ls -l
-rwsr-xr-- 1 scott admins ... backup_data
$ chmod 0754 backup_data
$ ls -l
-rwxr-xr-- 1 scott admins ... backup_data
```

> NOTE: As an ordinary user, it's not very likely that you'll need to change programs to suid. Most often it's associated with programs owned by root, but it's still good to know about it for that every-so-often case in which you need to use it.

Set and Then Clear sgid

```
chmod g[+-]s
```

Closely related to suid is sgid. sgid can apply to both files and directories. For files, sgid is just like suid, except that a user can now execute a file with the group's permissions instead of an owner's permissions. For example, on your system the crontab command is probably set as sgid, so that users can ask cron to run programs for them, but as the much more restricted crontab group rather than the all-powerful root user.

```
$ ls -l /usr/bin/crontab
-rwxr-sr-x 1 root crontab ... /usr/bin/crontab
```

When applied to directories, sgid does something interesting: Any subsequent files created in that directory belong to the group assigned to the directory. An example helps make this clearer.

Let's say you have three users—Alice, Bob, and Carol—who are all members of the admins group. Alice's username is alice, and her primary group is also alice, an extremely common occurrence on most Linux systems. Bob and Carol follow the same pattern, with their usernames and primary groups being, respectively, bob and carol. If Alice creates a file in a directory shared by the admins group, the owner and group for that file is alice, which means that the other members of the admins group are unable to write to that file. Sure, Alice could run chgrp admins document (or chown :admins document) after she creates a new file, but that quickly grows incredibly tedious.

If the shared directory is set to sgid, however, any new file created in that directory is still owned by the user who created the file, but it's also automatically assigned to the directory's group, in this case, admins. The result: Alice, Bob, and Carol can all read and edit any files created in that shared directory, with a minimum of tedium.

Unsurprisingly, you can set sgid with either letters or numbers. Using letters, sgid is just like suid, except that a g instead of a u is used. Let's look at sgid applied to a directory, but keep in mind that the same process is used on a file.

```
$ ls -1F
drwxr-xr-x 11 scott admins ... bin/
$ chmod g+s bin
$ ls -1F
drwxr-Sr-x 11 scott admins ... bin/
```

NOTE: You might see both an s and an S to indicate that sgid is set. You see an s if the group already had execute permissions (x) before you set sgid, and an S if the group didn't have execute set before sgid was put in place. The end result is the same, but the capitalization tells you what was in place originally.

Removing sgid is pretty much the opposite of adding it.

```
$ ls -1F
drwxr-Sr-x 11 scott admins ... bin/
```

```
$ chmod g-s bin
$ ls -1F
drwxr-xr-x 11 scott admins ... bin/
```

If you haven't already read the previous section, "Set and Then Clear suid," go back and do so, as it explains the otherwise mysterious fourth digit that appears just before the number representing the owner's permissions. In the case of suid, that number is 4; for sgid, it's 2.

```
$ ls -1F
drwxr-xr-x 11 scott admins ... bin/
$ chmod 2755 bin
$ ls -1F
drwxr-Sr-x 11 scott admins ... bin/
```

You remove sgid the same way you remove suid: with a 0 at the beginning, which takes sgid out of the picture.

```
$ ls -1F
drwxr-Sr-x 11 scott admins ... bin/
$ chmod 0755 bin
$ ls -1F
drwxr-xr-x 11 scott admins ... bin/
```

NOTE: You know what creating a new file in a sgid directory will do, but be aware that other file system processes
can also be affected by sgid. If you copy a file with cp
into the sgid directory, it acquires the group of that
directory. If you move a file with mv into the sgid directory, however, it keeps its current group ownership and does
not acquire that of the directory's group. Finally, if you
create a new directory inside the sgid directory using
mkdir, it not only inherits the group that owns the sgid
directory, but also becomes sgid itself.

Set and Then Clear the Sticky Bit

`chmod [+-]t`

Besides being a fun phrase that rolls off the tongue, what's the sticky bit? In the old days of Unix, if the sticky bit was set for an executable file, the OS knew that the file was going to be run constantly, so it was kept in swap space so it could be quickly and efficiently accessed. Linux is a more modern system, so it ignores the sticky bit when it's set on files.

That means that the sticky bit is used on directories. After it is set on a folder, users cannot delete or rename files in that folder unless they are that file's owner or the owner of the directory that has the sticky bit set on it. If the sticky bit isn't set and the folder is writable for users, that also means that those users can delete and rename any files in that directory. The sticky bit prevents that from happening. The most common place you'll see it is in your /tmp directory, which is world-writable by design, but the individual files and folders within /tmp are protected from other users by the sticky bit.

```
$ ls -l /
drwxrwxrwt 12 root root ... tmp
[Results truncated for length]
```

NOTE: You may see both a t and a T to indicate that the sticky bit is set. You see a t if the world already had execute permissions (x) before you set the sticky bit, and a T if the world didn't have execute set before the sticky bit was put in place. The end result is the same, but the capitalization tells you what was in place originally.

Like so many other examples using chmod in this chapter, it's possible to set the sticky bit with either letters or numbers.

```
$ ls -1F
drwxrwxr-x 2 scott family ... libby_pix/
$ chmod +t libby_pix
$ ls -1F
drwxrwxr-t 2 scott family ... libby_pix/
```

Two things might be a bit confusing here. First, although previous uses of the alphabetic method for setting permissions required you to specify who was affected by typing in a **u**, **g**, or **o**, for instance, that's not necessary with the sticky bit. A simple +t is all that is required.

Second, note that the t appears in the world's execute position, but even though the directory isn't world-writable, it still allows members of the family group to write to the directory, while preventing those members from deleting files unless they own them.

Removing the sticky bit is about as straightforward as you could hope.

```
$ ls -1F
drwxrwxr-t 2 scott family ... libby_pix/
$ chmod -t libby_pix
$ ls -1F
drwxrwxr-x 2 scott family ... libby_pix/
```

Setting the sticky bit using octal permissions involves the fourth digit already covered in "Set and Then Clear suid" and "Set and Then Clear sgid." Where suid uses 4 and sgid uses 2, the sticky bit uses 1 (see a pattern?).

```
$ ls -1F
drwxrwxr-x 2 scott family ... libby_pix/
$ chmod 1775 libby_pix
$ ls -1F
drwxrwxr-t 2 scott family ... libby_pix/
```

Once again, a 0 cancels out the sticky bit.

```
$ ls -1F
drwxrwxr-t 2 scott family ... libby_pix/
$ chmod 0775 libby_pix
$ ls -1F
drwxrwxr-x 2 scott family ... libby_pix/
```

The sticky bit isn't something you'll be using on many
directories on your workstation, but on a server it can be
incredibly handy. Keep it in mind, and you'll find that it
solves some otherwise thorny permission problems.

TIP: In the interest of speeding up your time on the command line, it's possible to set combinations of suid, sgid,
and the sticky bit at the same time. In the same way that
you add 4 (read), 2 (write), and 1 (execute) together to get
the numeric permissions for users, you can do the same for
suid, sgid, and the sticky bit.

Number	Meaning
0	Removes sticky bit, sgid, and suid
1	Sets sticky bit
2	Sets sgid
3	Sets sticky bit and sgid
4	Sets suid
5	Sets sticky bit and suid
6	Sets sgid and suid
7	Sets sticky bit, sgid, and suid

Be sure to note that using a 0 removes suid, `sgid`, and the sticky bit all at the same time. If you use 0 to remove `suid` but you still want the sticky bit set, you need to go back and reset the sticky bit.

Conclusion

Permissions are vitally important for the security and even sanity of a Linux system, and they can seem overwhelming at first. With a bit of thought and learning, however, it's possible to get a good handle on Linux permissions and use them to your advantage. The combination of `chgrp` to change group ownership, `chown` to change user ownership (and group ownership as well), and the powerful `chmod` gives a Linux user a wealth of tools at her disposal that enable her to set permissions in a powerful, effective way.

## 8

Archiving and Compression

Although the differences are sometimes made opaque in casual conversation, there is in fact a complete difference between archiving files and compressing them. Archiving means that you take 10 files and combine them into one file, with no difference in size. If you start with 10 100KB files and archive them, the resulting single file is 1000KB. On the other hand, if you compress those 10 files, you might find that the resulting files range from only a few kilobytes to close to the original size of 100KB, depending upon the original file type.

NOTE: In fact, you might end up with a bigger file during compression! If the file is already compressed, compressing it again adds extra overhead, resulting in a slightly bigger file.

All of the archive and compression formats in this chapter—zip, gzip, bzip2, and tar—are popular, but zip is probably the world's most widely used format. That's because of its almost universal use on Windows, but zip and unzip are well supported among all major (and most minor) operating systems, so things compressed using `zip` also work on Linux and Mac OS. If you're sending archives out to users and you don't know which operating systems they're using, `zip` is a safe choice to make.

`gzip` was designed as an open-source replacement for an older Unix program, `compress`. It's found on virtually every Unix-based system in the world, including Linux and Mac OS X, but it is much less common on Windows. If you're sending files back and forth to users of Unix-based machines, `gzip` is a safe choice.

The `bzip2` command is the new kid on the block. Designed to supersede `gzip`, `bzip2` creates smaller files, but at the cost of speed. That said, computers are so fast nowadays that most users won't notice much of a difference between the times it takes `gzip` or `bzip2` to compress a group of files.

NOTE: *Linux Magazine* published a good article comparing several different compression formats, which you can find at http://www.linux-mag.com/content/view/1678/43/.

`zip`, `gzip`, and `bzip2` are focused on compression (although `zip` also archives). The `tar` command does one thing—archive—and it has been doing it for a long time. It's found almost solely on Unix-based machines. You'll definitely run into tar files (also called tarballs) if you download source code, but almost every Linux user can expect to encounter a tarball some time in his career.

Archive and Compress Files Using zip

zip

zip both archives and compresses files, thus making it
great for sending multiple files as email attachments,
backing up items, or for saving disk space. Using it is
simple. Let's say you want to send a TIFF to someone
via email. A TIFF image is uncompressed, so it tends to
be pretty large. Zipping it up should help make the
email attachment a bit smaller.

NOTE: When using ls -l, I'm only showing the information needed for each example.

```
$ ls -lh
-rw-r--r-- scott scott 1006K young_edgar_scott.tif
$ zip grandpa.zip young_edgar_scott.tif
  adding: young_edgar_scott.tif (deflated 19%)
$ ls -lh
-rw-r--r-- scott scott 1006K young_edgar_scott.tif
-rw-r--r-- scott scott  819K grandpa.zip
➥grandpa.zip
```

In this case, you shaved off about 200KB on the resulting zip file, or 19%, as zip helpfully informs you. Not
bad. You can do the same thing for several images.

```
$ ls -l
-rw-r--r-- scott scott  251980 edgar_intl_shoe.tif
-rw-r--r-- scott scott 1130922 edgar_baby.tif
-rw-r--r-- scott scott 1029224 young_edgar_scott.tif
```

```
$ zip grandpa.zip edgar_intl_shoe.tif edgar_
➥baby.tif young_edgar_scott.tif
  adding: edgar_intl_shoe.tif (deflated 4%)
  adding: edgar_baby.tif (deflated 12%)
  adding: young_edgar_scott.tif (deflated 19%)
$ ls -l
-rw-r--r-- scott scott  251980 edgar_intl_shoe.tif
-rw-r--r-- scott scott 1130922 edgar_baby.tif
-rw-r--r-- scott scott 2074296 grandpa.zip
-rw-r--r-- scott scott 1029224 young_edgar_scott.tif
```

It's not too polite, however, to zip up individual files
this way. For three files, it's not so bad. The recipient
will unzip grandpa.zip and end up with three individual files. If the payload was 50 files, however, the user
would end up with files strewn everywhere. Better to
zip up a directory containing those 50 files so when
the user unzips it, he's left with a tidy directory instead.

```
$ ls -lF
drwxr-xr-x scott scott edgar_scott/
$ zip grandpa.zip edgar_scott
adding: edgar_scott/ (stored 0%)
adding: edgar_scott/edgar_baby.tif (deflated 12%)
adding: edgar_scott/young_edgar_scott.tif
➥(deflated 19%)
adding: edgar_scott/edgar_intl_shoe.tif
➥(deflated 4%)
$ ls -lF
drwxr-xr-x scott scott     160 edgar_scott/
-rw-r--r-- scott scott 2074502 grandpa.zip
```

Whether you're zipping up a file, several files, or a
directory, the pattern is the same: the zip command,
followed by the name of the Zip file you're creating,
and finished with the item(s) you're adding to the Zip
file.

Get the Best Compression Possible with zip

`-[0-9]`

It's possible to adjust the level of compression that zip uses when it does its job. The zip command uses a scale from 0 to 9, in which 0 means "no compression at all" (which is like tar, as you'll see later), 1 means "do the job quickly, but don't bother compressing very much," and 9 means "compress the heck out of the files, and I don't mind waiting a bit longer to get the job done." The default is 6, but modern computers are fast enough that it's probably just fine to use 9 all the time.

Say you're interested in researching Herman Melville's *Moby-Dick*, so you want to collect key texts to help you understand the book: *Moby-Dick* itself, Milton's *Paradise Lost*, and the Bible's book of Job. Let's compare the results of different compression rates.

```
$ ls -l
-rw-r--r-- scott scott  102519 job.txt
-rw-r--r-- scott scott 1236574 moby-dick.txt
-rw-r--r-- scott scott  508925 paradise_lost.txt
$ zip -0 moby.zip *.txt
adding: job.txt (stored 0%)
adding: moby-dick.txt (stored 0%)
adding: paradise_lost.txt (stored 0%)
$ ls -l
-rw-r--r-- scott scott  102519 job.txt
-rw-r--r-- scott scott 1236574 moby-dick.txt
-rw-r--r-- scott scott 1848444 moby.zip
-rw-r--r-- scott scott  508925 paradise_lost.txt
$ zip -1 moby.zip *txt
updating: job.txt (deflated 58%)
```

```
updating: moby-dick.txt (deflated 54%)
updating: paradise_lost.txt (deflated 50%)
$ ls -l
-rw-r--r-- scott scott  102519 job.txt
-rw-r--r-- scott scott 1236574 moby-dick.txt
-rw-r--r-- scott scott  869946 moby.zip
-rw-r--r-- scott scott  508925 paradise_lost.txt
$ zip -9 moby.zip *txt
updating: job.txt (deflated 65%)
updating: moby-dick.txt (deflated 61%)
updating: paradise_lost.txt (deflated 56%)
$ ls -l
-rw-r--r-- scott scott  102519 job.txt
-rw-r--r-- scott scott 1236574 moby-dick.txt
-rw-r--r-- scott scott  747730 moby.zip
-rw-r--r-- scott scott  508925 paradise_lost.txt
```

In tabular format, the results look like this:

Book	zip -0	zip -1	zip -9
Moby-Dick	0%	54%	61%
Paradise Lost	0%	50%	56%
Job	0%	58%	65%
Total (in bytes)	1848444	869946	747730

The results you see here would vary depending on the file types (text files typically compress well) and the sizes of the original files, but this gives you a good idea of what you can expect. Unless you have a really slow machine or you're just naturally impatient, you should just use -9 all the time to get the maximum compression.

NOTE: If you want to be clever, define an alias in your .bashrc file that looks like this:

```
alias zip='zip -9'
```

That way you'll always use -9 and won't have to think about it.

Password-Protect Compressed Zip Archives

```
-P
-e
```

The Zip program allows you to password-protect your Zip archives using the -P option. You shouldn't use this option. It's completely insecure, as you can see in the following example (the actual password is 12345678):

```
$ zip -P 12345678 moby.zip *.txt
```

Because you had to specify the password on the command line, anyone viewing your shell's history (and you might be surprised how easy it is for other users to do so) can see your password in all its glory. Don't use the -P option!

Instead, just use the -e option, which encrypts the contents of your Zip file and also uses a password. The difference, however, is that you're prompted to type the password in, so it won't be saved in the history of your shell events.

```
$ zip -e moby.zip *.txt
Enter password:
Verify password:
adding: job.txt (deflated 65%)
adding: moby-dick.txt (deflated 61%)
adding: paradise_lost.txt (deflated 56%)
```

The only part of this that's saved in the shell is `zip -e moby.zip *.txt`. The actual password you type disappears into the ether, unavailable to anyone viewing your shell history.

CAUTION: The security offered by the Zip program's password protection isn't that great. In fact, it's pretty easy to find a multitude of tools floating around the Internet that can quickly crack a password-protected Zip archive. Think of password-protecting a Zip file as the difference between writing a message on a postcard and sealing it in an envelope: It's good enough for ordinary folks, but it won't stop a determined attacker.

Also, the version of zip included with some Linux distros may not support encryption, in which case you'll see a zip error: "encryption not supported." The only solution: recompile zip from source. Ugh.

Unzip Files

`unzip`

Expanding a Zip archive isn't hard at all. To create a zipped archive, use the `zip` command; to expand that archive, use the `unzip` command.

```
$ unzip moby.zip
Archive:  moby.zip
inflating: job.txt
inflating: moby-dick.txt
inflating: paradise_lost.txt
```

The `unzip` command helpfully tells you what it's doing as it works. To get even more information, add the -v option (which stands, of course, for *verbose*).

```
unzip -v moby.zip
Archive:  moby.zip
 Length   Method   Size   Ratio  CRC-32   Name
 -------  ------  ------  -----  ------   ----
  102519  Defl:X   35747   65%   fabf86c9 job.txt
 1236574  Defl:X  487553   61%   34a8cc3a moby-dick.txt
  508925  Defl:X  224004   56%   6abe1d0f paradise_lost.t
 -------          ------   ---            -------
 1848018          747304   60%            3 files
```

There's quite a bit of useful data here, including the method used to compress the files, the ratio of original to compressed file size, and the cyclic redundancy check (CRC) used for error correction.

List Files That Will Be Unzipped

-l

Sometimes you might find yourself looking at a Zip file and not remembering what's in that file. Or perhaps you want to make sure that a file you need is contained within that Zip file. To list the contents of a zip file without unzipping it, use the -l option (which stands for "list").

```
$ unzip -l moby.zip
Archive:  moby.zip
  Length      Date    Time    Name
 --------    ----    ----    ----
        0  01-26-06 18:40   bible/
   207254  01-26-06 18:40   bible/genesis.txt
   102519  01-26-06 18:19   bible/job.txt
  1236574  01-26-06 18:19   moby-dick.txt
   508925  01-26-06 18:19   paradise_lost.txt
 --------                   -------
  2055272                   5 files
```

From these results, you can see that moby.zip contains two files—moby-dick.txt and paradise_lost.txt—and a directory (bible), which itself contains two files, genesis. txt and job.txt. Now you know exactly what will happen when you expand moby.zip. Using the -l command helps prevent inadvertently unzipping a file that spews out 100 files instead of unzipping a directory that contains 100 files. The first leaves you with files strewn pell-mell, while the second is far easier to handle.

Test Files That Will Be Unzipped

```
-t
```

Sometimes zipped archives become corrupted. The worst time to discover this is after you've unzipped the archive and deleted it, only to discover that some or even all of the unzipped contents are damaged and won't open. Better to test the archive first before you actually unzip it by using the -t (for test) option.

```
$ unzip -t moby.zip
Archive:  moby.zip
    testing: bible/                   OK
    testing: bible/genesis.txt        OK
    testing: bible/job.txt            OK
    testing: moby-dick.txt            OK
    testing: paradise_lost.txt        OK
No errors detected in compressed data of moby.zip.
```

You really should use -t every time you work with a zipped file. It's the smart thing to do, and although it might take some extra time, it's worth it in the end.

Archive and Compress Files Using gzip

gzip

Using gzip is a bit easier than zip in some ways. With zip, you need to specify the name of the newly created Zip file or zip won't work; with gzip, though, you can just type the command and the name of the file you want to compress.

```
$ ls -l
-rw-r--r-- scott scott 508925 paradise_lost.txt
$ gzip paradise_lost.txt
$ ls -l
-rw-r--r-- scott scott 224425 paradise_lost.txt.gz
```

You should be aware of a very big difference between zip and gzip: When you zip a file, zip leaves the original behind so you have both the original and the newly zipped file, but when you gzip a file, you're left with only the new gzipped file. The original is gone.

If you want gzip to leave behind the original file, you need to use the -c (or --stdout or --to-stdout) option, which outputs the results of gzip to the shell, but you need to redirect that output to another file. If you use -c and forget to redirect your output, you get nonsense like this:

```
$ gzip -c paradise lost.txt
w`
  I
�1�,(3 �집�i`+��M�S3�t1*f%eY□□'[q��
D�□}d]C%g�        R�@,r�e■trB3+3/��|*��0D@■s
➡BAqn��,Y8*#"]]RU
*b�U\����G���'t(-��x�Yz3-�o'~cnS겹K
 �c�
```

Not good. Instead, output to a file.

```
$ ls -l
-rw-r--r-- 1 scott scott 508925 paradise_lost.txt
$ gzip -c paradise_lost.txt > paradise_lost.txt.gz
$ ls -l
-rw-r--r-- 1 scott scott 497K paradise_lost.txt
-rw-r--r-- 1 scott scott 220K paradise_lost.txt.gz
```

Much better! Now you have both your original file and the zipped version.

TIP: If you accidentally use the -c option without specifying an output file, just start pressing Ctrl+C several times until gzip stops.

Archive and Compress Files Recursively Using gzip

`-r`

If you want to use gzip on several files in a directory, just use a wildcard. You might not end up gzipping everything you think you will, however, as this example shows.

```
$ ls -F
bible/  moby-dick.txt  paradise_lost.txt
$ ls -l *
-rw-r--r-- scott scott 1236574 moby-dick.txt
-rw-r--r-- scott scott  508925 paradise_lost.txt

bible:
-rw-r--r-- scott scott 207254 genesis.txt
-rw-r--r-- scott scott 102519 job.txt
$ gzip *
gzip: bible is a directory -- ignored
$ ls -l *
-rw-r--r-- scott scott 489609 moby-dick.txt.gz
-rw-r--r-- scott scott 224425 paradise_lost.txt.gz

bible:
-rw-r--r-- scott scott 207254 genesis.txt
-rw-r--r-- scott scott 102519 job.txt
```

Notice that the wildcard didn't do anything for the files inside the bible directory because gzip by default doesn't walk down into subdirectories. To get that behavior, you need to use the -r (or --recursive) option along with your wildcard.

```
$ ls -F
bible/  moby-dick.txt  paradise_lost.txt
$ ls -l *
-rw-r--r-- scott scott 1236574 moby-dick.txt
-rw-r--r-- scott scott  508925 paradise_lost.txt

bible:
-rw-r--r-- scott scott 207254 genesis.txt
-rw-r--r-- scott scott 102519 job.txt
$ gzip -r *
$ ls -l *
-rw-r--r-- scott scott 489609 moby-dick.txt.gz
```

```
-rw-r--r-- scott scott 224425 paradise_lost.txt.gz

bible:
-rw-r--r-- scott scott 62114 genesis.txt.gz
-rw-r--r-- scott scott 35984 job.txt.gz
```

This time, every file—even those in subdirectories—was gzipped. However, note that each file is individually gzipped. The gzip command cannot combine all the files into one big file, like you can with the zip command. To do that, you need to incorporate tar, as you'll see in "Archive and Compress Files with tar and gzip."

Get the Best Compression Possible with `gzip`

`-[0-9]`

Just as with zip, it's possible to adjust the level of compression that gzip uses when it does its job. The gzip command uses a scale from 0 to 9, in which 0 means "no compression at all" (which is like tar, as you'll see later), 1 means "do the job quickly, but don't bother compressing very much," and 9 means "compress the heck out of the files, and I don't mind waiting a bit longer to get the job done." The default is 6, but modern computers are fast enough that it's probably just fine to use 9 all the time.

```
$ ls -l
-rw-r--r-- scott scott 1236574 moby-dick.txt
$ gzip -c -1 moby-dick.txt > moby-dick.txt.gz
$ ls -l
-rw-r--r-- scott scott 1236574 moby-dick.txt
-rw-r--r-- scott scott  571005 moby-dick.txt.gz
```

```
$ gzip -c -9 moby-dick.txt > moby-dick.txt.gz
$ ls -l
-rw-r--r-- scott scott 1236574 moby-dick.txt
-rw-r--r-- scott scott  487585 moby-dick.txt.gz
```

Remember to use the -c option and pipe the output into the actual .gz file due to the way gzip works, as discussed in "Archive and Compress Files Using gzip."

NOTE: If you want to be clever, define an alias in your .bashrc file that looks like this:

```
alias gzip='gzip -9'
```

That way, you'll always use -9 and won't have to think about it.

Uncompress Files Compressed with gzip

`gunzip`

Getting files out of a gzipped archive is easy with the gunzip command.

```
$ ls -l
-rw-r--r-- scott scott  224425 paradise_lost.txt.gz
$ gunzip paradise_lost.txt.gz
$ ls -l
-rw-r--r-- scott scott  508925 paradise_lost.txt
```

In the same way that gzip removes the original file, leaving you solely with the gzipped result, gunzip removes the .gz file, leaving you with the final gunzipped result. If you want to ensure that you have both, you need to use the -c option (or --stdout or --to-stdout) and pipe the results to the file you want to create.

```
$ ls -l
-rw-r--r-- scott scott  224425 paradise_lost.txt.gz
$ gunzip -c paradise_lost.txt.gz > paradise_lost.txt
$ ls -l
-rw-r--r-- scott scott  508925 paradise_lost.txt
-rw-r--r-- scott scott  224425 paradise_lost.txt.gz
```

It's probably a good idea to use -c, especially if you plan to keep behind the .gz file or pass it along to someone else. Sure, you could use gzip and create your own archive, but why go to the extra work?

NOTE: If you don't like the gunzip command, you can also use gzip -d (or --decompress or --uncompress).

Test Files That Will Be Unzipped with gunzip

`-t`

Before gunzipping a file (or files) with gunzip, you might want to verify that they're going to gunzip correctly without any file corruption. To do this, use the -t (or --test) option.

```
$ gzip -t paradise_lost.txt.gz
$
```

That's right: If nothing is wrong with the archive, gzip reports nothing back to you. If there's a problem, you'll know, but if there's not a problem, gzip is silent. That can be a bit disconcerting, but that's how Unix-based systems work. They're generally only noisy if there's an issue you should know about, not if everything is working as it should.

Archive and Compress Files Using bzip2

```
bzip2
```

Working with bzip2 is pretty easy if you're comfortable with gzip, as the creators of bzip2 deliberately made the options and behavior of the new command as similar to its progenitor as possible.

```
$ ls -l
-rw-r--r-- scott scott 1236574 moby-dick.txt
$ bzip2 moby-dick.txt
$ ls -l
-rw-r--r-- scott scott 367248 moby-dick.txt.bz2
```

Just like gzip, bzip2 leaves you with just the .bz2 file. The original moby-dick.txt is gone. To keep the original file, use the -c (or --stdout) option and pipe the output to a filename that ends with .bz2.

```
$ ls -l
-rw-r--r-- scott scott 1236574 moby-dick.txt
$ bzip2 -c moby-dick.txt > moby-dick.txt.bz2
$ ls -l
-rw-r--r-- scott scott 1236574 moby-dick.txt
-rw-r--r-- scott scott 367248 moby-dick.txt.bz2
```

If you look back at "Archive and Compress Files Using gzip," you'll see that gzip and bzip2 are incredibly similar, which is by design.

Get the Best Compression Possible with bzip2

`-[0-9]`

Just as with zip and gzip, it's possible to adjust the level of compression that bzip2 uses when it does its job. The bzip2 command uses a scale from 0 to 9, in which 0 means "no compression at all" (which is like tar, as you'll see later), 1 means "do the job quickly, but don't bother compressing very much," and 9 means "compress the heck out of the files, and I don't mind waiting a bit longer to get the job done." The default is 6, but modern computers are fast enough that it's probably just fine to use 9 all the time.

```
$ ls -l
-rw-r--r-- scott scott 1236574 moby-dick.txt
$ bzip2 -c -1 moby-dick.txt > moby-dick.txt.bz2
$ ls -l
-rw-r--r-- scott scott 1236574 moby-dick.txt
-rw-r--r-- scott scott  424084 moby-dick.txt.bz2
$ bzip2 -c -9 moby-dick.txt > moby-dick.txt.bz2
$ ls -l
-rw-r--r-- scott scott 1236574 moby-dick.txt
-rw-r--r-- scott scott  367248 moby-dick.txt.bz2
```

From 424KB with 1 to 367KB with 9—that's quite a difference! Also notice the difference in ultimate file size between gzip and bzip2. At -9, gzip compressed moby-dick.txt down to 488KB, while bzip2 mashed it even further to 367KB. The bzip2 command is noticeably slower than the gzip command, but on a fast machine that means that bzip2 takes two or three seconds longer than gzip, which frankly isn't much to worry about.

NOTE: If you want to be clever, define an alias in your .bashrc file that looks like this:

`alias bzip2='bzip2 -9'`

That way, you'll always use -9 and won't have to think about it.

Uncompress Files Compressed with bzip2

`bunzip2`

In the same way that bzip2 was purposely designed to emulate gzip as closely as possible, the way bunzip2 works is very close to that of gunzip.

```
$ ls -l
-rw-r--r-- scott scott  367248 moby-dick.txt.bz2
$ bunzip2 moby-dick.txt.bz2
$ ls -l
-rw-r--r-- scott scott 1236574 moby-dick.txt
```

You'll notice that bunzip2 is similar to gunzip in another way: Both commands remove the original compressed file, leaving you with the final uncompressed result. If you want to ensure that you have both the compressed and uncompressed files, you need to use the -c option (or --stdout or --to-stdout) and pipe the results to the file you want to create.

```
$ ls -l
-rw-r--r-- scott scott  367248 moby-dick.txt.bz2
$ bunzip2 -c moby-dick.txt.bz2 > moby-dick.txt
$ ls -l
-rw-r--r-- scott scott 1236574 moby-dick.txt
-rw-r--r-- scott scott  367248 moby-dick.txt.bz2
```

It's a good thing when commands copy each other's options and behavior, as it makes them easier to learn. In this, the creators of bzip2 and bunzip2 showed remarkable foresight.

NOTE: If you're not feeling favorable toward bunzip2, you can also use bzip2 -d (or --decompress or --uncompress).

Test Files That Will Be Unzipped with bunzip

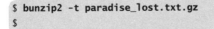

Before bunzipping a file (or files) with bunzip, you might want to verify that they're going to bunzip correctly without any file corruption. To do this, use the -t (or --test) option.

```
$ bunzip2 -t paradise_lost.txt.gz
$
```

Just as with gunzip, if there's nothing wrong with the archive, bunzip2 doesn't report anything back to you. If there's a problem, you'll know, but if there's not a problem, bunzip2 is silent.

Archive Files with tar

-cf

Remember, tar doesn't compress; it merely archives (the resulting archives are known as tarballs, by the way). Instead, tar uses other programs, such as gzip or bzip2, to compress the archives that tar creates. Even if you're not going to compress the tarball, you still create it the same way with the same basic options: -c (or --create), which tells tar that you're making a tarball, and -f (or --file), which is the specified filename for the tarball.

```
$ ls -l
scott scott  102519 job.txt
scott scott 1236574 moby-dick.txt
scott scott  508925 paradise_lost.txt
$ tar -cf moby.tar *.txt
$ ls -l
scott scott  102519 job.txt
scott scott 1236574 moby-dick.txt
scott scott 1853440 moby.tar
scott scott  508925 paradise_lost.txt
```

Pay attention to two things here. First, add up the file sizes of job.txt, moby-dick.txt, and paradise_lost.txt, and you get 1848018 bytes. Compare that to the size of moby.tar, and you see that the tarball is only 5422 bytes bigger. Remember that tar is an archive tool, not a compression tool, so the result is at least the same size as the individual files put together, plus a little bit for overhead to keep track of what's in the tarball. Second, notice that tar, unlike gzip and bzip2, leaves the original files behind. This isn't a surprise, considering the tar command's background as a backup tool.

What's really cool about tar is that it's designed to compress entire directory structures, so you can archive a large number of files and subdirectories in one fell swoop.

```
$ ls -1F
drwxr-xr-x scott scott 168 moby-dick/
$ ls -l moby-dick/*
scott scott  102519 moby-dick/job.txt
scott scott 1236574 moby-dick/moby-dick.txt
scott scott  508925 moby-dick/paradise_lost.txt

moby-dick/bible:
scott scott 207254 genesis.txt
scott scott 102519 job.txt
$ tar -cf moby.tar moby-dick/
$ ls -1F
scott scott      168 moby-dick/
scott scott 2170880 moby.tar
```

The tar command has been around forever, and it's obvious why: It's so darn useful! But it gets even more useful when you start factoring in compression tools, as you'll see in the next section.

Archive and Compress Files with tar and gzip

-zcvf

If you look back at "Archive and Compress Files Using gzip" and "Archive and Compress Files Using bzip2" and think about what was discussed there, you'll probably start to figure out a problem. What if you want to compress a directory that contains 100 files, contained in various subdirectories? If you use gzip or bzip2 with

the -r (for *recursive*) option, you'll end up with 100
individually compressed files, each stored neatly in its
original subdirectory. This is undoubtedly not what you
want. How would you like to attach 100 .gz or .bz2
files to an email? Yikes!

That's where tar comes in. First you'd use tar to
archive the directory and its contents (those 100 files
inside various subdirectories) and then you'd use gzip
or bzip2 to compress the resulting tarball. Because gzip
is the most common compression program used in
concert with tar, we'll focus on that.

You could do it this way:

```
$ ls -l moby-dick/*
scott scott  102519 moby-dick/job.txt
scott scott 1236574 moby-dick/moby-dick.txt
scott scott  508925 moby-dick/paradise_lost.txt

moby-dick/bible:
scott scott 207254 genesis.txt
scott scott 102519 job.txt
$ tar -cf moby.tar moby-dick/ | gzip -c >
moby.tar.gz
$ ls -l
scott scott  168 moby-dick/
scott scott   20 moby.tar.gz
```

That method works, but it's just too much typing!
There's a much easier way that should be your default.
It involves two new options for tar: -z (or --gzip),
which invokes gzip from within tar so you don't have
to do so manually, and -v (or --verbose), which isn't
required here but is always useful, as it keeps you noti-
fied as to what tar is doing as it runs.

```
$ ls -l moby-dick/*
scott scott  102519 moby-dick/job.txt
scott scott 1236574 moby-dick/moby-dick.txt
scott scott  508925 moby-dick/paradise_lost.txt

moby-dick/bible:
scott scott 207254 genesis.txt
scott scott 102519 job.txt
$ tar -zcvf moby.tar.gz moby-dick/
moby-dick/
moby-dick/job.txt
moby-dick/bible/
moby-dick/bible/genesis.txt
moby-dick/bible/job.txt
moby-dick/moby-dick.txt
moby-dick/paradise_lost.txt
$ ls -l
scott scott    168 moby-dick
scott scott 846049 moby.tar.gz
```

The usual extension for a file that has had the tar and then the gzip commands used on it is .tar.gz; however, you could use .tgz and .tar.gzip if you like.

NOTE: It's entirely possible to use bzip2 with tar instead of gzip. Your command would look like this (note the -j option, which is where bzip2 comes in):

```
$ tar -jcvf moby.tar.bz2 moby-dick/
```

In that case, the extension should be .tar.bz2, although you may also use .tar.bzip2, .tbz2, or .tbz. Yes, it's very confusing that using gzip or bzip2 might both result in a file ending with .tbz. This is a strong argument for using anything but that particular extension to keep confusion to a minimum.

Test Files That Will Be Untarred and Uncompressed

`-zvtf`

Before you take apart a tarball (whether or not it was also compressed using gzip), it's a really good idea to test it. First, you'll know if the tarball is corrupted, saving yourself hair pulling when files don't seem to work. Second, you'll know if the person who created the tarball thoughtfully tarred up a directory containing 100 files, or instead thoughtlessly tarred up 100 individual files, which you're just about to spew all over your desktop.

To test your tarball (once again assuming it was also zipped using gzip), use the -t (or --list) option.

```
$ tar -zvtf moby.tar.gz
scott/scott 0 moby-dick/
scott/scott 102519 moby-dick/job.txt
scott/scott 0 moby-dick/bible/
scott/scott 207254 moby-dick/bible/genesis.txt
scott/scott 102519 moby-dick/bible/job.txt
scott/scott 1236574 moby-dick/moby-dick.txt
scott/scott 508925 moby-dick/paradise_lost.txt
```

This tells you the permissions, ownership, file size, and time for each file. In addition, because every line begins with moby-dick/, you can see that you're going to end up with a directory that contains within it all the files and subdirectories that accompany the tarball, which is a relief.

Be sure that the -f is the last option because after that you're going to specify the name of the .tar.gz file. If you don't, tar complains:

```
$ tar -zvft moby.tar.gz
tar: You must specify one of the `-Acdtrux' options
Try `tar --help' or `tar --usage' for more
information.
```

Now that you've ensured that your .tar.gz file isn't corrupted, it's time to actually open it up, as you'll see in the following section.

NOTE: If you're testing a tarball that was compressed using bzip2, just use this command instead:

```
$ tar -jvtf moby.tar.bz2
```

Untar and Uncompress Files

```
-zxvf
```

To create a .tar.gz file, you used a set of options: -zcvf. To untar and uncompress the resulting file, you only make one substitution: -x (or --extract) for -c (or --create).

```
$ ls -l
rsgranne rsgranne 846049 moby.tar.gz
$ tar -zxvf moby.tar.gz
moby-dick/
moby-dick/job.txt
moby-dick/bible/
moby-dick/bible/genesis.txt
moby-dick/bible/job.txt
moby-dick/moby-dick.txt
moby-dick/paradise_lost.txt
$ ls -l
rsgranne rsgranne    168 moby-dick
rsgranne rsgranne 846049 moby.tar.gz
```

Make sure you always test the file before you open it,
as covered in the previous section, "Test Files That Will
Be Untarred and Uncompressed." That means the order
of commands you should run will look like this:

```
$ tar -zvtf moby.tar.gz
$ tar -zxvf moby.tar.gz
```

NOTE: If you're opening a tarball that was compressed
using bzip2, just use this command instead:

```
$ tar -jxvf moby.tar.bz2
```

Conclusion

Back in the days of slow modems and tiny hard drives,
archiving and compression was a necessity. These days,
it's more of a convenience, but it's still something you'll
find yourself using all the time. For instance, if you ever
download source code to compile it, more than likely
you'll find yourself face-to-face with a file such as
sourcecode.tar.gz. In the future, you'll probably see
more and more of those files ending with .tar.bz2.
And if you exchange files with Windows users, you're
going to run into files that end with .zip. Learn how
to use your archival and compression tools because
you're going to be using them far more than you
think.

9

Finding Stuff: Easy

Every year, hard drives get bigger and cheaper, a nice combination. With all the technical toys we have in our lives now—digital cameras, video cameras, MP3 players, as well as movies and music we find on the Net—we certainly have plenty of stuff to fill those hard drives. Every digital pack rat has to pay the price, however, and that too often tends to be an inability to find the stuff you want. It can be hard to find that one photo of your brother in the midst of 10,000 other pictures, or that paper you wrote when you have to dig through 600 other documents. Fortunately, Linux has powerful tools at your disposal that can help make retrieving a necessary file a quick and efficient activity.

Search a Database of Filenames

locate

Know the name of a file, or even part of the name, but don't know where it resides on your system? That's what `locate` is for. The `locate` command looks for files, programs, and directories matching your search term. Any matching results are printed to your terminal, one after the other.

NOTE: In order to save space, I've replaced the first part of the path – /home/scott – with an ellipses.

```
$ locate haggard
.../txt/rider_haggard
.../txt/rider_haggard/Queen_of_the_Dawn.txt
.../txt/rider_haggard/Allan_and_the_Ice-Gods.txt
.../txt/rider_haggard/Heu-Heu_or_The_Monster.txt
```

Your search results show up quickly because locate isn't searching your system in real time. Instead, locate searches a database of filenames that is automatically updated daily (more about that in "Update the Database Used by locate" later in this chapter). Because locate searches a precreated database, its results appear almost instantaneously.

On your computer, though, you're probably using slocate instead of locate—you're just not aware of it. The slocate command (which stands for *secure locate*) is a more recent version that won't search directories that the user running slocate doesn't have permission to view (for instance, if you're not root, results from /root shouldn't show up when you search with locate). Before slocate, locate would spit back many errors complaining about permission problems; with slocate, those errors are a thing of the past.

To verify how slocate works, try the following. Note that the first search, done when you're a normal user and not root, fails. Use su to become root, run locate again, and bingo! Search results appear (slocate.db is the database file used by slocate, by the way).

```
$ locate slocate.db
$ su -
# locate slocate.db
/var/lib/slocate/slocate.db.tmp
/var/lib/slocate/slocate.db
```

To make things easy on users, however, most systems
create a soft link for /usr/bin/locate that points to
/usr/bin/slocate. To verify that your Linux distribution
does this, try the following (these particular results are
from a box running K/Ubuntu 5.10, a Debian-based
distribution, and I've removed some data so I can focus
on the important information):

```
$ ls -l /usr/bin/locate
root root /usr/bin/locate -> slocate
```

Because it's transparent to the user that she's running
slocate, and because locate uses fewer letters and is
therefore quicker to type, we're going to refer to locate
in this book, even though slocate is the actual command that's being run.

Search a Database of Filenames Without Worrying About Case

```
locate -i
```

In the previous section, you tested locate by searching
for any files or directories with the word *haggard* in the
name, so you could find your collection of public
domain H. Rider Haggard novels. The results looked
like this:

```
$ locate haggard
.../txt/rider_haggard
.../txt/rider_haggard/Queen_of_the_Dawn.txt
.../txt/rider_haggard/Allan_and_the_Ice-Gods.txt
.../txt/rider_haggard/Heu-Heu_or_The_Monster.txt
```

This worked because the directory containing the novels had the word *haggard* in it. But if that directory had instead been named H_Rider_Haggard, the search would have failed due to Linux's case sensitivity (discussed in Chapter 1, "Things to Know About Your Command Line"). Sure enough, when you use the -i option, a case-insensitive search is performed, finding files with both *haggard* and *Haggard* (and, in fact, *HAGGARD*, *HaGgArD*, and so on) in the path.

```
$ locate -i haggard
/txt/rider_haggard
/txt/rider_haggard/Queen_of_the_Dawn.txt
/txt/rider_haggard/Allan_and_the_Ice-Gods.txt
/txt/rider_haggard/Heu-Heu_or_The_Monster.txt
/txt/Rider_Haggard
/txt/Rider_Haggard/King_Solomons_Mines.txt
/txt/Rider_Haggard/Allan_Quatermain.txt
```

It turns out that there were more Haggard novels available than it first seemed. Remember to use -i when you want to maximize your locate results, as you can otherwise miss important files and folders that you wanted to find.

NOTE: For more on H. Rider Haggard, see http://en.wikipedia. org/wiki/Rider_Haggard. He's a fun, if dated, read.

Manage Results Received When Searching a Database of Filenames

`-n`

If you use `locate` very much, eventually you're going to run into something like this:

```
$ locate pdf
/etc/cups/pdftops.conf
/etc/xpdf
/etc/xpdf/xpdfrc-latin2
```

On this computer, we get 2,373 results. Far too many! Better to use this construction instead:

```
$ locate pdf | less
```

Pipe the output of your `locate` search to the pager `less` (which was covered in "View Text Files a Screen at a Time," in Chapter 5, "Viewing Files"), and you get your 2,373 results one manageable screen at a time.

If you just want to see the first x results, where x is an integer of your choice, use the -n option, followed by the number of results you want to see.

```
$ locate -n 3 pdf
/etc/cups/pdftops.conf
/etc/xpdf
/etc/xpdf/xpdfrc-latin2
```

This is far more manageable, and might be all you need. Don't let `locate` just spew a flood of results at you; instead, take control of the `locate` command's output and use it to your favor.

Update the Database Used by `locate`

`updatedb`

The first section of this chapter that introduced `locate`, "Search a Database of Filenames," mentioned that the reason the command is so fast is because it is actually searching a database containing your machine's file and directory names. When `locate` is installed, it automatically sets itself up to scan your hard drive and update that database, usually in the middle of the night. That's great for convenience, but not so great if you need to find a file you just placed on your computer.

For instance, what if you install Rootkit Hunter, a program that looks for rootkits (used by bad guys to take control of your Linux box), and then you want to look at the files the program has installed? The `locate` command won't be able to help you because it doesn't know about those files and won't know about them until its database is updated at a later time. You can, however, manually update the database used by `locate` at any time by running `updatedb`. Because that command indexes virtually every file and folder on your computer, you need to be root to run it (or use `sudo` on distributions like K/Ubuntu that discourage root use).

```
# apt-get install rkhunter
# exit
$ locate rkhunter
$ su -
# updatedb
# exit
$ locate rkhunter
```

```
/usr/local/rkhunter
/usr/local/rkhunter/bin
/usr/local/rkhunter/etc
```

In the preceding commands, you first install `rkhunter`, the package name for Rootkit Hunter, and then exit root. You search for `rkhunter`, but it's nowhere to be seen. You become root again, run `updatedb` to scan your hard drive and let the `locate` database know about any changes, and then exit root. Finally, you search for `rkhunter` with `locate` again, and this time you're successful.

One thing you should be aware of, however: The speed with which `updatedb` works is directly proportional to the amount of stuff on your hard drive and the speed of your computer. Got a fast processor, a fast hard drive, and few files? Then `updatedb` will work quickly. Do you have a slow CPU, 5,400RPM drive, and a million files? Expect `updatedb` to take quite a while. If you're interested in knowing just how long it takes to run, preface `updatedb` with the time command, like this:

```
# time updatedb
```

When `updatedb` finishes, `time` tells you how long it took to get the `locate` database squared away. That is useful information to have in your head in case you ever need to use `updatedb` and you're in a hurry.

NOTE: The `updatedb` command is exactly the same as running `slocate -u`, and `updatedb` is actually just a link to `slocate`, as you can easily see for yourself.

```
$ ls -l /usr/bin/updatedb
root root /usr/bin/updatedb -> slocate
```

Searching Inside Text Files for Patterns

`grep`

The `locate` command searches the names of files and directories, but it can't search inside those files. To do that, you use `grep`. Essentially, you give `grep` a pattern for which you want to search, point it at a file or a group of files (or even a whole hard drive) that you want to search, and then `grep` outputs a list of lines that match your pattern.

```
$ grep pain three_no_more_forever.txt
all alone and in pain
```

In this case you used `grep` to see if the word *pain* was in a file containing a poem by Peter Von Zer Muehlen titled "Three No More Forever." Sure enough, the word *pain* is in the file, so `grep` prints the line containing your search term on the terminal. But what if you want to look in several of Peter's poems at once? Wildcards to the rescue!

```
$ grep pain *
fiery inferno in space.txt:watch the paint peel,
three_no_more_forever.txt:all alone and in pain
the speed of morning.txt:of a Chinese painting.
8 hour a day.txt:nice paint job too
ghost pain.txt:Subject: ghost pain
```

Notice that `grep` finds all uses of the string `pain`, including `paint` and `painting`. Also pay attention to how grep shows you the filename for each file that contains the search term, as well as the line containing that term. So far, it's been pretty easy to search inside files with grep. So it's a perfect time to complicate matters, as you'll discover in the following sections.

The Basics of Searching Inside Text Files for Patterns

In the previous section, you learned that grep works by looking for the existence of a pattern in a group of files. Your first use of grep was extremely basic, but now you need to get a bit more complex, and to do that you need to understand the patterns for which grep searches. Those patterns are built using one of the most powerful tools in the Linux toolbox: regular expressions, or regex. To take full advantage of grep, you really need to grok regex; however, regex is a book all in itself, so we're only going to cover the basics here.

TIP: Want to learn more about regular expressions? You can search the Internet, and you'll find quite a bit of great stuff there, but *Sams Teach Yourself Regular Expressions in 10 Minutes* (by Ben Forta; ISBN: 0672325667) is a great book that'll really help you as you explore and learn regex.

One thing that confuses new users when they start playing with grep is that the command has several versions, as shown in Table 9.1.

Table 9.1   Different Versions of grep

Interpret Pattern As	grep Command Option	Separate Command
Basic regular expression	grep -G (or --basic-regexp)	grep
Extended regular expression	grep -E (or --extended-regexp)	egrep
List of fixed strings, any of which can be matched	grep -F (or --fixed-strings)	fgrep
Perl regular expression	grep -P (or --perl-regexp)	Not applicable

To summarize this table, grep all by itself works with basic regex. If you use the -E (or --extended-regexp) option or the egrep command, you can use extended regex. Much of the time, this is probably what you'll want to do, unless you're performing a very simple search. Two more complicated choices are grep with the -F (or --fixed-strings) option or the fgrep command, which allows you to use multiple search terms that could be matched, and grep with the -P (or --perl-regexp) option, which allows Perl programming mavens to use that language's sometimes unique approach to regex.

NOTE: In this book, unless otherwise stated, we're using just plain grep for basic regex.

A few possible points of confusion need to be covered before you continue. If you're unclear about any of these, use the listed resources as a jumping-off point to learn more.

Wildcards are not equivalent to regex. Yes, both wildcards and regular expressions use the * character, for instance, but they have completely different meanings. Where certain characters (? and *, for example) are used as wildcards to indicate substitution, the same characters in regex are used to indicate the number of times a preceding item is to be matched. For instance, with wildcards, the ? in c?t replaces one and only one letter, matching cat, cot, and cut, for instance, but not ct. With regex, the ? in c[a-z]?t indicates that the letters *A* through *Z* are to be matched both zero or one time(s), thereby corresponding to cat, cot, cut, and also ct.

TIP: To learn more about differences between wildcards and regular expressions, see "What Is a Regular Expression" (http://docs.kde.org/stable/en/kdeutils/KRegExpEditor/whatIsARegExp.html), "Regular Expressions Explained" (www.castaglia.org/proftpd/doc/contrib/regexp.html), and "Wildcards Gone Wild" (www.linux-mag.com/2003-12/power_01.html).

Another potentially confusing thing about grep is that you need to be aware of special characters in your grep regex. For instance, in regular expressions, the string [a-e] indicates a regex range, and means any one character matching a, b, c, d, or e. When using [or] with grep, you need to make it clear to your shell whether the [and] are there to delimit a regex range or are part of the words for which you're searching. Special characters of which you need to keep aware include the following:

. ? [ ] ^ $ | \

Finally, there is a big difference between the use of single quotes and double quotes in regex. Single quotes (' and ') tell the shell that you are searching for a string of characters, while double quotes (" and ") let your shell know that you want to use shell variables. For instance, using grep and regex in the following way to look for all usages of the phrase "hey you!" in a friend's poetry wouldn't work:

```
$ grep hey you! *
grep: you!: No such file or directory
txt/pvzm/8 hours a day.txt:hey you! let's run!
txt/pvzm/friends & family.txt:in patience they wait
txt/pvzm/speed of morning.txt:they say the force
```

Because you simply wrote out "hey you!" with nothing around it, grep was confused. It first looked for the search term *hey* in a file called "you!" but it was unsuccessful, as that isn't the actual name of a file. Then it searched for *hey* in every file contained in the current working directory, as indicated by the * wildcard, with three good results. It's true that the first of those three contained the phrase you were searching for, so in that sense your search worked, but not really. This search was crude and does not always deliver the results you'd like. Let's try again.

This time you'll use double quotes around your search term. That should fix the problem you had when you didn't use anything at all.

```
$ grep "hey you!" *
bash: !" *: event not found
```

Even worse! Actually, the quotation marks also cause a big problem and give even worse results than you just saw. What happened? The ! is a shell command that references your command history. Normally you'd use the ! by following it with a process ID (PID) number that represents an earlier command you ran, like !264.

Here, though, bash sees the !, looks for a PID after it, and then complains that it can't find an earlier command named " * (a double quote, a space, and an asterisk), which would be a very weird command indeed.

It turns out that quotation marks indicate that you are using shell variables in your search term, which is in fact not what you wanted at all. So double quotes don't work. Let's try single quotes.

```
$ grep 'hey!' *
txt/pvzm/8 hours a day.txt:hey you! let's run!
```

Much better results! The single quotes told grep that your search term didn't contain any shell variables, and was just a string of characters that you wanted to match. Lo and behold, there was a single result, the exact one you wanted.

The lesson? Know when to use single quotes, when to use double quotes, and when to use nothing. If you're searching for an exact match, use single quotes, but if you want to incorporate shell variables into your search term (which will be rare indeed), use double quotes. If you're searching for a single word that contains just numbers and letters, though, it's safe to leave off all quotes entirely. If you want to be safe, go ahead and use single quotes, even around a single word—it can't hurt.

Search Recursively for Text in Files

`-R`

The * wildcard allows you to search several files in the same directory, but to search in several subdirectories at once, you need the -R (or --recursive) option. Let's look for the word *hideous*, a favorite of horror writers of the nineteenth and early twentieth centuries, amongst a collection of old-fashioned (but still wonderful!) tales.

```
$ grep -R hideous *
machen/great_god_pan.txt:know, not in
your most fantastic, hideous dreams can you have
machen/great_god_pan.txt:hideously
contorted in the entire course of my practice, and I
machen/great_god_pan.txt:death was
horrible. The blackened face, the hideous form upon
lovecraft/Beyond the Wall of Sleep.txt:some hideous
but unnamed wrong, which
lovecraft/Beyond the Wall of Sleep.txt:blanket over
the hideous face, and awakened the nurse.
lovecraft/Call of Cthulhu.txt:hideous a chain. I
think that the professor, too, intended to
lovecraft/Call of Cthulhu.txt:voodoo meeting;
and so singular and hideous were the rites
lovecraft/Call of Cthulhu.txt:stated, a very
crude bas-relief of stone, comprising a hideous...
```

TIP: Of course, if you get too many results, you should pipe the results to less, as you did previously with locate in "Manage Results Received When Searching a Database of Filenames":

```
$ grep -R hideous * | less
```

Another tactic would be to send the output of the command into a text file, and then open that file in whatever text editor you prefer:

```
$ grep -R hideous * > hideous_in_horror.txt
```

That's a great way to search and store your results in case you need them later.

Search for Text in Files, Ignoring Case

```
-i
```

By default, searches performed with `grep` are case-sensitive. In the previous section, you searched amongst H.P. Lovecraft stories for the word `hideous` (a favorite of that author). But what about *Hideous*?

```
$ grep Hideous h_p_lovecraft/*
h_p_lovecraft/the_whisperer_in_darkness.txt: them.
Hideous though the idea was, I knew...
```

Your earlier search for *hideous* found 463 results (wow!) and *Hideous* returned one. Is there any way to combine them? Yes, with the `-i` (or `--ignore-case`) option, which searches for both, and also searches for *HiDeOuS*, *HIDEOUS*, and all other possible combinations.

```
$ grep -i hideous h_p_lovecraft/*
h_p_lovecraft/Call of Cthulhu.txt:voodoo meeting;
and so singular and hideous were the rites
h_p_lovecraft/Call of Cthulhu.txt:stated, a very
crude bas-relief of stone, comprising a hideous
h_p_lovecraft/the_whisperer_in_darkness.txt: them.
Hideous though the idea was, I knew...
```

Keep in mind that you're probably increasing the number of results you're going to get, perhaps by an order of magnitude. If that's a problem, check the tip at the end of the previous section for some advice about dealing with it.

Search for Whole Words Only in Files

`-w`

Think back to the earlier section "The Basics of Searching Inside Text Files for Patterns," in which you first learned about grep. You searched for the word *pain*, and grep obediently returned a list showing you where *pain* had been used.

```
$ grep pain *
fiery inferno in space.txt:watch the paint peel,
three_no_more_forever.txt:all alone and in pain
the speed of morning.txt:of a Chinese painting.
8 hour a day.txt:nice paint job too
ghost pain.txt:Subject: ghost pain
```

By default, grep searches for all occurrences of the string pain, showing you lines that contain *pain*, but also *paint* and *painting*. If *painless*, *Spain*, or *painstaking* had been in one of the files that were searched, those lines would have shown up as well. But what if you only wanted lines in which the exact word *pain* appeared? For that, use the -w (or --word-regexp) option.

```
$ grep -w pain *
three_no_more_forever.txt:all alone and in pain
ghost pain.txt:Subject: ghost pain
```

This option can really help narrow your search results when you receive too many to easily sort through.

Show Line Numbers Where Words Appear in Files

```
-n
```

The grep command shows you the line containing the term for which you're searching, but it doesn't really tell you where in the file you can find that line. To find out the line number, utilize the -n (or --line-number) option.

```
$ grep -n pain *
fiery inferno in space.txt:56:watch the paint peel,
three_no_more_forever.txt:19:all alone and in pain
the speed of morning.txt:66:of a Chinese painting.
8 hour a day.txt:78:nice paint job too
ghost pain.txt:32:Subject: ghost pain
```

Now that you know the line numbers for each instance of the string pain, it is a simple matter to go directly to those lines in virtually any text editor. Nice!

Search the Output of Other Commands for Specific Words

```
$ ls -1 | grep 1960
```

The grep command is powerful when used by itself, but it really comes alive when you use it as a filter for the output of other programs. For instance, let's say you have all your John Coltrane MP3s organized in separate subfolders for each album (66 in all...yes, Coltrane is that good), with the year at the beginning. A partial listing might look like this (the -1 option is used with ls so there is one result on each line):

```
$ ls -1
1956_Coltrane_For_Lovers
1957_Blue_Train
1957_Coltrane_[Prestige]
1957_Lush_Life
1957_Thelonious_Monk_With_John_Coltrane
```

Now, what if you just wanted to see a list of the albums you own that Coltrane released in 1960? Pipe the results of ls -1 to grep, and you'll get your answer in seconds.

```
$ ls -1 | grep 1960
1960_Coltrane_Plays_The_Blues
1960_Coltrane's_Sound
1960_Giant_Steps
1960_My_Favorite_Things
```

After you start thinking about it, you'll find literally hundreds of uses for grep in this way. Here's another powerful one. The ps command lists running processes, while the -f option tells ps to give the full listing, with lots of information about each process, and the -U option, followed by a username, restricts the output to processes owned by that user. Normally ps -fU scott would result in a long list, too long if you're looking for information about a specific process. With grep, however, you can easily restrict the output.

NOTE: To save space, some of the information you'd normally see with ps has been removed.

```
$ ps -fU scott | grep firefox
scott 17623 /bin/sh /opt/firefox/firefox
scott 17634 /opt/firefox/firefox-bin
scott  1601 grep firefox
```

The ps command lists all commands owned by the
scott user (64, in fact), but pipes that output to grep,
which lists only those lines that contain the word *firefox*
in them. Unfortunately, the last line of output is erro-
neous: You only care about the actual Firefox program,
not the search for firefox using grep. To hide the
search for firefox in the grep results, try this instead:

```
$ ps -fU scott | grep [f]irefox
scott 17623 /bin/sh /opt/firefox/firefox
scott 17634 /opt/firefox/firefox-bin
```

Now your grep search term used a regex range, from f
to f, that found firefox on those lines output by ps in
which Firefox was running; however, it didn't match
the line for grep because that line was actually
[f]irefox, which wouldn't match. The grep command
here can't match the original string ps -ef | grep
[f]irefox because it contained [and], and the grep
search for [f]irefox resolves to searching for the exact
word *firefox*. This is a bit confusing, but if you try it
yourself and think about it a bit, it'll make some sense.
At any rate, it works. Give it a try!

See Context for Words
Appearing in Files

-A, -B, -C

When dealing with data, context is everything. As
you've learned, grep outputs the actual line containing
the search term, but you can also tell grep to include
lines before and after the match. In the last section,
"Search the Output of Other Commands for Specific

Words," you used grep to work with a list of John
Coltrane albums. One of his best was *A Love Supreme*.
What three albums came out before that one? To get
the answer, use the -B (or --before-context=#) option.

```
$ ls -1 | grep -B 3 A_Love_Supreme
1963_Impressions
1963_John_Coltrane_&_Johnny_Hartman
1963_Live_At_Birdland
1964_A_Love_Supreme
```

If you want to find out what came after *A Love Supreme*,
use the -A (or --after-context=#) option instead.

```
$ ls -1 | grep -A 3 'A_Love_Supreme'
1964_A_Love_Supreme
1964_Coltrane's_Sound
1964_Crescent
1965_Ascension
```

To get the full historical context for *A Love Supreme*,
try the -C (or --context=#) option, which combines
before and after.

```
$ ls -1 | grep -C 2 'A_Love_Supreme'

1963_John_Coltrane_&_Johnny_Hartman
1963_Live_At_Birdland
1964_A_Love_Supreme
1964_Coltrane's_Sound
1964_Crescent
```

This can be a bit confusing when you have more than
one match in a file or group of files. For instance,
Coltrane released several live albums, and if you want
to see the albums just before and after those, you're
going to get more complex results.

```
$ ls -1 | grep -C 1 Live
1963_John_Coltrane_&_Johnny_Hartman
1963_Live_At_Birdland
1964_A_Love_Supreme
--
1965_Last_Trane
1965_Live_in_Seattle
1965_Major_Works_of_John_Coltrane
--
1965_Transition
1966_Live_at_the_Village_Vanguard_Again!
1966_Live_in_Japan
1967_Expression
1967_Olatunji_Concert_Last_Live_Recording
1967_Stellar_Regions
```

The -- characters separate each matched group. The
first two groups of results are obvious—an album with
Live in the title, preceded and followed by another
album—but the last section is a bit more complicated.
Several albums containing the word *Live* in the title are
right next to each other, so the results are bunched
together. It might look a bit weird, but if you look at
each instance of *Live*, you'll notice that the album
before and after it is in fact listed.

The results are even more informative if you incorporate
the -n option, which lists line numbers (because you're
using ls -1, it's the line number of that ls listing).

```
$ ls -1 | grep -n -C 1 Live
37-1963_John_Coltrane_&_Johnny_Hartman
38:1963_Live_At_Birdland
39-1964_A_Love_Supreme
--
48-1965_Last_Trane
49:1965_Live_in_Seattle
```

```
50-1965_Major_Works_of_John_Coltrane
--
52-1965_Transition
53:1966_Live_at_the_Village_Vanguard_Again!
54:1966_Live_in_Japan
55-1967_Expression
56-1967_Olatunji_Concert_Last_Live_Recording
57-1967_Stellar_Regions
```

Now -C gives you even more information about each line, as indicated by the character after the line number. A : indicates that the line matches, while a - means that it's a line before or after a match. Line 54, 1966_Live_in_Japan, does double duty. It comes after 1966_Live_at_the_Village_Vanguard_Again!, which should mean it has a -, but it is itself a match, which necessitates a :. Because a match is more important, that wins, and a : is ultimately used.

Show Lines Where Words Do Not Appear in Files

-v

In the jazz world, John Coltrane still rules nearly 40 years after his death; likewise, Led Zeppelin is recognized as one of the great all-time rock 'n' roll bands. While they were together, Led Zeppelin released nine albums; however, many of them had the band's name in the album title (yes, the fourth release didn't really have a title, but most critics still recognize it as *Led Zeppelin IV*, so humor me). What if you want to see a list of MP3 folders containing Led Zeppelin's albums, but exclude those that actually have the words *Led Zeppelin* in the title? With the -v (or --invert-match) option, you can show only results that *do not* match the given pattern.

```
$ ls -1
1969_Led_Zeppelin
1969_Led_Zeppelin_II
1970_Led_Zeppelin_III
1971_Led_Zeppelin_IV
1973_Houses_Of_The_Holy
1975_Physical_Graffiti
1976_Presence
1979_In_Through_The_Out_Door
1982_Coda
$ ls -1 | grep -v Led_Zeppelin
1973_Houses_Of_The_Holy
1975_Physical_Graffiti
1976_Presence
1979_In_Through_The_Out_Door
1982_Coda
```

With -v, you can really start to funnel your results to show only the exact items you need. You won't use -v all the time, but when you need it, you'll be glad it's available.

List Files Containing Searched-for Words

-1

The grep command lists the lines containing the term for which you searched, but there might be times when you don't want to know the lines; instead, you want to know the names of the files that contain those matched lines. Previously in "Search for Text in Files, Ignoring Case," you looked for lines in H.P. Lovecraft stories that contained the word *hideous*. With the -l (or --files-with-matches) option, you can instead produce a list of those files (the -i is for case-insensitive searches, remember).

```
$ grep -il hideous h_p_lovecraft/*
h_p_lovecraft/Call of Cthulhu.txt
h_p_lovecraft/From Beyond.txt
h_p_lovecraft/The Case of Charles Dexter Ward.txt
```

This type of result is particularly useful when combined with other commands. For example, if you wanted to print a list of Lovecraft's stories containing the word *hideous*, you could combine grep with the lpr command as follows:

```
$ grep -il hideous h_p_lovecraft/* | lpr
```

Keep in mind that this command would print out the list of stories, not the stories themselves (there is a way to do that, though, and here's a hint: It involves cat).

Search for Words Inside Search Results

grep | grep

What if you want a list of albums released by John Coltrane in the last two years of his career? Simple enough.

```
$ ls -1 | grep 196[6-7]

1966_Live_at_the_Village_Vanguard_Again!
1966_Live_in_Japan
```

```
1967_Expression
1967_Olatunji_Concert_Last_Live_Recording
1967_Stellar_Regions
```

The range [5-7] limits what would otherwise be a
much longer list to the years 1966–1967. So far, so
good, but what if you don't want to include any of his
live albums (which would normally be a horrible mistake, but let's pretend here)? Here's how to do it:

```
$ ls -1 | grep 196[6-7] | grep -v Live
1967_Expression
1967_Stellar_Regions
```

The -v option (which you learned about previously in
"Show Lines Where Words Do Not Appear in Files")
worked to strip out lines containing Live, but the really
interesting thing here is how you took the output of
ls -1, piped that to grep 196[6-7], and then piped the
output from that filter to a second instance of grep, this
one with -v Live. The final results are exactly what you
wanted: a list of all John Coltrane's albums, released
between 1966–1967, that do not contain Live in the
title. And that, my friends, shows you the power of the
Linux command line in a nutshell!

Conclusion

This chapter focused on two commands that you'll be
using often: locate and grep. Though they're related—
both assist the Linux user in finding files and information on his computer—they go about it in different
ways. The locate command searches the names of files
using a database of filenames to speed up its work,

while the grep command looks in real time within the contents of files to pull out the search terms.

As cool as both locate and grep are, they're just the beginning when it comes to searching your file system. The next chapter is about one of the most powerful and versatile commands on a Linux system, a command that perfectly complements, and in fact can work in tandem with, locate and grep. That command? The mighty find. Turn that page and let's get going!

10

The find **Command**

In the last chapter, we covered commands that let you search for files (locate) and data within files (grep). The third command in the powerful triumvirate is find. While locate searches a database for files, which makes it fast but dependent upon a constantly updated database, find searches for files on the fly using criteria that you specify. Since find has to parse through your file structure, it's much slower than locate, but you can do things with find that aren't possible with locate.

Throughout this chapter, we look for files on an external hard drive that contains music mounted at /media/music. You can see that find allows us to slice and dice the files in a variety of ways.

Find Files by Name

```
find -name
```

find is basically used to look for files by name, or part of a name (hence the -name option). By default, find is automatically recursive and searches down through a directory structure. Let's look for all MP3 files sung by the unique group the Shaggs on the music drive:

```
$ cd /media/music
$ find . -name Shaggs
./Outsider/Shaggs
```

What? This can't be correct! The find command found the folder, but not the songs. Why? Because we didn't use any wildcards, find looked for files specifically named "Shaggs." There is only one item with that precise name: the folder that contains the songs. (Since a folder is a special kind of file, it's counted!)

We need to use wildcards, but in order to prevent the shell from interpreting the wildcards in ways we don't intend, we need to surround what we're searching for with quotation marks. Let's try the search again with our new improvements:

```
$ find . -name "*Shaggs*"
./Outsider/Shaggs
./Outsider/Shaggs/Gimme_Dat_Ting_(Live).mp3
./Outsider/Shaggs/My_Pal_Foot_Foot.ogg
./Outsider/Shaggs/I_Love.mp3
./Outsider/Shaggs/Things_I_Wonder.ogg
```

We surrounded the wildcards with quotation marks; lo and behold, we found the folder and the files.

NOTE: Another option to find that you've been using without realizing it is -print. The -print option tells find to list the results of its search on the terminal. The -print option is on by default, so you don't need to include it when you run find.

Another important aspect of find is that the format of your results is dependent upon the path searched. Previously, we used a relative path, so our results were given to us as relative paths. What would happen if we used an absolute path—one that begins with a /—instead?

```
$ find / -name "*Shaggs*"
/music/Outsider/Shaggs
/music/Outsider/Shaggs/Gimme_Dat_Ting_(Live).mp3
/music/Outsider/Shaggs/My_Pal_Foot_Foot.ogg
/music/Outsider/Shaggs/I_Love.mp3
/music/Outsider/Shaggs/Things_I_Wonder.ogg
```

If you search using a relative path, your results use a relative path; if you search using an absolute path, your results use an absolute path. We'll see other uses of this principle later in the chapter. For now, just keep this important idea in mind.

NOTE: To find out more about the Shaggs, see www.allmusic.com/cg/amg.dll?p=amg&sql=11:qyk9kett7q7q, or just search www.allmusic.com for "Shaggs." You haven't lived until you've played "My Pal Foot Foot" at your next party!

Find Files by Ownership

```
find -user
```

In addition to searching for files by name, you can also search for files by owner. Do you want to find the files on the music drive owned by scott? Use find with the -user option, followed by the user name (or the user number, which you can find in /etc/passwd):

```
$ find . -user scott
```

Whoa! There are way too many results! It might be easier to look for files that are *not* owned by scott. To do so, put a ! in front of the option you wish to reverse:

NOTE: In order to conserve space, some of the data you'd normally see with ls -l has been removed.

```
$ find . ! -user scott
./Outsider/Wing/01_-_Dancing_Queen.mp3
$ ls -l ./Outsider/Wing/01_-_Dancing_Queen.mp3
gus music ./Outsider/Wing/01_-_Dancing_Queen.mp3
```

Ah... one song by Wing is owned by gus instead of scott. To fix this problem, we need to use chown (covered in Chapter 7, "Ownerships and Permissions"). Keep in mind that you can always use the ! as a NOT operator (which is saying, for example, "find files where the user is *not* scott").

NOTE: Ah, Wing. First introduced to the world at large in an episode of *South Park*, her website can be found at www. wingtunes.com. Wing's version of "Dancing Queen" is highly recommended, as is her rendition of "I Want to Hold Your Hand."

Find Files by Group Ownership

`file -group`

If an option that allows you to work with users is available for a command, you know that an option for groups is also probably present. The find command is no different: If you want to look for files owned by a particular group, just use -group, followed by the group's name or number. On the music drive, scott should be the owner and music should be the group. Let's see if there are any files that aren't in the music group:

```
$ find . ! -group music
./Disco/Brides_of_Funkenstein_-_Disco_to_Go.mp3
./Disco/Sister_Sledge_-_He's_The_Greatest_Dancer.mp3
./Disco/Wild_Cherry_-_Play_That_Funky_Music.mp3
./Electronica/New_Order/Bizarre_Love_Triangle.mp3
```

There are only four files out of a large number of files that aren't in the music group. Now we need to run chgrp (see Chapter 7) on these files to make everything on the drive exactly the same.

Notice that, once again, we used ! to say, "Find the files that are *not* owned by the music group."

Find Files by File Size

file -size

Sometimes you'll want to find files based on their size. The find command can assist here as well. To specify a size, use the -size option, followed by a letter representing the size scheme you wish to use. If you don't provide a letter, the default is used; however, you should understand that you probably won't find what you want. If you don't append a letter after the number, the default is in bytes (which is then divided by 512 and rounded up to the next integer). This is too much math. It's easier to use a suffix after the number that represents the size in more common terms, as shown in Table 10.1.

TABLE 10.1   Find Files by Size

Suffix	Meaning
b	512-byte blocks (the default)
c	Bytes
k	Kilobytes (KB)
M	Megabytes (MB)
G	Gigabytes (GB)

Let's say we want to find every Clash song from their immortal album, *London Calling*, that is 10MB. (Yes, these were encoded at a super-high rate.) This job is easy enough with find:

```
$ cd Punk/Clash/1979_London_Calling
$ find . -size 10M
./07_-_The_Right_Profile.ogg
./08_-_Lost_In_The_Supermarket.ogg
./09_-_Clampdown.ogg
./12_-_Death_Or_Glory.ogg
```

That's weird. Only four songs? Here's where you need to understand a "gotcha" associated with using find: If you say 10M, then find looks for files that are exactly 10MB in size (rounded to 10MB, of course). If you want files larger than 10MB, you need to place a plus sign (+) in front of the given size; if you want files smaller than 10MB, use a minus sign (-) in front of the size:

```
$ find . -size +10M
./Jimmy_Jazz.ogg
./ Lover's_Rock.ogg
./ Revolution_Rock.ogg
```

Now we have a problem. Specifying 10M gives us files that are exactly 10MB, excluding those that are bigger, while specifying +10M gives us files that are larger than 10MB, excluding those that are exactly 10MB. How do we get both? If you want to learn how to obtain files that are 10MB and larger, see the "Show Results If Either Expression Is True (OR)" section later in this chapter.

TIP: If you want to find large text files, use c after your number. As Table 10.1 shows, c changes the search size to bytes. Every character in a text file is a byte, so an easy way to remember c is to associate it with the "characters" in a text file.

For instance, to find enormous text files, you can use this code:

```
$ find /home/scott/documents -size +500000c
```

Find Files by File Type

`find -type`

One of the most useful options for find is -type, which allows you to specify the type of object you wish to look for. Remember that everything on a UNIX system is a file (covered back in Chapter 1, "Things to Know About Your Command Line," in the "Everything Is a File" section), so what you're actually indicating is the type of file you want find to ferret out for you. Table 10.2 lists the file types you can use with find.

TABLE 10.2   Finding Files by Type

File Type Letter	Meaning
f	Regular file
d	Directory
l	Symbolic (soft) link

TABLE 10.2   Continued

File Type Letter	Meaning
b	Block special file
c	Character special file
p	FIFO (First In First Out)
s	Socket

Let's say we want a quick list of the Steely Dan albums we have on the music drive. Since all songs are placed into directories by album, look for folders with -type d:

```
$ cd /media/music/Rock
$ find Steely_Dan/ -type d
Steely_Dan/
Steely_Dan/1980_Gaucho
Steely_Dan/1975_Katy_Lied
Steely_Dan/1974_Pretzel_Logic
Steely_Dan/1976_The_Royal_Scam
Steely_Dan/2000_Two_Against_Nature
Steely_Dan/1972_Can't_Buy_A_Thrill
Steely_Dan/1973_Countdown_To_Ecstasy
Steely_Dan/1977_Aja
```

This list is helpful, but since the name of every album directory begins with the year the album was released, we can sort by year for more precise information:

```
$ cd /media/music/Rock
$ find Steely_Dan/ -type d | sort
Steely_Dan/
Steely_Dan/1972_Can't_Buy_A_Thrill
Steely_Dan/1973_Countdown_To_Ecstasy
Steely_Dan/1974_Pretzel_Logic
Steely_Dan/1975_Katy_Lied
Steely_Dan/1976_The_Royal_Scam
```

```
Steely_Dan/1977_Aja
Steely_Dan/1980_Gaucho
Steely_Dan/2000_Two_Against_Nature
```

It can be incredibly beneficial to use a pipe to filter the list you generate with find; as you get better with find, you'll see that you do this more and more.

Show Results If the Expressions Are True (AND)

```
find -a
```

A key feature of find is the ability to join several options to more tightly focus your searches. You can link together as many options as you'd like with -a (or -and). For example, if you want to list every song performed by the world's greatest rock 'n' roll band, the Rolling Stones, you might use just -name "Rolling_Stones*" at first, but that wouldn't necessarily work. Some folders have Rolling_Stones in them, and there may be a soft link or two with the band's name in it as well. We, therefore, also need to use -type f. Combine them as follows:

```
$ find . -name "Rolling_Stones*" -a -type f
1968_Beggars_Banquet/03_-_Dear_Doctor.mp3
1968_Beggars_Banquet/01_-_Sympathy_For_The_Devil.mp3
1968_Beggars_Banquet/02_-_No_Expectations.mp3
1968_Beggars_Banquet/04_-_Parachute_Woman.mp3
1968_Beggars_Banquet/05_-_Jig-Saw_Puzzle.mp3
1968_Beggars_Banquet/06_-_Street_Fighting_Man.mp3
```

That's cool, but how many Stones tunes do we have? Pipe the results of find to wc (which stands for "word count"), but also use the -1 option, which gives you the number of lines instead of the word count:

```
$ find . -name "Rolling_Stones*" -a -type f | wc -l
317
```

Three hundred and seventeen Rolling Stones songs. Sweet. In this case, you *can* always get what you want.

NOTE: If you have no idea what that last sentence means, get yourself a copy of the album *Let It Bleed* now. Don't forget to play it loud.

Show Results If Either Expression Is True (OR)

`find -o`

Earlier, in the section "Find Files by File Size," we saw that we could use find to list every Clash song on *London Calling* that was exactly 10MB, and we could use find to list songs on *London Calling* that were more than 10MB, but we couldn't do both at the same time with -size. In the previous section, we saw that -a combines options using AND; however, we can also utilize -o (or -or) to combine options using OR.

So, in order to find songs from *London Calling* that are 10MB or larger, we use the following command:

```
$ cd London_Calling
$ find . -size +10M -o -size 10M
03_-_Jimmy_Jazz.ogg
07_-_The_Right_Profile.ogg
08_-_Lost_In_The_Supermarket.ogg
```

```
09_-_Clampdown.ogg
12_-_Death_Or_Glory.ogg
15_-_Lover's_Rock.ogg
18_-_Revolution_Rock.ogg
(25th_Anniversary)_-_18_-_Revolution_Rock.mp3
(25th_Anniversary)_-_37_-_Heart_And_Mind.mp3
(25th_Anniversary)_-_ 39_-_London_Calling_(Demo).mp3
```

Oops...we also got results from the 25th Anniversary release of *London Calling* as well, which we didn't want. We need to do two things: exclude results from the 25th Anniversary edition and make sure that our OR statement works correctly.

To exclude the 25th Anniversary songs, we add ! -name "*25*" at the end of our command. To make sure that OR works, we need to surround it with parentheses, which combines the statements. However, you need to escape the parentheses with backslashes so the shell doesn't misinterpret them, and you also need to put spaces before and after your statement. The combination gives us this command:

```
$ cd London_Calling
$ find . \( -size +10M -o -size 10M \) ! -name
"*25*"
03_-_Jimmy_Jazz.ogg
07_-_The_Right_Profile.ogg
08_-_Lost_In_The_Supermarket.ogg
09_-_Clampdown.ogg
12_-_Death_Or_Glory.ogg
15_-_Lover's_Rock.ogg
18_-_Revolution_Rock.ogg
```

Perfect. Seven songs are 10MB or greater in size.

NOTE: Read about *London Calling* at Allmusic.com (www.allmusic.com/cg/amg.dll?p=amg&sql=10:aeu1z82ajyvn) or Pitchfork (www.pitchforkmedia.com/record-reviews/c/clash/london-calling.shtml).

We can also use -o to find out how many songs we have on the music drive. We might start with this command, which we run from the root of /media/music, and which uses -a (be patient; we'll get to -o):

```
$ find . -name "*mp3*" -a -type f | wc -l
23407
```

Twenty-three thousand? That's not right. Ah, now it's obvious. We were only searching for mp3 files, and an enormous amount of songs was encoded in the superior Ogg Vorbis format, a patent-free, open source alternative to mp3. Let's look for mp3 or ogg files and count the results with wc -l:

```
$ find . \( -name "*mp3*" -o -name "*.ogg*" \) -a
➥-type f | wc -l
41631
```

That sounds much better, but there are also some FLAC files on there. Let's add another -o to the mix:

```
$ find . \( -name "*mp3*" -o -name "*.ogg*" -o -name
➥"*.flac*" \) -a -type f | wc -l
42187
```

Now that's more like it: 42,000 songs and growing!

Show Results If the Expression Is Not True (NOT)

```
find -n
```

We have already used ! to negate expressions in earlier sections in this chapter (see "Find Files By Ownership" and "Show Results If Either Expression Is True (OR)"), but let's take another, longer look at this operator. In the previous section, we used find to determine how many mp3, ogg, and flac files we have on the music drive. But how many total files do we have on the drive?

```
$ find . -name "*" | wc -l
52111
```

Hmm…52,000 total files, but only 42,000 are mp3, ogg, or flac. What are the others? Let's construct a find command that excludes files that end in .mp3, .ogg, or .flac while also excluding directories. Wrap these four conditions in parentheses, and then place ! before the command to indicate our wish to negate these items and instead look for things that do not match these specifications:

```
$ find . ! \( -name "*mp*" -o -name "*ogg" -o
➥-name "*flac" -o -type d \)
./Folk/Joan_Baez/Joan_Baez_-_Imagine.m3u
./500_Greatest_Singles/singles.txt
./Blues/Muddy_Waters/Best_Of.m3u
./Blues/Robert_Johnson/Hellhound_On_My_Trail.MP3
./Blues/Johnny_Winter/Johnny_Winter.m3u [Results
truncated for length]
```

Now we have the answer, or at least we're starting to get an answer. We have m3u (playlist) files, text files, and files that end in MP3 instead of mp3 (we also have

JPEGs, GIFs, and even music videos). The find command, like all of Linux, is case-sensitive (as discussed in Chapter 1), so a search for "*mp3*" will not turn up songs that have the .MP3 suffix. Is there any quick and easy way to change these files so that they have the correct, lowercase extension? Sure. And we'll use find to do it.

Execute a Command on Every Found File

```
find -exec
```

Now we enter the area in which find really shows off its power: the ability to execute commands on the files that it, uh, finds. After listing the options that help narrow down your search—such as -name, -type, or -user—append -exec along with the commands you want to run on each individual file. You use the symbols {} to represent each file, and end your command with \ to escape the semicolon so your shell doesn't interpret it as an indication of command stacking (which we discussed in Chapter 4, "Building Blocks").

In the previous section, for example, we discovered that some of the files on the music drive ended with MP3. Since we prefer lowercase extensions, we need to convert all instances of MP3 to mp3 to make the files consistent. We can do this with the -exec option for find. First, let's verify that there are files that end with MP3:

```
$ find . -name "Robert_Johnson*MP3"
./Blues/Robert_Johnson/Judgment_Day.MP3
./Blues/Robert_Johnson/Dust_My_Broom.MP3
./Blues/Robert_Johnson/Hellhound_On_My_Trail.MP3
```

Let's use find with -exec to change the file extension. The program we can use with -exec is rename, which changes parts of filenames:

```
$ find . -name " *MP3" -exec rename
➥'s/MP3/mp3/g' {} \;
```

The rename command is followed with instructions for the name change in this format: s/old/new/g. (The s stands for "substitute," while the g stands for "global.") Now let's see if our command works:

```
$ find . -name "Robert_Johnson*MP3"
$ ls -1 Blues/Robert_Johnson/
Hellhound_On_My_Trail.mp3
Judgment_Day.mp3
Dust_My_Broom.mp3
Love_in_Vain.mp3
Me_and_the_Devil_Blues.mp3
```

The command appears to work. Let's try a similar process with another situation. In the previous section, we noticed that many of the results discovered were m3u, or playlist, files. Unfortunately, many of these files had spaces in the filenames, which we try to avoid. Let's first generate a list of m3u files that have spaces. We can search for * *m3u, which uses wildcards around a space to discover files that include spaces in their name:

```
$ find . -name "* *m3u"
./Christmas/Christmas With The Rat Pack.m3u
./Christmas/Holiday_Boots_4_Your_Stockings.m3u
./Classical_Baroque/Handel/Chamber Music.m3u
./Classical_Opera/Famous Arias.m3u
./Doo_Wop/Doo Wop Box.m3u
./Electronica/Aphex_Twin/I Care Because You Do.m3u
```

Now let's find m3u files with spaces in their names; when one is found, we can run rename against it. We're substituting "\ " (we escape the space so that find understands what we're looking for and the shell doesn't get confused) with "_" to fix the problem:

```
$ find . -name "* *m3u" -exec rename 's/\ /_/g' {}
\;
$ find . -name "* *m3u"
$
```

The command worked as planned.

NOTE: Note that before running commands on the files, we must always first figure out which files are going to be changed. That's just good prudence. You don't want to change the wrong files!

Print Find Results into a File

`find -fprint`

Every time we've used find, we have assumed that the -print option isn't necessary because it's on by default. If you want to print to a file instead of the terminal, you use the -fprint option, followed by the name of the file you want to create.

```
$ find . ! \( -name "*mp*" -o -name "*ogg" -o -name
➥"*flac" -o -type d \) -fprint non_music_files.txt
$ cat non_music_files.txt
./Folk/Joan_Baez/Joan_Baez_-_Imagine.m3u
./500_Greatest_Singles/singles.txt
./Blues/Muddy_Waters/Best_Of.m3u
./Blues/Robert_Johnson/Hellhound_On_My_Trail.MP3
./Blues/Johnny_Winter/Johnny_Winter.m3u
```

You can then use these results in scripts, or send them to a printer if that would be helpful.

Conclusion

As you can tell, you can do a lot with find. There are still plenty of things that find can do, so you really should look at man find or read several of the excellent tutorials available on the World Wide Web that cover the more arcane—yet useful—aspects of the command. You can use find to search for and list files and folders using an amazing variety of options. It really becomes invaluable, however, when you use the -exec option to run commands on the discovered files, or when you pipe the output to other commands. This is one of the greatest commands available to you on your Linux box, so start using it!

11

Your Shell

So far in this book you've been running commands in your bash shellbut you haven't focused on the shell itself. In this chapter, you look at two commands that affect your use of the shell: history, which lists everything you've entered on the command line, and alias, which allows you to create shortcuts for commands. Both are useful, and both can save you lots of time when you're using the command line. Laziness is a good thing when it comes to computer users, and these are definitely two commands that will help you be as lazy as possible when using your Linux box.

View Your Command-Line History

`history`

Every time you type a command in your shell, that command is saved in a file named .bash_history in your home directory (the dot in front of the filename means that it's hidden unless you use ls -a). By default, that file holds the last 500 lines entered on the command line. If you want to view that list of commands, just enter the **history** command.

```
$ history

  496  ls
  497  cd rsync_ssh
  498  ls
  499  cat linux
  500  exit
```

Because you're looking at 500 results, they're going to stream by so fast that you can't see any until you get to the end. Want to step through the results one screen at a time? Turn to your old friend less:

```
$ history | less
```

Now you can jump through your results much more easily.

CAUTION: Now you understand why you need to be careful typing passwords and other sensitive information on the command line: Anyone who can view your .bash_history file is able to see those passwords. Be careful and think about what you enter directly on the command line!

Run the Last Command Again

```
!!
```

If you want to run the last command you used a second time, enter two exclamation points. That looks in the history file and runs the last command in the list.

```
$ pwd
/home/scott
$ !!
pwd
/home/scott
```

Notice that you first see the actual command that's
going to run, and then the results of that command.
This is a truly useful way to have your computer do
tedious work for you.

Run a Previous Command
Using Numbers

`![##]`

When you run history, it automatically places a number in front of every previous command. If you'd like
to run a previous command and you know the number
that history has assigned to it, just enter an exclamation point immediately followed by that command's
history number, and it will run again.

```
$ pwd
/home/scott
$ whoami
scott
$ !499
pwd
/home/scott
```

If you're unsure about the number, run history again
to find out. Be aware that the pwd command in this
example was number 499 the first time, but after I ran
it again using !499, it became 498 because it was
pushed down on the list by my new command.

Run a Previous Command Using a String

`![string]`

The capability to run a command again by referencing its number is nice, but it requires that you know the command's number in history, which can be tedious to discover (piping the output of history to grep would help, but it's still not optimal). Often a better way to reference a previously entered command is by the actual command's name. If you follow the exclamation point by the first few letters of that command, your shell runs the first command it finds when looking backward in .bash_history.

```
$ cat /home/scott/todo
Buy milk
Buy dog food
Renew Linux Magazine subscription
$ cd /home/scott/pictures
$ !cat
cat /home/scott/todo
Buy milk
Buy dog food
Renew Linux Magazine subscription
```

If the cat command is found three times in your history—at 35 (cat /home/scott/todo), 412 (cat /etc/apt/sources.list), and 496 (cat /home/scott/todo)—and you enter !cat, the one found at 496 is the one that runs. If you want to run the cat found at 412, you need to run either !412 or follow the exclamation mark with enough information so it can tell you're referencing the command listed as 412.

```
$ !cat /etc
cat /etc/apt/sources.list
deb http://us.archive.ubuntu.com/ubuntu breezy main
➥restricted
deb-src http://us.archive.ubuntu.com/ubuntu breezy
➥main restricted
```

Because humans have a far easier time remembering words instead of numbers, you'll probably end up using this method for invoking past commands. If you're ever unsure, run history and take a look.

Display All Command Aliases

alias

If you use a command all the time, or if a command is just particularly long and onerous to type, it behooves you to make that command an alias. After you've created an alias, you type its name, and the command referenced by the alias runs. Of course, if a command is particularly complicated or involves several lines, you should instead turn it into a script or function. But for small things, aliases are perfect.

Aliases are stored in a file in your home directory. You might find them in .bashrc, but more likely (or more properly, rather) they're in .bash_aliases. Most Linux distributions come with several aliases already defined for you; to see that list, just enter **alias** on the command line.

```
$ alias
alias la='ls -a'
alias ll='ls -l'
```

Most distributions purposely keep the default aliases to a minimum. It's up to you to add new ones, as you'll shortly see.

View a Specific Command Alias

```
alias [alias name]
```

After you've defined several aliases, it can be hard to find a specific one if you type in the **alias** command. If you want to review what a specific alias does, just follow alias by the name of the specific alias about which you want to learn more.

```
$ alias wgetpage
alias wgetpage='wget --html-extension --recursive
➥--convert-links --page-requisites --no-parent $1'
```

Now you know exactly what the wgetpage alias does, quickly and easily.

NOTE: You'll learn more about wget in Chapter 15, "Working on the Network."

Create a New Temporary Alias

```
alias [alias]='[command]'
```

If you find yourself typing a command over and over again, maybe it's time to make it an alias. For instance, to see just the subdirectories in your current working directory, you'd use ls -d */. To create a temporary alias for that command, use the following:

```
$ ls -d */
by_pool/  libby_pix/  on_floor/
$ alias lsd='ls -d */'
$ lsd
by_pool/  libby_pix/  on_floor/
```

You should realize a couple of things about using alias
in this way. Your alias name can't have an = in it, which
makes sense, because it's immediately followed by an =
when you're defining it. You can, however, have an = in
the actual alias itself. Also, an alias created in this fashion only lasts as long as this shell session is active. Log
out, and your alias is gone.

Want to create an alias that lasts past when you log out?
Then read the next section, "Create a New Permanent
Alias."

Create a New Permanent Alias

```
alias [alias name]='[command]'
```

If you want your aliases to stick around between shell ses-
sions, you need to add them to the file your shell uses to
store aliases. Most of the time that file is either .bashrc or
.bash_aliases; in this case, you're going to use .bash_
aliases. No matter which file it is, be careful editing it, as
you can cause yourself problems later when logging in. If
you want to be really careful, create a backup of the file
before editing it. Better safe than sorry.

NOTE: How can you find out which file you should use?
Simple: Type ls -a ~. If you see .bash_aliases, use that;
otherwise, look in .bashrc and see if other aliases are
defined in there. If you don't see any aliases in there, take
a look at .profile, which is occasionally used.

To add an alias to .bash_aliases, open it with your favorite text editor and add a line like the following:

```
alias lsd='ls -d */'
```

The same rule discussed in "Create a New Temporary Alias" applies here as well: Your alias name can't have an = in it. After adding your alias to .bash_aliases, save the file and close it. But the alias doesn't work yet. The .bash_aliases file (or .bashrc if that's what you used) needs to be reloaded for the new alias to work. You can do this in two ways. You can either log out and then log in again, which is a pain and not recommended, or you can just reload the file by running this command:

```
$ . .bash_aliases
```

That's a dot, followed by a space, followed by the name of the file, which begins with a dot. Now your new alias will work. Because you have to reload the file every time you add an alias, it's a good idea to add several at a time to lessen the hassle.

Remove an Alias

unalias

All good things must come to an end, and sometimes an alias outlives its usefulness. To remove an alias, use the unalias command.

```
$ ls -d */
by_pool/  libby_pix/  on_floor/
$ alias lsd='ls -d */'
$ lsd
by_pool/  libby_pix/  on_floor/
$ unalias lsd
```

```
$ lsd
$
```

Note, though, that this command only works permanently for temporary shell aliases, discussed previously in "Create a New Temporary Alias." The lsd alias in the previous example is gone for good. If you use the unalias command on an alias found in .bash_aliases, it too will be gone, but only as long as you're logged in. When you log out and log back in, or reload .bash_aliases, the alias is back.

To remove aliases from .bash_aliases, you need to edit the file and manually remove the line containing the alias. If you think there's a chance you might want to reuse the alias again sometime, just put a pound sign (which comments it out) in front of the alias, like this:

```
# alias lsd='ls -d */'
```

Save .bash_aliases, reload it with the . .bash_aliases command, and the alias won't work any longer. But if you ever need it again, open .bash_aliases, remove the pound sign, save and reload the file, and it's good to go again.

Conclusion

One of your goals as a Linux user should be reducing the amount of characters you have to type to accomplish your goals. The original developers of Unix were strong believers in that concept—that's why you enter ls instead of list and mkdir instead of makedirectory.

The commands you've learned about in this chapter—
history and alias—both aid in that process. Tired of
typing a long and complicated command? Reference it
with history, or create an alias for it. Either way, you'll
save keystrokes, and your keyboard (and, more importantly, your hands and wrists) will thank you for it.

## 12

Monitoring System Resources

A good computer user has to be a bit of a systems administrator, always checking the health of her machine to make sure that everything is running smoothly. To help achieve that goal, Linux has several commands to monitor system resources. In this chapter, you're going to look at several of those commands. Many of them have multiple uses, but all—in the best Unix tradition of small tools that solve a single task well—are especially good at one particular aspect of system monitoring. Their tasks range from keeping track of the programs running on your computer (ps and top) to ending errant processes (kill) to listing all open files (lsof) to reporting your system's usage of RAM (free) and hard disk space (df and du). Learn these tools well. You'll find yourself using them in all sorts of situations.

View All Currently Running Processes

```
ps aux
```

Every once in a while a program you're running locks up and stops responding, requiring that you close it. Or you might want to know what programs a certain user is running. Or you might just want to know about the processes currently running on your machine. In any of those cases and many others, you want to use the ps command that lists open processes on your computer.

Unfortunately, ps has many versions, and they have different types of options. They can even have different meanings, depending on whether those options are preceded by a hyphen, so that u and -u mean completely different things. Up to now, this book has been pretty strict about preceding all options with a hyphen, but for ps, it's not, as it makes things a bit easier and more uniform.

To see all the processes that any user is running on your system, follow ps with these options: a (which means *all users*), u (*user-oriented*, or show the user who owns each process), and x (*processes without controlling ttys, or terminal screens*, another way of saying "show every process"). Be forewarned that a fairly long list is going to zoom by on your screen: 132 lines on this computer.

```
$ ps aux
USER      PID %CPU %MEM    VSZ   RSS TTY   STAT START
➥TIME COMMAND

scott 24224  4.1  4.2 1150440 44036 ?     R     11:02
➥12:03 /home/scott/.cxoffice/bin/wine-preloader
```

```
scott  5594  0.0  0.1   3432  1820 pts/6 S+  12:14
➥0:00 ssh scott@humbug.machine.com

scott 14957  0.3  7.5 171144 78628 ?      S1  13:01
➥0:35 /usr/lib/openoffice2/program/soffice.bin
➥-writer

scott 12369  0.0  0.0      0     0 ?      Z   15:43
➥0:00 [wine-preloader] <defunct>

scott 14680  0.0  0.1   3860  1044 pts/5 R+  15:55
➥0:00 ps aux
```

The ps command gives you a lot of information,
including the user who owns the process, the unique
process ID number (PID) that identifies the process,
the percentage of the CPU (%CPU) and memory (%MEM)
that the process is using, the current status (STAT) of the
process, and the name of the process itself.

The STAT column can have different letters in it, with
the following being the most important:

STAT Letter	Meaning
R	Running
S	Sleeping
T	Stopped
Z	Zombie

A Z is bad news because it means that the process has
basically hung and cannot be stopped (fortunately, it
does *not* mean that it will try to eat your brain). If
you're having a problem with a program and ps indicates that it has a status of Z, you're probably going to
have to reboot the machine to completely kill it.

Because ps aux provides you with a lot of data, it can be
difficult to find the program for which you're searching.

Piping the output of ps aux to grep can be an easy way to limit the results to a particular command.

```
$ ps aux | grep [f]irefox
scott 25205  0.0  0.0   4336      8 ?          S
➥Feb08   0:00 /bin/sh /opt/firefox/firefox

scott 25213  1.1 10.9 189092 113272 ?         Rl
➥Feb08  29:42 /opt/firefox/firefox-bin
```

Now you know just the instances of Firefox running on this machine, including who's running the program, how much of a load on the machine that program is, and how long that program has been running. Useful!

TIP: Why did you search for [f]irefox instead of firefox? To find the answer, take a look in Chapter 9, "Finding Stuff: Easy," in the "Search the Output of Other Commands for Specific Words" section.

View a Process Tree

`ps axjf`

In the Linux world, processes don't just appear out of thin air. Often, starting one program starts other programs. All processes on a Linux system, for instance, ultimately come from init, the mother of all processes, which always has a PID of 1. The ps command can provide you with a text-based representation of this process tree so you can visually see what processes have spawned others. To see the process tree, use the a, u, and x options, used in the previous section, along with the f (the evocatively named *ASCII art forest*) option.

NOTE: Normally you'd see the following columns:

PPID PID PGID SID TTY TPGID STAT UID TIME
➥COMMAND

In the interests of making the command tree easier to understand, most of the columns you'd actually see with ps axuf have been removed in the following code listing.

```
$ ps axuf
PPID    PID  COMMAND
   1   7558  /usr/sbin/gdm
7558   7561  \_ /usr/sbin/gdm
7561   7604      \_ /usr/X11R6/bin/X :0
7561   8225      \_ /bin/sh /usr/bin/startkde
8225   8279          \_ /usr/bin/ssh-agent
8225   8341          \_ kwrapper ksmserver
   1   8316  kdeinit Running...
8316  10842  \_ konqueror [kdeinit] --silent
8316  29663  \_ quanta
8316  30906  \_ /usr/bin/kwrite /home/scott/analysis
8316  17893  \_ /usr/lib/opera/9.0-20060206.1/opera
17893 17960  |   \_ /usr/lib/opera/pluginwrapper
17893 17961  |   \_ /usr/lib/opera/plugincleaner
```

Note that ps axjf introduces a key new column, PPID. PPID, the Parent Process ID number, is the number of the process that spawned the PID. Armed with the PID or PPID, you can end runaway processes, as you'll see soon in "End a Running Process."

View Processes Owned by a Particular User

```
ps U [username]
```

Up to now you've been looking at how ps gives you a list of all processes on your system. If you want to limit the results to those owned by a single user, simply use the U option, followed by the username or number.

```
$ ps U scott
  PID TTY    STAT TIME COMMAND
14928 ?      S    0:00 /opt/ooo2/program/soffice
➡-writer
14957 ?      Sl   0:42 /opt/ooo2/program/soffice.bin
➡-writer
 4688 pts/4 S+   0:00 ssh scott@humbug.machine.com
26751 ?      Z    0:00 [wine-preloader] <defunct>
27955 pts/5 R+   0:00 ps U scott
```

Of course, ps doesn't include the username in the listing because it was already part of the command.

TIP: Remember, if you don't know the user's number, just look in /etc/passwd. Find the username, and the user number is in the third column.

End a Running Process

```
kill
```

Sometimes a program goes rogue, and it won't react to normal attempts to close it. In the GUI, you click repeatedly on the Close button, but nothing happens, or, in the shell, you press Ctrl+C but it fails to stop a running command. When this happens, it's time for the `kill` command.

You can use several signals with the `kill` command, ranging from "Please shut yourself down, cleaning up your mess as you do so" to "Shut yourself down as soon as you can" to "Die *now!*" You're going to focus on the three most important. When you use `kill`, you can specify the intensity of the process's death with a number or a word, as Table 12.1 shows.

Table 12.1   Common Signals Associated with `kill`

Signal Number	Signal Word	Meaning
-1	-HUP (*hang up*)	Controlling process has died. Shut down (if applied to a system service, reload configuration files and restart).
-15	-TERM	Terminate gracefully, cleaning up stray processes and files.
-9	-KILL	Stop whatever you're doing and die now!

Normally, you should first try -15 (in fact, it's the default if you run `kill` without any option). That way, you give the program a chance to shut down any other programs depending upon it, close files opened by it, and so on. If you've been patient and waited a while ("a while" is completely subjective, of course), and the process is still running completely out of control or still failing to respond, you can bring out the big guns and use -9. The -9 option is equivalent to yanking the rug out from under a running program, and while it does the job, it could leave stray files and processes littering your system, and that's never a good idea.

As for -1, or -HUP, that's primarily for services such as Samba or wireless connectivity. You won't use it much, but you should know what it means.

Here's what you would do if gvim (which normally behaves just fine; this is just for demonstration purposes) seemed to freeze on your system.

```
$ ps U scott
  PID TTY    STAT TIME COMMAND
14928 ?      S    0:00 /opt/ooo2/program/soffice
➥-writer
14957 ?      Sl   0:42 /opt/ooo2/program/soffice.bin
➥-writer
 4688 pts/4 S+   0:00 ssh scott@humbug.machine.com
26751 ?      Z    0:00 [wine-preloader] <defunct>
27921 ?      Ss   0:00 /usr/bin/gvim
27955 pts/5 R+   0:00 ps U scott
$ kill 27921
$ ps U scott
  PID TTY    STAT TIME COMMAND
14928 ?      S    0:00 /opt/ooo2/program/soffice
➥-writer
14957 ?      Sl   0:42 /opt/ooo2/program/soffice.bin
➥-writer
 4688 pts/4 S+   0:00 ssh scott@humbug.machine.com
26751 ?      Z    0:00 [wine-preloader] <defunct>
27955 pts/5 R+   0:00 ps U scott
```

To kill gvim, you use ps to find gvim's PID, which in this case is 27921. Next you kill that PID (and remember that kill uses the TERM signal by default) and then check again with ps. Yes, gvim is no more.

> **NOTE:** Why didn't you kill PID 26751, which has a STAT of
> Z, indicating that it's a zombie? Because even -9 doesn't
> work on a zombie—it's already dead, hence the kill com-
> mand won't work. A reboot is the only way to fix that
> (usually unimportant) problem.

View a Dynamically Updated List of Running Processes

top

On occasion you'll find that your Linux machine suddenly slows down, apparently for no reason. Something
is running on your computer at full tilt, and it's using
up the processor. Or perhaps you'll start running a
command, only to find that it's using far more of your
CPU's cycles than you thought it would. To find out
what's causing the problem, or if you just want to find
out what's running on your system, you could use ps,
except that ps doesn't update itself. Instead, it provides
a snapshot of your system's processes, and that's it.

The top command, on the other hand, provides a
dynamically updated view of what's running on your
system and how many system resources each process is
using. It's a bit hard to see in a book because you can't
see top update its display every second, but here's what
you would see at one moment while top is running.

```
$ top
top - 18:05:03 up 4 days, 8:03, 1 user, load
➥average: 0.83, 0.82, 0.97
Tasks: 135 total, 3 running, 126 sleeping, 2
➥stopped, 4 zombie
```

```
Cpu(s): 22.9% us, 7.7% sy, 3.1% ni, 62.1% id,
➥3.5% wa, 0.1% hi, 0.7% si
Mem:    1036136k total, 987996k used,   48140k free,
➥27884k buffers
Swap: 1012084k total, 479284k used, 532800k free,
➥179580k cached
  PID USER   PR NI  VIRT  RES  SHR S %CPU %MEM
➥TIME+  COMMAND
25213 scott  15  0  230m 150m  15m S 11.1 14.9
➥33:39.34 firefox-bin
 7604 root   15  0  409m 285m 2896 S 10.8 28.2
➥749:55.75 Xorg
 8378 scott  15  0 37084  10m 7456 S  1.0  1.1
➥13:53.99 kicker
 8523 scott  15  0 69416  13m 3324 S  0.7  1.3
➥63:35.14 skype
29663 scott  15  0 76896  13m 4048 S  0.7  1.3
➥13:48.20 quanta
```

The top command gives you a great deal of information about your system in the first five lines of its output, and then it focuses on listing each running process. Note that top automatically sorts the output by the numbers in the %CPU column, so as programs use more and then less of your processor, their position in top changes as well.

If you want to kill programs from within top, just press k. At the top of the listings, just after the line that begins with Swap:, you'll see the following:

```
PID to kill:
```

Enter the PID for the process you want to end (let's say 8026), press Enter, and you're asked what signal number (discussed in the previous "End a Running Process" section) you want to use:

```
Kill PID 8026 with signal [15]:
```

By default, top wants to use 15. If you're happy with that, just press Enter; if not, enter the signal number you want to use and then press Enter. A second or so later, that process will disappear from top.

To exit top, press q.

The top command is incredibly useful, and you'll find yourself turning to it often, just to find out what's happening on your Linux machine. When you have questions about your computer's activity, top often provides the answers.

List Open Files

lsof

Chapter 1, "Things to Know About Your Command Line," discussed the fact that everything is a file to a Linux machine, including directories, network connections, and devices. That means that even though from your perspective you only have one file open—a letter to your Mom—your system actually has thousands of files open at any one time. That's right—thousands. To see the complete list of those open files, use the lsof command (short for *list open files*).

Actually, don't. If you just run lsof by itself (to get the full list of results, you need to be root), you'll receive as output that list of thousands of files. On this system, there were 5,497 files open and being used. Still, lsof can be a useful way to get an idea of just how much is going on with your computer at any one time.

Piping the output of lsof to less gives you the results one screen at a time.

```
# lsof | less
COMMAND PID USER FD TYPE DEVICE SIZE NODE NAME
init      1 root cwd DIR 3,1     656   2 /
init      1 root rtd DIR 3,1     656   2 /
init      1 root txt REG 3,1   31608 2072 /sbin/init
```

Still, with 5,497 results, that's many screens to page through. You can also pipe the output of lsof to grep. As you'll see in the next few sections, however, lsof contains within itself ways to filter out the data you don't want to see so you can focus only on a particular subset of open files that interest you.

List a User's Open Files

lsof -u

If you want to look at the files a particular user has open (and remember that those include network connections and devices, among many others), add the -u option to lsof, followed by the username (remember that lsof must be run as root).

NOTE: In order to save space, some of the data you'd normally see when you run lsof has been removed in this and further examples.

```
# lsof -u scott
COMMAND     PID  USER NAMEP
evolution  8603 scott /home/scott/.evolution/
➥addressbook/local/system/addressbook.db
opera     11638 scott /usr/lib/opera/9.0/opera
opera     11638 scott /usr/share/fonts/truetype/
➥msttcorefonts/Arial_Bold.ttf
```

Even filtering out all users except one, you're left with 3,039 lines in this list. Still, some interesting items are here. For one, it appears that Evolution (an email and personal information manager program) is running all the time, without your knowledge or intention. Also, the Opera web browser is running, which is expected, and one of the web pages it's on is requiring the use of the Arial Bold font, among other files.

If you administer a box used by more than person, try out lsof -u for your users. You might find that they are running programs that they shouldn't. If you're the sole user on your Linux machine, try lsof -u on yourself— you might find that you're running programs of which you were unaware!

List Users for a Particular File

```
lsof [file]
```

In the previous section, you saw what files a particular user had open. Let's reverse that, and see who's using a particular file. To do so, simply follow lsof with the path to a file on your system. For instance, let's take a look at who's using the SSH daemon, used to connect remotely to this computer (remember that lsof must be run as root).

```
# lsof /usr/sbin/sshd
COMMAND    PID  USER TYPE NAME
sshd      7814  root  REG /usr/sbin/sshd
sshd     10542  root  REG /usr/sbin/sshd
sshd     10548 scott  REG /usr/sbin/sshd
```

That's the result you wanted: two users, root and scott. If an unexpected user had shown up here—say, 4ackordood—you'd know that you've been compromised.

NOTE: Yes, sshd is a program, but remember, that's from your human perspective. To Linux, /usr/sbin/sshd is just another file.

List Processes for a Particular Program

```
lsof -c [program]
```

In the previous section, you saw who was using /usr/sbin/sshd. The results you received, however, don't tell the whole story. Any particular program is actually comprised of calls to several (perhaps many) other processes, programs, sockets, and devices, all of which appear to Linux as more files. To find out the full universe of other files associated with a particular running program, follow lsof with the -c option, and then the name of a running (and therefore "open") program. For example, lsof /usr/sbin/sshd said that there were only two users and three open files associated with that exact file. But what about the entire sshd command?

```
# lsof -c sshd
COMMAND   PID   USER NAME
sshd      10542 root /lib/ld-2.3.5.so
sshd      10542 root /dev/null
sshd      10542 root 192.168.0.170:ssh-
>192.168.0.100:4577
➥(ESTABLISHED)
sshd      10548 scott /usr/sbin/sshdp
sshd      10548 scott 192.168.0.170:ssh-
>192.168.0.100:4577
➥(ESTABLISHED)
```

In the preceding code, you can see a few of the 94 lines (representing 94 open files) somehow connected with the sshd program. One is a .so file (*shared object*, akin to a DLL on Windows), and a few even show you that a network connection has occurred between this and another machine (actually, that another machine on this network has connected via SSH to this machine; for more on that process, see "Securely Log In to Another Computer" in Chapter 15, "Working on the Network").

You can find out a tremendous amount by applying lsof to various commands on your computer; at the least, you'll learn just how complicated modern programs are. Try it out with the software you use every day, and you might gain a fresh appreciation for the programmers who worked hard to make it available to you.

NOTE: The lsof command has an amazing number of options, and you're only going to look at a tiny subset. The source code for lsof includes a file named 00QUICKSTART (that's two zeroes at the beginning) that is a tutorial for some of the command's more powerful features. Search Google for that filename and start reading.

Display Information About System RAM

Nowadays most computers come with hundreds of megabytes or even gigabytes of RAM, but it's still possible to find your machine slowing down due to a lot of memory usage or virtual memory swapping. To see the current state of your system's memory, use the free command.

```
$ free
        total    used    free shared buffers cached
Mem:   1036136 995852   40284      0   80816 332264
-/+ buffers/cache:    582772 453364
Swap: 1012084 495584 516500
```

By default, free shows the results in kilobytes, the same
as if you'd used the -k option. You can change that,
however. The -b option shows you memory usage in
bytes, and -m (which you should probably use most of
the time) uses megabytes.

```
$ free -m
               total used free shared buffers
cached
Mem:            1011  963   48      0      78    316
-/+ buffers/cache: 569 442
Swap:            988  483  504
```

From free's output, you can see that this machine has
1011MB of available physical RAM (actually 1024MB,
but free displays it as 1011MB because the kernel takes
up the remaining 13MB, so it could never be made
available for other uses). The first line makes it appear
that 963MB of that is in use, leaving only 48MB of
RAM free. There's nearly a gigabyte of swap, or virtual
memory, in place, too, and about half of that, or 483MB,
has already been used. That's how it appears, anyway.

It's not that simple, however. The important row is the
middle one, labeled -/+ buffers/cache. Hard drives use
buffers and cache to speed up access, and if a program
needs that memory, it can be quickly freed up for that
program. From the point of view of the applications
running on this Linux machine, 442MB of memory is
free right now for use, with 569MB cached but available if needed. And that's in addition to the swap space

you have available. Linux is nothing if not efficient when it comes to managing memory.

TIP: An excellent page with more information on free and Linux memory management can be found on the Gentoo Wiki, at http://gentoo-wiki.com/FAQ_Linux_Memory_ Management. Even though it's purportedly for Gentoo (a unique Linux distribution), it still applies to all versions of Linux.

Show File System Disk Usage

`df`

The `free` command deals with the RAM you have on your system; likewise, the `df` command (think *disk free*) deals with the amount of hard drive space you have. Run `df`, and you get a list of the disk space that is available to, and used by, every mounted filesystem.

```
$ df
Filesystem 1Kblocks     Used Available Use% Mounted
➥on
/dev/hda1   7678736  5170204   2508532  68% /
tmpfs        518068        0    518068   0%
➥/dev/shm
tmpfs        518068    12588    505480   3%
➥/lib/modules/2.6.12-10-386/volatile
/dev/hda2 30369948 24792784   5577164  82% /home
```

Before looking at these results in a more detail, let's make them a little easier to read. The `df` command shows results in kilobytes by default, but it's usually easier to comprehend if you instead use the -h (or --human-readable) option.

```
$ df -h
Filesystem Size Used Avail Use% Mounted on
/dev/hda1  7.4G 5.0G  2.4G 68% /
tmpfs      506M   0   506M  0% /dev/shm
tmpfs      506M  13M  494M  3% /lib/modules/
➥2.6.12-10-386/volatile
/dev/hda2   29G  24G  5.4G 82% /home
```

"Human-readable" (which is a wonderful term, by the way) means that kilobytes are indicated by K, megabytes by M, and gigabytes by G. You can see those last two in the preceding listing.

So what do the results mean? You have two partitions on the hard drive: /dev/hda1, mounted at /, and /dev/hda2, mounted at /home. The /home partition had 29GB allocated to it, of which 82% is currently used, leaving about 5.4GB free. It's not panic time yet when it comes to disk space for that partition, but a few more CDs worth of MP3s and it might be time to delete some unnecessary files.

The root partition, or /, has less space available: only 2.4GB out of 7.4GB. That partition isn't as likely to grow, however, because it contains programs and other relatively static files. Granted, /var is found there, and that's where software installers (as you'll discover in Chapter 13, "Installing Software") and other files that change size and contents, such as logs, are located. But overall, there's still plenty of space left on that partition, especially if you're not planning to install enormous applications or start running a web or database server on this machine.

The other two partitions are both labeled as tmpfs, which means they are temporary file systems used by the virtual memory, or swap space, on your computer. When you shut down your computer, the contents of those partitions disappear.

TIP: For more on tmpfs, see the Wikipedia article at http://en.wikipedia.org/wiki/TMPFS.

Report File Space Used by a Directory

`du`

The df command tells you about your entire hard drive, but what if you just want to know how much space a directory and its contents are using? The du command (short for *disk usage*) answers that question. First you use the cd command to change directories to the directory in question, and then run du.

```
$ cd music
$ du
36582    ./Donald_Fagen
593985   ./Clash
145962   ./Hank_Mobley/1958_Peckin'_Time
128200   ./Hank_Mobley/1963_No_Room_For_Squares
108445   ./Hank_Mobley/1961_Workout
2662185  .
```

As with df, results for du are given in kilobytes, but also like df, you can view them in a more comprehensible fashion with the -h (or --human-readable) option.

```
$ cd music
$ du -h
36M    ./Donald_Fagen
581M   ./Clash
143M   ./Hank_Mobley/1958_Peckin'_Time
126M   ./Hank_Mobley/1963_No_Room_For_Squares
```

```
106M    ./Hank_Mobley/1961_Workout
2.6G    .
```

This output shows you the space used by each subdirectory, but directories that contain other directories also show the total for those contents. Look at the Hank_Mobley directory, which takes up 374MB on this filesystem. That total comes from the three subdirectories contained within Hank_Mobley (since the actual amount in kilobytes was rounded to display megabytes, the totals are just a bit off); if the total for Hank_Mobley was substantially bigger than the total of its three subdirectories, that would mean that the Hank_Mobley directory contained within it several loose files that were outside of a subdirectory.

Finally, you get a total for the entire music/ directory at the end: 2.6GB.

Report Just the Total Space Used for a Directory

```
du -s
```

If you don't want information about all of a directory's subdirectories, it's possible to ask du to simply report back the grand total by using the -s option.

```
$ cd music
$ du -hs
2.6G    .
```

Short and sweet.

Conclusion

Virtually every command you've looked at in this chapter has GUIs. But if your system is non-responsive, if you're connecting to a machine via SSH (covered in Chapter 15) and can't use a GUI, or if you just want to use the speediest tool, you'll need to use the command line. The commands in this chapter are easy to remember, thanks to well-chosen names:

- ps (view running **p**rocesses)
- kill (kill processes)
- top (top listing of running processes)
- lsof (list [**ls**] **o**pen **f**iles)
- free (free, or available, memory)
- df (**d**isk **f**ree space)
- du (**d**isk **u**sage)

Practice with them on your computer, and don't forget to read the man pages for each one because this chapter could only cover a fraction of their capabilities. There are many options to several of them—in particular, ps, top, and lsof—that allow you to do some truly amazing detective work on the computers under your watch.

13

Installing Software

Linux distributions by default contain thousands of great software packages. Immediately after completing a basic install, you can surf the Net, write reports, create spreadsheets, view and manipulate images, and listen to music. Even with that plethora of software, you're still going to want to add new tools that you run across. Fortunately, Linux makes it easy to install new software onto your computer.

Conventional wisdom about Linux said you had to compile any software you wanted to install. You can still do that if you'd like (and many people do), but that's rarely necessary in this day and age. Instead, you can install any of thousands of packages easily and quickly using some simple tools.

You need to understand one important thing before proceeding, however. In the Linux world, software packages come in a variety of formats, with two in particular dominating: RPM and DEB (not surprisingly, those are the two we're going to cover in this chapter). RPM is used by distributions such as Red Hat (in fact, RPM stands for Red Hat Package Manager), Fedora Core, SUSE, and other RPM-based distributions. DEB is used by Debian-based distributions such as Debian itself, K/Ubuntu, Linspire, Xandros, and many others. You should know how both work, but focus on the system that matches your distribution.

TIP: For a great breakdown of the various package management systems and the distributions that use them, see DistroWatch's "Linux Distributions—Facts and Figures: What Is Your Distribution's Package Management?," at http://distrowatch.com/stats.php?section=packagemanagement. Note that DEB leads the pack (note also that I'm biased because this is being written using K/Ubuntu, also known as "Debian Done Right").

Install Software Packages for RPM-Based Distributions

```
rpm -ihv [package]
rpm -Uhv [package]
```

The rpm command installs software installers that end in .rpm, which seems entirely logical. To install an RPM package, you need to download it first. Let's use the industry-standard open-source network port scanner nmap as the example. You can download the RPM package for nmap from www.insecure.org/nmap/download.html; after it's on your system, you simply run rpm along with three options: -i (for *install*), -h (to show hash marks so you can watch the progress of the install), and -v (be verbose and tell me what you're doing). The command, which must be run as root, would look like this:

```
# rpm -ihv nmap-4.01-1.i386.rpm
```

This is actually *not* the command you should run, however. A better choice is -Uhv, where -U stands for *upgrade*. Why is -U better than -i? Because -i only installs, while -U upgrades *and* installs. If a package already exists on your system and you're trying to put a newer one on your machine, -U performs an upgrade; if a package doesn't already exist on your system, -U notices that and instead installs it. Therefore, just use -U all the time, and it won't matter if you're upgrading or installing: -U does what needs to be done, and you won't need to worry about it.

```
# rpm -Uhv nmap-4.01-1.i386.rpm
Preparing...    ############################ [100%]
   1:nmap        ############################ [100%]
```

If you want to install more than one RPM, just list them separated by spaces, one after the other:

```
# rpm -Uhv nmap-4.01-1.i386.rpm nmap-frontend-4.01-
➥1.i386.rpm
```

You can also use wildcards if you have many RPMs to install. For instance, if you have 20 .rpm files in a subdirectory named software, just run this command to install them all:

```
# rpm -Uhv software/*.rpm
```

CAUTION: The -U option is always better, except when installing a kernel. Then you want to use -i instead. If you upgrade with -U and the new kernel doesn't work, you're in a world of hurt. On the other hand, if you install a new kernel with -i, the old one is still on your machine as a backup if the new one blows up.

Remove Software Packages for RPM-Based Distributions

rpm -e [package]

Getting rid of installed RPMs is even easier than installing them. Instead of -Uhv to place RPMs on your computer, use -e (for *erase*) to remove them.

```
# rpm -e nmap
```

And that's it. The -e option is silent, so there's no output. Notice, however, that when you install software using rpm -Uhv, you need to specify the filename, otherwise rpm has no way to know what you want to install. When you remove software with rpm -e, however, you specify the package name because the files used for installation are now long gone, and rpm knows software by the package name.

Install Software Packages and Dependencies for RPM-Based Distributions

yum install [package]

The rpm command is powerful, but after you use it for a while you'll quickly run into a problem when you try to install a package that has dependencies (otherwise known as "dependency hell"). In order to install package A, you also need to download and install packages B and C, but in order to install C you also need to download and install packages D and E, but in order to install E…aaaaaggh!

Debian-based distributions (that you'll read about later in this chapter) solved this problem years ago with the powerful and useful apt; RPM-based distributions can use apt, but more commonly they use the relatively new and still immature yum. Originally developed for the RPM-based Yellow Dog Linux distribution (hence the name, which stands for Yellow Dog Updater, Modified), yum is now widely used but still lags behind apt in features and usability. Still, that's what's available, so that's what we're going to cover.

The yum command installs, upgrades, and uninstalls software packages by acting as a wrapper around rpm. In addition, yum automatically handles dependencies for you. For example, if you're trying to install package A from the example in the introductory paragraph, yum downloads and installs A, B, and C for you. Later, if you decide that you no longer want A on your system, yum can uninstall it for you, along with B and C, as long as other software packages don't require them.

Installing software with yum is pretty easy. Let's say you want to install XMMS, a media player (not surprising, since the name stands for X Multimedia System). To install XMMS, you also need to install several other dependencies. With yum, this process becomes much less painful than it would be if you were attempting to install manually using rpm. To start with, you don't need to find and download the xmms package yourself; instead, yum downloads XMMS and any other necessary dependencies for you.

Unfortunately, yum is incredibly verbose as it goes about its work. The following output has been cut drastically, yet it's still lengthy. Nevertheless, this gives you a rough approximation of what you'd see if you were using yum.

```
# yum install xmms
Setting up Install Process
Setting up repositories
update 100% |=====================| 951 B    00:00
base   100% |=====================| 1.1 kB   00:00


Resolving Dependencies
--> Populating transaction set with selected
➥packages. Please wait.
---> Downloading header for xmms to pack into
➥transaction set.
xmms-1.2.10-9.i386.rpm 100% |==========| 24 kB 00:00
--> Restarting Dependency Resolution with new
➥changes.

---> Downloading header for gtk+ to pack into
➥transaction set.
gtk%2B-1.2.10-33.i386.rpm 100% |==========| 23 kB
➥00:00

Dependencies Resolved

 Package    Arch Version      Repository    Size

Installing:
 xmms       i386 1:1.2.10-9   base          1.9 M
Installing for dependencies:

 libogg     i386 2:1.1.2-1    base          16 k
 libvorbis  i386 1:1.1.0-1    base          185 k




Total download size: 3.3 M
Is this ok [y/N]:
```

After you enter **y**, yum downloads and installs the packages, continuing to inform you about what it's doing, every step of the way.

```
Downloading Packages:
...

(5/6): libogg-1.1.2-1.i38 100% |==========|  16 kB
➥00:00
(6/6): libvorbis-1.1.0-1. 100% |==========| 185 kB
➥00:00
Running Transaction Test

Running Transaction
  Installing: libogg     ########## [1/6]
  Installing: libvorbis  ########## [2/6]

...
Installed: xmms.i386 1:1.2.10-9
Dependency Installed: gdk-pixbuf.i386
➥1:0.22.0-17.el4.3 gtk+.i386 1:1.2.10-33 libogg.i386
➥2:1.1.2-1 libvorbis.i386 1:1.1.0-1
➥mikmod.i386 0:3.1.6-32.EL4
```

Whew! XMMS is finally installed and available for use. Now find out how to get rid of XMMS if you decide you don't like it.

Remove Software Packages and Dependencies for RPM-Based Distributions

`yum remove [package]`

One thing in yum's favor: Its command syntax is very user friendly. Want to install a package? yum install.

Want to remove? yum remove. So if you're tired of
XMMS, just run this command:

```
# yum remove xmms
Setting up Remove Process
Resolving Dependencies

---> Package xmms.i386 1:1.2.10-9 set to be erased

Dependencies Resolved

 Package  Arch  Version       Repository  Size

Removing:
 xmms     i386  1:1.2.10-9    installed   5.2 M

Is this ok [y/N]:
```

Even for something as simple as removing a software
package, yum continues its habit of grabbing you by the
lapels and telling you at length about its day. Press y to
approve the uninstall, and you get a bit more data
thrown at you:

```
Running Transaction Test

Running Transaction
  Removing  : xmms        ################### [1/1]
Removed: xmms.i386 1:1.2.10-9
Complete!
```

And now XMMS is gone. Notice that the dependencies
that were installed by yum (detailed in the previous section, "Install Software Packages and Dependencies for
RPM-Based Distributions") are not removed along
with the xmms package. XMMS needed those dependencies to run, but they can still work on your computer

with different programs, so yum allows them to remain (this is the default behavior of apt as well, as you'll see soon in "Remove Software Packages and Dependencies for Debian").

Upgrade Software Packages and Dependencies for RPM-Based Distributions

yum update

Your Linux system contains hundreds, if not thousands, of software packages, and upgrades come out constantly for one package or another. It would be a full-time job for you to manually keep track of every new version of your software and install updates, but yum makes the process easy. A simple yum update command tells yum to check for any upgrades to the software it's tracking. If new packages are available, yum shows you what's available and asks your permission to proceed with an install.

```
# yum update
Setting up Update Process
Setting up repositories
update 100% |=====================|   951 B    00:00
base   100% |=====================|   1.1 kB    00:00


Resolving Dependencies
--> Populating transaction set with selected
➥packages. Please wait.
---> Downloading header for cups-libs to pack into
➥transaction set.
```

```
cups-libs-1.1.22-0.rc1.9. 100% |==========|  22 kB
➡00:00
---> Package cups-libs.i386 1:1.1.22-0.rc1.9.10 set
➡to be updated

--> Running transaction check
Dependencies Resolved
Package Arch Version              Repository Size

Installing:
openssl i686 0.9.7a-43.4          update    1.1 M
pam     i386 0.77-66.13           update    1.8 M
perl    i386 3:5.8.5-24.RHEL4     update     11 M
udev    i386 039-10.10.EL4.3      update    830 k
wget    i386 1.10.2-0.40E         update    567 k
Transaction Summary

Install      1 Package(s)
Update      11 Package(s)
Remove       0 Package(s)
Total download size: 30 M
Is this ok [y/N]:
```

If you press y at this point, you're giving yum approval
to download and install 12 packages. After lots of output, yum completes its job, and your computer is now
up to date. Want to live on the bleeding edge? Run yum
update daily. If you're not desirous of always using the
latest and greatest, run yum update at a longer interval,
but be sure to run it regularly. Security updates for
software come out all the time, and it's a good idea to
keep up-to-date.

Find Packages Available for Download for RPM-Based Distributions

```
yum search [string]
yum list available
```

So you know how to install and remove software using yum, but how do you find software in the first place? Let's say you're interested in the GIMP, the GNU Image Manipulation Program. You want to know if any packages related to the GIMP are available to install using yum. You could try using yum search gimp, but it wouldn't be a good idea. That command looks for matches to your search term in all package names, descriptions, summaries, and even the list of packagers' names. You'll end up with a list about as long as Bill Gates's bank statement.

A better choice is to query the list of packages available through yum (which would normally produce another crazily long list), but then pipe the results through a grep search for your term.

```
$ yum list available | grep gimp
gimp.i386                1:2.0.5-5    base
gimp-devel.i386          1:2.0.5-5    base
gimp-help.noarch         2-0.1.0.3    base
gimp-print.i386          4.2.7-2      base
```

Eleven results show up—now that's workable. If you really want to perform the complete search, use yum search; otherwise, use yum list available and grep. Most of the time, the latter choice is what you'll really want, and it'll be far easier to work with to boot.

Install Software Packages for Debian

```
dpkg -i [package]
```

Installing new software is one of the most fun things you can do with a Linux machine. As you'll learn in upcoming sections, Debian has apt, the most powerful and easiest-to-use system for installing software of any Linux distribution. As powerful as apt is, much of it is a wrapper around the dpkg program (in the same way yum is a wrapper around rpm), which does the grunt work of installing and removing software on a Debian-based machine. Before learning how to use apt, you should learn how to use dpkg because apt can't be used to install everything.

Here's a case in point: One of the most popular Voice over IP (VoIP) programs out now is Skype. Due to licensing issues, however, Skype isn't included in the default installs of most distributions. If you want Skype, you have to first download it from the company's site, and then manually install it. To get Skype, head over to the Linux download page, at www.skype.com/products/skype/linux, and find the package for your distribution. In this case, you're going to use the Debian package, which at this time is named skype_1.2.0.18-1_i386.deb.

After the .deb file is downloaded onto your system, it's time to install it. First use cd to change directories to the directory that contains the .deb file, and then use dpkg to install it.

NOTE: On most Debian-based distributions, this and all other dpkg commands are run as root. The wildly popular K/Ubuntu distribution, however, doesn't use root. Instead, commands normally run as root are prefaced with sudo. In other words, Debian would use this:

```
# dpkg -i skype_1.2.0.18-1_i386.deb
```

K/Ubuntu and other sudo-based distributions would instead use this:

```
$ sudo dpkg -i skype_1.2.0.18-1_i386.deb
```

This book was written using several machines running K/Ubuntu, so if you see sudo instead of root, now you know why.

```
# ls
skype_1.2.0.18-1_i386.deb
# dkpg -i skype_1.2.0.18-1_i386.deb
sudo dpkg -i skype_1.2.0.18-1_i386.deb
Selecting previously deselected package skype.
(Reading database ... 97963 files and directories
➥currently installed.)
Unpacking skype (from skype_1.2.0.18-1_i386.deb) ...
Setting up skype (1.2.0.18-1) ...
```

That's it. The dpkg command is a model of brevity, telling you the important information and nothing more.

Remove Software Packages for Debian

dpkg -r [package]

The -i option, used to install software on Debian-based machines, stands for *install*; in a similar bit of happy obviousness, the -r option, used to uninstall software on Debian-based machines, stands for *remove*. If you get tired of Skype, it's a simple matter to get it off your computer.

```
# dpkg -r skype
(Reading database ... 98004 files and directories
➥currently installed.)
Removing skype ...
```

When you install software using dpkg -i, you need to
specify the filename, otherwise dpkg has no way to
know what you want to install. When you remove software with dpkg -r, however, you specify the package
name because the files used for installation are now long
gone, and apt knows software by the package name.

Install Software Packages and Dependencies for Debian

`apt-get install [package]`

The dkpg command is powerful, but after you use it for
a while you'll quickly run into a problem when you
try to install a package that has dependencies (otherwise known as "dependency hell"). In order to install
package A, you also need to download and install packages B and C, but in order to install C you also need to
download and install packages D and E, but in order to
install E...aaaaaggh! You need apt!

The apt command and its accessories install, upgrade,
and uninstall software packages. Best of all, apt automatically handles dependencies for you. For example, if
you're trying to install package A from the example in
the previous paragraph, apt downloads and installs A, B,
and C for you. Later, if you decide that you no longer
want A on your system, apt can uninstall it for you,
along with B and C, as long as other software packages
don't require them.

The apt command was originally developed for use on the Debian distribution as a front end to dpkg. It's now found on every Debian-based distribution—which includes Debian itself, K/Ubuntu, Linspire, Xandros, and a whole host of others—and it's one of the features that make Debian so easy to use and powerful. Other, non-Debian distributions realized how great apt was, and eventually Connectiva ported apt to work with RPMs. (This chapter focuses on apt as it is used with Debian.)

TIP: For a good overview of apt as it is used with RPM-based distros, see my "A Very Apropos apt" in the October 2003 issue of *Linux Magazine*, available at www.linux-mag.com/2003-10/apt_01.html. In addition to that article, however, you should also check out http://apt.freshrpms.net for the latest in RPM repositories. Note that free registration is required to access *Linux Magazine*'s content.

Let's say you want to install the awesome tool sshfs using apt. To do it, you go through the following process (and remember that these commands must be run as root):

```
# apt-get update
Get:1 http://us.archive.ubuntu.com breezy
➥Release.gpg [189B]
Get:2 http://archive.ubuntu.com breezy Release.gpg
➥[189B]


Hit ftp://ftp.free.fr breezy/free Sources
Hit ftp://ftp.free.fr breezy/non-free Sources
Fetched 140kB in 1m4s (2176B/s)
Reading package lists... Done
[Results truncated for length]
# apt-get install sshfs
```

```
Reading package lists... Done
Building dependency tree... Done
The following extra packages will be installed:
  fuse-utils libfuse2
The following NEW packages will be installed:
  fuse-utils libfuse2 sshfs

Need to get 96.9kB of archives.
After unpacking 344kB of additional disk space
➥will be used.
Do you want to continue [Y/n]? y
Get:1 http://us.archive.ubuntu.com breezy/universe
➥sshfs 1.1-1 [19.3kB]
...
Fetched 96.9kB in 10s (9615B/s)
Reading package fields... Done
Reading package status... Done
Preconfiguring packages ...
...
Selecting previously deselected package sshfs.
Unpacking sshfs (from .../archives/sshfs_1.1-
➥1_i386.deb) ...

Setting up sshfs (1.1-1) ...
```

Let's go over what you just did because you actually
ran two commands. apt-get update downloads a list of
current software packages from apt servers—known as
repositories—that are listed in your apt configuration
file, found at /etc/apt/sources.list (if you want to see
where your repositories are, run cat /etc/apt/sources.
list). If you saw Get at the beginning of a line after
running apt-get update, it means that apt saw that the
list on the repository is newer, so it's downloading that
particular list; Ign, on the other hand, means that the

list on the repository and on your computer are in sync, so nothing is downloaded. By running `apt-get update` before you do anything else, you ensure that your list of packages is correct and up-to-date.

The command `apt-get install sshfs` retrieves the specified package, as well as any necessary dependencies (in this case, `fuse-utils` and `libfuse2`). After they're on your computer, `apt` (really `dpkg` acting at the behest of `apt`) installs all of the software for you. Keep in mind that you always use the package name, not the filename. In other words, use `apt-get install sshfs`, not `apt-get install sshfs_1.1-1_i386.deb`. As you saw, if `apt` does discover additional dependencies for the requested package, as it did for sshfs, you'll have to confirm that you want them installed before `apt` grabs them.

If you want to install more than one package at the same time, just list them all on the command line. For example, if you wanted to install `sshfs` and `shfs-utils`, you'd do the following:

```
# apt-get install sshfs shfs-utils
```

Any dependencies for either `sshfs` or `shfs-utils` are discovered, and you are asked if you want to install them as well. Yes, it's that simple.

TIP: Don't know what `sshfs` is? Oh, but you should! Read my blog posting "Mount Remote Drives via SSH with SSHFS," which you can find on The Open Source Weblog at http://opensource.weblogsinc.com/2005/11/03/mount-remote-drives-via-ssh-with-sshfs/.

Remove Software Packages and Dependencies for Debian

```
apt-get remove [package]
```

If you no longer want a package on your system, apt makes it easy to uninstall it: Instead of apt-get install, you use apt-get remove. This command works exactly contrary to apt-get install: It uninstalls the packages you specify, along with any dependencies. Once again, reference the package name, not the filename, so run apt-get remove sshfs, not apt-get remove sshfs_1.1-1_i386.deb.

```
# apt-get remove sshfs
Password:

The following packages will be REMOVED:
  sshfs


After unpacking 98.3kB disk space will be freed.
Do you want to continue [Y/n]?
```

Removing a package actually doesn't remove every vestige of a package, however, because configuration files for the removed package stick around on your computer. If you're sure that you want to remove everything, use the --purge option.

```
# apt-get --purge remove sshfs
Password:

The following packages will be REMOVED:
  sshfs*
```

```
After unpacking 98.3kB disk space will be freed.
Do you want to continue [Y/n]?
```

Using --purge, the packages that apt is about to remove are marked with asterisks, indicating that associated configuration files are going to be removed as well.

Upgrade Software Packages and Dependencies for Debian

apt-get upgrade

A modern Linux system has several thousand software packages on it, and it's a sure bet that at least one of those is upgraded by its maintainer every day. With apt, it's quite simple to keep your system up-to-date. The process looks like this (and remember, this command must be run as root):

```
# apt-get update
Get:1 http://us.archive.ubuntu.com breezy
➥Release.gpg [189B]
Get:2 http://archive.ubuntu.com breezy Release.gpg
➥[189B]

Hit ftp://ftp.free.fr breezy/free Sources
Hit ftp://ftp.free.fr breezy/non-free Sources
Fetched 140kB in 1m4s (2176B/s)
Reading package lists... Done
[Results truncated for length]
# apt-get upgrade
Reading package lists... Done
Building dependency tree... Done
The following packages have been kept back:
  koffice
```

```
The following packages will be upgraded:
  kalzium kamera kanagram karbon kbruch kchart
➥ kcoloredit kdegraphics kdegraphics-kfile-plugins
...
53 upgraded, 0 newly installed, 0 to remove and 1
➥not upgraded.
Need to get 58.3MB of archives.
After unpacking 28.7kB of additional disk space will
➥be used.
Do you want to continue [Y/n]?
```

Let's figure out what was going on here. Once again, you want to run apt-get update first so your computer is in sync with your apt repositories. Then apt-get upgrade looks for any differences between what you have installed and what's available on the repositories. If differences exist, apt shows you a list of all of the packages that it would like to download and install on your computer. Of course, the actual list of packages varies depending on how up-to-date your system is. In this case, enough time had passed that there were 53 packages to upgrade.

If you type y, apt downloads the 53 software packages to /var/cache/apt/archives and then installs them after they're all on your machine. If you don't want to go through with the upgrade, just type **n** instead.

That's easy enough, but the most efficient way to use apt to update your Linux box is to just join the commands together:

```
# apt-get update && apt-get upgrade
```

The && makes sure that apt-get upgrade doesn't run unless apt-get update finishes without errors. Better yet, make an alias for that command in your .bash_aliases file, as was discussed in the "Create a New Permanent Alias" section of Chapter 11, "Your Shell."

```
alias upgrade='apt-get update && apt-get upgrade'
```

Reload your .bash_aliases file, and now you just need to type in **upgrade**, press Enter, press Y to accept any new packages, and you're done. Windows Update, eat your heart out!

Find Packages Available for Download for Debian

apt-cache search

We've been talking a lot about installing software using apt, but how do you know what software packages are available in the first place? There's another tool in the apt toolbox that helps you do that: apt-cache search, which searches the lists of packages available in your apt repositories. In a nice change of pace, you don't need to be root at all to use apt-cache search.

```
$ apt-cache search dvdcss
libdvdread3 - Simple foundation for reading DVDs
ogle - DVD player with support for DVD menus
libdvdcss2 - portable library for DVD decryption
libdvdcss2-dev - development files for libdvdcss2
```

Keep in mind several things about how this command searches. It looks for matches to your string—in this case, dvdcss—and not for exact words. Also, your search pattern might appear in the package name or description. Finally, apt-cache search looks through the entire package list of both installed and uninstalled packages, so you might already have installed a package that shows up.

TIP: Synaptic is a GUI for apt that allows you to do virtually everything discussed here, but via point-and-click instead of typing. In particular, its search tools are very nice, so much so that I usually use Synaptic solely for searching, and do everything else via the command line. That seems to maximize the effectiveness of each tool best.

Clean Up Unneeded Installation Packages for Debian

`apt-get clean`

When packages are downloaded and installed using apt, the .deb files are left behind in /var/cache/apt/archives/. Over time, you can take up a lot of disk space with those unnecessary installers. To remove all of the unneeded .deb files, use apt-get clean (once again, this command is run as root):

```
$ ls -1 /var/cache/apt/archives/
fuse-utils_2.3.0-1ubuntu1.1_i386.deb
libfuse2_2.3.0-1ubuntu1.1_i386.deb
lock
partial/
sshfs_1.1-1_i386.deb
# apt-get clean
$ ls -1 /var/cache/apt/archives/
lock
partial/
```

If a download is interrupted for whatever reason, you might find a partial .deb file in /var/cache/apt/archives/partial/. If you know that all of the updates and upgrades are complete and installed, it's safe to delete the contents of that directory, should you find anything in it.

Troubleshoot Problems with apt

Of course, as great as apt is, you might run into problems. Here are some problems and their workarounds.

One simple problem that will result in a smack to your own forehead is the "Could not open lock file" error. You'll try to run apt-get, but instead of working, you get this error message:

```
E: Could not open lock file /var/lib/dpkg/lock -
↪open (13 Permission denied)
E: Unable to lock the administration directory
↪(/var/lib/dpkg/), are you root?
```

The solution to this issue is right there in the second line: You're not logged in as root! Simply log in as root and try again, and everything should work.

NOTE: If you're running K/Ubuntu, or any other distribution that uses sudo instead of root, the error means that you didn't preface the command with sudo. In other words, you ran this:

```
$ apt-get upgrade
```

You're seeing the error message because you should have run this instead:

```
$ sudo apt-get upgrade
```

The next common issue occurs when `apt` complains about broken dependencies. You'll know this one's happening when `apt` encourages you to run `apt-get -f install`. This suggestion is the program's way of telling you that your system has some broken dependencies that prevent `apt` from finishing its job.

There are a couple of possible solutions. You can follow `apt`'s advice, and run `apt-get -f install`, which tries to fix the problem by downloading and installing the necessary packages. Normally, this solves the problem, and you can move on.

If you don't want to do that, you can instead try running `apt-get -f remove`, which tries to fix the problem by removing packages that `apt` deems troublesome. These might sound like potentially dangerous steps to take—and they could be if you don't pay attention—but each option gives you the chance to review any proposed changes and give your assent. Just be sure to examine `apt`'s proposals before saying yes.

Finally, `apt` might warn you that some packages "have been kept back." This warning tells you that `apt` has found a conflict between the requested package or one of its dependencies and another package already installed on your system. To resolve the issue, try to install the package that was kept back with the `-u` option, which gives you information about exactly what needs to be upgraded.

Conclusion

RPM-based and Debian-based distributions, despite their differences, share some similarities when it comes to package management, in that both are designed to simplify the installation, removal, and management of software. RPM-based distributions use the `rpm` command to install, upgrade, and remove software, while Debian-based distributions use `dpkg` for the same purposes. To solve the headaches of dependency hell, RPM-based distributions have `yum`, a wrapper around `rpm`, while Debian-based distributions have `apt`, a wrapper around `dpkg`. Still, there are differences, principally in maturity and ease of use. In those areas, `apt` is definitely superior to `yum`, but `yum` is improving constantly.

In the end, both are still better than what Windows users have to put up with. Windows Update only updates Microsoft's own software and a few third-party hardware drivers, while both `apt` and `yum` handle virtually every piece of software on a Linux system. That's a huge advantage that Linux users have over their Microsoft cousins, and it's one that should make us proud.

Connectivity

Networking has been part of Linux since the OS's beginning as a humble kernel hacked on by a small group of programmers, and it's completely central to what makes Linux great. Linux networking most of the time just works, providing you with a rock-solid connection that can be endlessly tweaked and tuned to meet your exact needs.

This chapter is all about testing, measuring, and managing your networking devices and connections. When things are working correctly—and they will for the vast majority of the time—you can use the tools in this chapter to monitor your system's network connections; should you experience problems, this chapter will help you resolve some of the most irksome.

TIP: The information in this chapter assumes that you're using IPv4 addressing, in the format of xxx.xxx.xxx.xxx. IPv6 will eventually replace IPv4, but that's still quite a while in the future. At that time, route and many of the other commands you'll be examining will change. For now, though, the information in this chapter is what you need. For more on IPv6, see Wikipedia's "IPv6" (http://en.wikipedia.org/wiki/Ipv6).

View the Status of Your Network Interfaces

ifconfig

Everything in this chapter depends on your network connection. At the end of this chapter, in "Trouble-shooting Network Problems," you're going to learn ways to fix problems with your network connection. Here at the beginning, let's find out what network connections you have in place and their status.

To get a quick look at all of your network devices, whether they're running or not, use ifconfig (which stands for *interface configuration*) with the -a (for *all*) option. Here's what you might see on a laptop (note that some distributions require you to log on as root to use ifconfig):

```
$ ifconfig -a
ath0 Link encap:Ethernet  HWaddr 00:14:6C:06:6B:FD
 inet addr:192.168.0.101  Bcast:192.168.0.255
➥Mask:255.255.255.0
 inet6 addr: fe80::214:6cff:fe06:6bfd/64 Scope:Link
 UP BROADCAST RUNNING MULTICAST  MTU:1500 Metric:1
 RX packets:1257 errors:7557 dropped:0
➥overruns:0 frame:7557
 TX packets:549 errors:2 dropped:0 overruns:0
➥carrier:0
 collisions:0 txqueuelen:200
 RX bytes:195869 (191.2 KiB) TX bytes:95727
➥(93.4 KiB)
 Interrupt:11 Memory:f8da0000-f8db0000

eth0 Link encap:Ethernet  HWaddr 00:02:8A:36:48:8A
 BROADCAST MULTICAST  MTU:1500  Metric:1
```

```
 RX packets:0 errors:0 dropped:0 overruns:0 frame:0
 TX packets:0 errors:0 dropped:0 overruns:0
➥carrier:0
 collisions:0 txqueuelen:1000
 RX bytes:0 (0.0 b)   TX bytes:0 (0.0 b)

lo    Link encap:Local Loopback
 inet addr:127.0.0.1  Mask:255.0.0.0
 inet6 addr: ::1/128 Scope:Host
 UP LOOPBACK RUNNING  MTU:16436  Metric:1
 RX packets:11092 errors:0 dropped:0 overruns:0
➥frame:0
 TX packets:11092 errors:0 dropped:0 overruns:0
➥carrier:0
 collisions:0 txqueuelen:0
 RX bytes:982629 (959.5 KiB)   TX bytes:982629
➥(959.5 KiB)
```

Three interfaces are listed here: ath0 (a wireless card), eth0 (an Ethernet card), and lo (the loopback interface—more on that in a moment). For each of those, you're told the type of connection, the Media Access Control (MAC) or hardware address, the IP address, the broadcast and subnet mask addresses, and information about received and transmitted packets, among other data. If a connection is disconnected, much of that information is missing. In fact, that's one way you can see that ath0 and lo are up, and eth0 is down: eth0 is missing an IP address, among other important details. Of course, an easier way to tell is that the fourth line of the ath0 and lo interfaces begins with UP, while eth0 does not.

Let's take the three interfaces in reverse order. lo is the loopback address, which enables a machine to refer to itself. The loopback address is always represented by the IP address of 127.0.0.1. Basically, your system needs it to work correctly. If you have it, don't worry about it;

if you don't have it, you'll know it because you will find yourself in a world of hurt.

TIP: For more on the loopback interface and address, see Wikipedia's "Loopback" at http://en.wikipedia.org/wiki/Loopback.

---

eth0 is an Ethernet card, into which you actually plug cables. No cables are plugged into the Ethernet card's port currently, so it's not activated, hence the lack of any addresses: IP, broadcast, and subnet mask. It's possible to have both a wired and wireless interface running at the same time, although it's usually not necessary.

Finally there is ath0, a wireless PCMCIA card. You might also see a wireless card with a name like eth0 if it's the primary network interface, or eth1 if it's secondary. When the wireless card was inserted, K/Ubuntu automatically recognized it and configured the system to work with it, giving it the ath0 identifier. Because wireless interfaces are just Ethernet interfaces with some extra wireless goodies, the information you get with ifconfig is similar to what you'd see for eth0 if it was up.

NOTE: You may see other names for your network devices, such as wlan0 for wireless cards.

---

ifconfig -a shows all interfaces, even those that are down; ifconfig by itself shows just those connections that are up. It's a quick way to check the status of your network interfaces, especially if you need to find your IP address quickly.

NOTE: You can also configure your network interfaces using ifconfig, a process described later in "Configure a Network Interface."

Verify That a Computer Is Running and Accepting Requests

```
ping
ping -c
```

The ping command sends a special kind of packet—an ICMP ECHO_REQUEST message—to the specified address. If a machine at that address is listening for ICMP messages, it responds with an ICMP ECHO_REPLY packet. (It's true that firewalls can block ICMP messages, rendering ping useless, but most of the time it's not a problem.) A successful ping means that network connectivity is occurring between the two machines.

```
$ ping www.google.com
ping www.google.com
PING www.l.google.com (72.14.203.99) 56(84) bytes of
➥data.
64 bytes from 72.14.203.99: icmp_seq=1 ttl=245
➥time=17.1 ms
64 bytes from 72.14.203.99: icmp_seq=2 ttl=245
➥time=18.1 ms


[Results truncated for length]--- www.l.google.com
ping statistics ---
```

```
6 packets transmitted, 5 received, 16% packet loss,
➥time 5051ms
rtt min/avg/max/mdev = 16.939/17.560/18.136/0.460 ms
```

The ping command won't stop until you press Ctrl+C.
This can cause problems if you forget that you're using
ping because it will continue forever until it is stopped
or your machine's network connection stops. I once
forgot and left a ping session running for 18 days, sending nearly 1.4 million pings to one of my servers. Oops!

If you want to give ping a limit, you can set the number of packets that ping is to send with the -c option,
followed by a number. After ping sends out that number of packets, it stops, reporting its results.

```
$ ping -c 3 www.granneman.com
PING granneman.com (216.23.180.5) 56(84) bytes of
➥data.
64 bytes from 216.23.180.5: icmp_seq=1 ttl=44
➥time=65.4 ms
64 bytes from 216.23.180.5: icmp_seq=2 ttl=44
➥time=64.5 ms
64 bytes from 216.23.180.5: icmp_seq=3 ttl=44
➥time=65.7 ms
--- granneman.com ping statistics ---
3 packets transmitted, 3 received, 0% packet loss,
time 4006ms
rtt min/avg/max/mdev = 64.515/65.248/65.700/0.510 ms
```

The ping command is a standard and speedy way to
determine basic network connectivity; even better, if
you include the -c option, you'll never forget and leave
ping running accidentally for 18 days.

For more about using ping to diagnose network connectivity issues, see "Troubleshooting Network
Problems."

Trace the Route Packets Take Between Two Hosts

traceroute

The traceroute command shows every step taken on the route from your machine to a specified host. Let's say you want to know why you can't get to www. granneman.com. You were able to load it just fine yesterday, but today's attempts to load the web page are timing out. Where's the problem?

```
$ traceroute www.granneman.com
traceroute to granneman.com (216.23.180.5), 30 hops
➥max, 38 byte packets
 1  192.168.0.1 (192.168.0.1)  1.245 ms  0.827 ms
➥0.839 ms
 2  10.29.64.1 (10.29.64.1)  8.582 ms  19.930 ms
➥7.083 ms
 3  24.217.2.165 (24.217.2.165)  10.152 ms  25.476
➥ms  36.617 ms
 4  12.124.129.97 (12.124.129.97)  9.203 ms  8.003
➥ms  11.307 ms
 5  12.122.82.241 (12.122.82.241)  52.901 ms  53.619
➥ms  51.215 ms
 6  tbr2-p013501.sl9mo.ip.att.net (12.122.11.121)
➥51.625 ms  52.166 ms  50.156 ms
 7  tbr2-cl21.la2ca.ip.att.net (12.122.10.14)
➥50.669 ms  54.049 ms  69.334 ms
 8  gar1-p3100.lsnca.ip.att.net (12.123.199.229)
➥50.167 ms  48.703 ms  49.636 ms
 9  * * *
10  border20.po2-bbnet2.lax.pnap.net
➥(216.52.255.101)  59.414 ms  62.148 ms  51.337 ms
11  intelenet-3.border20.lax.pnap.net
➥(216.52.253.234)  51.930 ms  53.054 ms  50.748 ms
```

```
12   v8.core2.irv.intelenet.net (216.23.160.66)
➥50.611 ms   51.947 ms   60.694 ms
13   * * *
14   * * *
15   * * *
```

What do those * * * mean? Each one indicates a five-second timeout at that hop. Sometimes that could indicate that the machine simply doesn't understand how to cope with that traceroute packet due to a bug, but a consistent set of * indicates that there's a problem somewhere with the router to which v8.core2.irv.intelenet.net hands off packets. If the problem persists, you need to notify the administrator of v8.core2.irv.intelenet.net and let him know there's a problem. (Of course, it might not hurt to let the administrator of gar1-p3100.lsnca.ip.att.net know that his router is having a problem getting to border20.po2-bbnet2.lax.pnap.net as well, but it's not nearly the problem that intelenet.net is having.)

One other way to get around a problematic traceroute is to increase the number of hops that the command will try. By default, the maximum number of hops is 30, although you can change that with the -m option, as in traceroute -m 40 www.bbc.co.uk.

TIP: Actually, a better traceroute is mtr, which stands for Matt's traceroute. Think of it as a combination of ping and traceroute. If mtr is available for your Linux distribution, download and try it out. For more information, head over to www.bitwizard.nl/mtr.

Perform DNS Lookups

`host`

The Domain Name System (DNS) was created to make it easier for humans to access resources on the Internet. Computers work beautifully with numbers—after all, everything a computer does is really a number—but humans can remember and process words much more efficiently. A website might be located at 72.14.203.99, but it would be hard for most people to remember that. Instead, it's much easier to keep in memory that you want to go to www.google.com. DNS is basically a giant database that keeps track of the relationship between 72.14.203.99 and www.google.com, and millions of other IP addresses and domain names as well.

TIP: DNS is a large, complicated, and fascinating topic. For more details, see Wikipedia's "Domain Name System" (http://en.wikipedia.org/wiki/Dns) to start, and then jump into Paul Albitz and Cricket Liu's seminal *DNS and BIND*.

To quickly find the IP address associated with a domain name, use the host command:

```
$ host www.granneman.com
www.granneman.com is an alias for granneman.com.
granneman.com has address 216.23.180.5
www.granneman.com is an alias for granneman.com.
www.granneman.com is an alias for granneman.com.
granneman.com mail is handled by 30 bhoth.pair.com.
```

There are five responses because host performs several types of DNS lookups. It's easy, however, to see what you wanted: www.granneman.com can be found at 216.23.180.5.

You can also reverse the process, and find out a domain name associated with an IP.

```
$ host 65.214.39.152
152.39.214.65.in-addr.arpa domain name pointer
➥web.bloglines.com.
```

NOTE: Many other commands will reveal a host's IP address, but host is the most efficient way to perform this task. Not to mention, you can do reverse lookups with host, which is not always possible with other commands.

Find out more about how host can help you at the end of this chapter in "Troubleshooting Network Problems."

Configure a Network Interface

`ifconfig`

In the first section of this chapter, "View the Status of Your Network Interfaces," you saw how you could use ifconfig to get details about the status of your network interfaces. The ifconfig command is more powerful than that, however, as you can also use it to configure your network interfaces.

NOTE: You can make quite a few changes with ifconfig, but you're only going to look at a few (for more details, see man ifconfig).

To change the IP address for the Ethernet card found at eth0 to 192.168.0.125, run this command (virtually all commands associated with ifconfig need to be run as root):

```
# ifconfig eth0 192.168.0.125
```

In order to run certain types of network-sniffing tools, such as the awesome Ethereal, you first need to set your network card to promiscuous mode. By default, eth0 only listens for packets sent specifically to it, but in order to sniff all the packets flowing by on a network, you need to tell your card to listen to everything, which is promiscuous mode.

```
# ifconfig eth0 promisc
```

After you've done that, running ifconfig shows you that your card is now looking at every packet it can. See the PROMISC in the fourth line?

```
# ifconfig eth0
eth0 Link encap:Ethernet  HWaddr 00:02:8A:36:48:8A
 inet addr:192.168.0.143  Bcast:192.168.0.255
➥Mask:255.255.255.0
 inet6 addr: fe80::202:8aff:fe36:488a/64 Scope:Link
 UP BROADCAST PROMISC MULTICAST MTU:1500 Metric:1
[Results truncated for length]
```

When you're done using Ethereal, don't forget to turn off promiscuous mode.

```
# ifconfig eth0 -promisc
# ifconfig eth0
eth0 Link encap:Ethernet  HWaddr 00:02:8A:36:48:8A
inet addr:192.168.0.143  Bcast:192.168.0.255
➥Mask:255.255.255.0
```

```
inet6 addr: fe80::202:8aff:fe36:488a/64 Scope:Link
UP BROADCAST MULTICAST  MTU:1500  Metric:1
```

You can even change (or "spoof") the hardware MAC address for your network device. This is usually only necessary to get around some ISPs' attempts to link Internet service to a specific machine. Be careful with spoofing your MAC address because a mistake can conflict with other network devices, causing problems. If you do decide to spoof your MAC, make sure you use ifconfig by itself to first acquire the default MAC address so you can roll back to that later (by the way, the MAC address shown in this command is completely bogus, so don't try to use it).

```
# ifconfig eth0 hw ether 00:14:CC:00:1A:00
```

The ifconfig command is a cornerstone of working with network interfaces. Make sure you understand how it works so you can take maximum advantage of all it has to offer.

View the Status of Your Wireless Network Interfaces

`iwconfig`

The ifconfig command shows the status of your network interfaces, even wireless ones. However, it can't show all the data associated with a wireless interface because ifconfig simply doesn't know about it. To get the maximum data associated with a wireless card, you want to use iwconfig instead of ifconfig.

```
$ iwconfig
lo   no wireless extensions.
eth0 no wireless extensions.
ath0 IEEE 802.11g  ESSID:"einstein"
Mode:Managed  Frequency:2.437 GHz  Access
➥Point: 00:12:17:31:4F:C6
 Bit Rate:48 Mb/s    Tx-Power:18 dBm Sensitivity=0/3
 Retry:off    RTS thr:off    Fragment thr:off
 Power Management:off
 Link Quality=41/94  Signal level=-54 dBm  Noise
➥level=-95 dBm
 Rx invalid nwid:1047  Rx invalid crypt:0  Rx
➥invalid frag:0
 Tx excessive retries:73  Invalid misc:73
➥Missed beacon:21
```

You can see the data unique to wireless interfaces that
iwconfig provides, including the type of card (802.11g in
this case), the ESSID or network name (this network's
ESSID is einstein), the mode or kind of network to
which you're connected, the MAC address of the wireless
access point (here 00:12:17:31:4F:C6), and various details
about the quality of the wireless connection.

The combination of ifconfig and iwconfig tells you
everything you need to know about your wireless network
interface. And, just as you can also use ifconfig to configure your wired cards, you can also use iwconfig to configure your wireless cards, as you'll see in the next section.

Configure a Wireless Network
Interface

iwconfig

In the previous section, "View the Status of Your
Wireless Network Interfaces," you used iwconfig to see

important details about your wireless card and its connection. You can also use iwconfig, however, to configure that wireless card and its connections. If this sounds like ifconfig, it should, as iwconfig was based on ifconfig and its behaviors.

NOTE: You can make several changes with iwconfig, but you're only going to look at a few (for more details, see man iwconfig).

The network topologies associated with wired networks, such as star, bus, and ring, to name a few, have been known and understood for quite some time. Wireless networks introduce some new topologies to the mix, including the following:

- Managed (an access point creates a network to which wireless devices can connect; the most common topology for wireless networking)

- Ad-Hoc (two or more wireless devices form a network to work with each other)

- Master (the wireless device acts as an access point)

- Repeater (the wireless device forwards packets to other wireless devices)

There are others, but those are the main ones. Using iwconfig, you can tell your wireless card that you want it to operate differently, in accordance with a new topology.

TIP: For more on stars, busses, rings, and the like, see Wikipedia's "Network Topology" at http://en.wikipedia.org/wiki/Network_topology.

```
# iwconfig ath0 mode ad-hoc
```

After specifying the interface, simply use the mode option following the name of the mode you want to use.

> **NOTE:** Remember that the card you're using in these examples has an interface name of ath0; yours might be eth1, wlan0, or something else entirely. To find out your interface's name, use iwconfig by itself, as discussed in the previous section.

The Extended Service Set Identifier (ESSID) is the name of the wireless network to which you're joined or you want to join. Most of the time an ESSID name of any will work just fine, assuming that you can meet the network's other needs, such as encryption, if that's necessary. Some networks, however, require that you specify the exact ESSID.

```
# iwconfig ath0 essid lincoln
```

Here you are joining a wireless network with an ESSID of lincoln. Simply use the essid option, followed by the name of the ESSID, and you're good.

More and more networks are using encryption to protect users' communications from sniffers that capture all the traffic and then look through it for useful information. The simplest form of network encryption for wireless networks is Wired Equivalent Privacy (WEP). Although this provides a small measure of security, it's just that: small. WEP is easily cracked by a knowledgeable attacker, and it has now been superseded by the much more robust Wi-Fi Protected Access (WPA). Unfortunately, getting WPA to work with wireless cards on Linux can be a real bear, and is beyond the scope of this book. Besides, WEP, despite its flaws, is still far more common, and it *is* better than nothing. Just don't expect complete and total security using it.

TIP: For more on WEP and WPA, see Wikipedia's "Wired Equivalent Privacy" (http://en.wikipedia.org/wiki/WEP) and "Wi-Fi Protected Access" (http://en.wikipedia.org/wiki/Wi-Fi_Protected_Access). You can find information about getting WPA to work with your Linux distribution at "Linux WPA/WPA2/IEEE 802.1X Supplicant" (http://hostap.epitest.fi/wpa_supplicant). If you're using Windows drivers via ndiswrapper, also be sure to check out "How to Use WPA with ndiswrapper" (http://ndiswrapper.sourceforge.net/mediawiki/index.php/WPA).

WEP works with a shared encryption key, a password that exists on both the wireless access point and your machine. The password can come in two forms: hex digits or plain text. It doesn't really matter which because iwconfig can handle both. If you've been given hex digits, simply follow the enc option with the key.

```
# iwconfig ath0 enc 646c64586278742a6229742f4c
```

If you've instead been given plain text to use, you still use the enc option, but you must preface the key with s: to indicate that what follows is a text string.

```
# iwconfig ath0 enc s:dldXbxt*b)t/L
```

TIP: I created those WEP keys using the very nice WEP Key Generator found at www.andrewscompanies.com/tools/wep.asp.

If you have several options to change at one time, you probably would like to perform all of them with one command. To do so, follow iwconfig with your device name, and then place any changes you want to make one after the other.

```
# iwconfig ath0 essid lincoln enc
➥646c64586278742a6229742f4c
```

The preceding listing changes the ESSID and sets WEP encryption using hex digits for the wireless device ath0. You can set as many things at one time as you'd like.

Grab a New Address Using DHCP

```
dhclient
```

Most home networks and many business networks use the Dynamic Host Control Protocol (DHCP) to parcel out IP addresses and other key information about the network to new machines joining it. Without DHCP, any new machine must have all of its networking information hard-coded in; with DHCP, a new machine simply plugs in to the network, asks the DHCP server to provide it with an IP address and other necessary items, and then automatically incorporates the DHCP server's reply into its networking configurations.

NOTE: The following discussion assumes that you've already configured your network device to use DHCP instead of hard-coded settings. Various Linux distributions expect that information to be found in different configuration files. Debian-based distributions look for the line iface [interface] inet dhcp in /etc/network/interfaces. Red Hat–derived distributions instead want to see BOOT-PROTO=dhcp in /etc/sysconfig/network-scripts/ifcfg-[interface]. In these examples, substitute [interface] with the name of your interface. For more inforamtion, search Google for "dhcp *your-distro*."

Sometimes your machine can't connect at boot to the DHCP server, so you need to manually initiate the

DHCP request. Or you might have networking problems that require a new IP address. No matter the reason, the dhclient command attempts to query any available DHCP server for the necessary data (dhclient must be run as root).

```
# dhclient eth0

Listening on LPF/eth0/00:0b:cd:3b:20:e2
Sending on   LPF/eth0/00:0b:cd:3b:20:e2
Sending on   Socket/fallback
DHCPDISCOVER on eth0 to 255.255.255.255 port 67
➥interval 8
DHCPOFFER from 192.168.0.1
DHCPREQUEST on eth0 to 255.255.255.255 port 67
DHCPACK from 192.168.0.1
bound to 192.168.0.104 -- renewal in 37250 seconds.
# ifconfig eth0
eth0 Link encap:Ethernet  HWaddr 00:0B:CD:3B:20:E2
inet addr:192.168.0.104  Bcast:192.168.0.255
➥Mask:255.255.255.0
 inet6 addr: fe80::20b:cdff:fe3b:20e2/64 Scope:Link
```

To release, or give up, the IP address that the DHCP server has assigned you, use the -r (for *release*) option.

```
# dhclient -r eth0

sit0: unknown hardware address type 776
sit0: unknown hardware address type 776
Listening on LPF/eth0/00:0b:cd:3b:20:e2
Sending on   LPF/eth0/00:0b:cd:3b:20:e2
Sending on   Socket/fallback
```

Ideally, the dhclient command should run automatically when you boot your computer, plug in a wireless PCMCIA card, or connect an Ethernet cable to your wired jack, but sometimes it doesn't. When DHCP doesn't work like it's supposed to, turn to dhclient. It's especially nice how dhclient is automatically verbose, so you can see what's going on and diagnose as necessary.

NOTE: Some Linux distributions are still using an older program to perform DHCP—pump—instead of dhclient. For info on pump, take a look at man pump, or read a brief HOWTO for Red Hat and Mandrake at www.faqs.org/docs/ Linux-mini/DHCP.html#REDHAT6.

Make a Network Connection Active

```
ifup
```

You actually use the ifup command all the time without realizing it. When you boot your computer to find that you're successfully connected to the Internet, you can thank ifup. If you plug in an Ethernet cable to the port on the back of your Linux box, and a few seconds later you're able to get email again, it's ifup that did the heavy lifting. In essence, ifup runs when it detects a network event, such as a reboot or a cable plugged in, and then executes the instructions found in your network interface configuration files (if you're curious, a note in the preceding section discussed the names and locations of those files).

Sometimes, though, you might experience networking problems and need to run ifup manually. It's incredibly easy to do so: Log on as root, and then follow ifup with the name of the network interface you want to activate.

```
# ifconfig
lo Link encap:Local Loopback
   inet addr:127.0.0.1  Mask:255.0.0.0
...
# ifup eth0
# ifconfig
eth0 Link encap:Ethernet  HWaddr 00:0B:CD:3B:20:E2
inet addr:192.168.0.14  Bcast:192.168.0.255
➥Mask:255.255.255.0
 inet6 addr: fe80::20b:cdff:fe3b:20e2/64 Scope:Link
 UP BROADCAST RUNNING MULTICAST  MTU:1500
➥Metric:1
...

lo    Link encap:Local Loopback
 inet addr:127.0.0.1  Mask:255.0.0.0
```

Notice that ifup doesn't tell you that it was successful. Indeed, like most Unix apps, ifup is silent upon success, and only noisy if it experiences failure or error. To see what ifup has accomplished, use ifconfig, as shown in the preceding listing.

NOTE: You can also use ifconfig [interface] up or iwconfig [interface] up to make wired or wireless connections active.

Bring a Network Connection Down

`ifdown`

The ifup command makes network connections active, and the ifdown command brings them down. Why would you need to bring down your network connection? Most often, it's because you're trying to bring it up, and ifconfig reports that it's already up, but erroneously configured. So you first bring it down, and then bring it back up.

```
# ifup eth0
ifup: interface eth0 already configured
# ifdown eth0
# ifup eth0
```

Notice that ifdown, like ifup, is silent upon success. If you don't see anything after entering ifdown, the command was successful, and that network interface is no longer going to work.

NOTE: You can also use ifconfig eth0 down or iwconfig ath0 down to bring wired or wireless connections down.

Display Your IP Routing Table

route

When you try to use Secure Shell (SSH) to connect to another computer on your LAN (something you'll learn about in Chapter 15, "Working on the Network"), how does your computer know that it should confine the packets to your LAN and not send them to your router to be sent out on the Internet? And if you point your web browser to www.ubuntu. com, how does your Linux box know to send that request to your router and not to another machine next to you?

The answer is that your Linux kernel has a routing table that keeps track of those things. To view your current routing table, simply enter **route** in your shell (no, you don't have to be root to *view* the routing table, but you do have to be root to *change* it, as you'll see in the next section).

```
$ route
Kernel IP routing table
Destination Gateway      Genmask         Flags Metric
➥Ref         Use Iface
192.168.0.0 *            255.255.255.0 U     0
➥0          0 eth0
default      192.168.0.1 0.0.0.0         UG    0
➥0          0 eth0
```

NOTE: There's only one network interface on this machine, so this is a pretty simple routing table. On a laptop that has both an Ethernet port and a wireless card, you'll see additional entries.

An IP address is composed of four octets, giving it the appearance of xxx.xxx.xxx.xxx, as in 192.168.0.124. When you send a packet out of your machine, the IP address that is the destination of that packet is compared to the Destination column in the routing table. The Genmask column works with the Destination column to indicate which of the four octets should be examined to determine the packet's destination.

For example, let's say you enter **ping 192.168.0.124** in your shell. A Genmask of 255.255.255.0 indicates that only the last octet—the number represented by 0—matters. In other words, when looking at 192.168.0.124, only the .124 is important to route packets to that address. Any packets intended for 192.168.0.1

through 192.168.0.255 (the limits of an IP address) match the Genmask and the Destination, so they stay on the Local Area Network and avoid the router. That's why there's an * in the Gateway column next to 192. 168.0.0: No Gateway is needed because that traffic is local.

On the other hand, everything else is by default intended for the router, which in this instance is at 192.168.0.1 in the Gateway column. The Genmask in this row is 0.0.0.0, indicating that any IP address not matching 192.168.0.1 through 192.168.0.255 should be sent through 192.168.0.1 (because 192.168.0.1 *is* the Gateway, it's a special case). 72.14.203.99, 82.211.81.166, and 216.23.180.5 all match with 0.0.0.0, so they must all go through the Gateway for the Net.

The other interesting thing about the routing table exposed by `route` is the Flags column, which gives information about the route. There are several possible flags, but the most common are U (the route is up) and G (use the gateway). In the preceding table, you can see that both routes are up, but only the second is the Gateway.

Change Your IP Routing Table

`route`

The `route` command can be used not only to view your routing table, but to alter it as well. You need to be careful here, however, as you can break the network and effectively landlock your computer.

Let's say your machine keeps dropping the Gateway, effectively making it impossible for any packets to leave your LAN for the Internet (this really happened to me once with a box). Run the `route` command, verify that

the Gateway is missing, and then add it in with route
(although viewing the route can be done as a normal
user, changes to route requires root access).

```
# route
Kernel IP routing table
Destination Gateway Genmask        Flags Metric Ref
➥Use Iface
192.168.0.0 *        255.255.255.0 U     0      0
➥0 eth0
# route add -net default gw 192.168.0.1 dev eth0
# route
Kernel IP routing table
Destination Gateway      Genmask        Flags Metric
➥Ref   Use Iface
192.168.0.0 *            255.255.255.0 U     0
➥0       0 eth0
default     192.168.0.1 0.0.0.0        UG    0
➥0       0 eth0
```

Let's break down that command. add indicates that
you're adding a new route (to remove one, use del).
The -net option tells the kernel that the target you're
adding is a network, in this case the default destination. gw indicates that you want to route packets matching the destination (here the default, therefore utilizing
a Genmask of 0.0.0.0) using a gateway at 129.168.0.1.
Finally, dev eth0 specifies the device to use, in this case
the Ethernet card at eth0.

Let's say that in addition to your Ethernet card at eth0,
you also have a wireless card at ath0. You want that
wireless card to access resources on a LAN that uses
10.1.xxx.xxx as its base. You don't want the wireless
card to be able to access the Internet at all. To add a
route matching those criteria, you'd use these commands:

```
# route
Kernel IP routing table
Destination Gateway       Genmask         Flags Metric
➥Ref    Use Iface
192.168.0.0 *             255.255.255.0 U       0
➥0        0 eth0
default    192.168.0.1 0.0.0.0           UG      0
➥0        0 eth0
# route add -net 10.1.0.0 netmask 255.255.0.0 dev
➥ath0
# route
Kernel IP routing table
Destination Gateway       Genmask         Flags Metric
➥Ref    Use Iface
192.168.0.0 *             255.255.255.0 U       0
➥0        0 eth0
10.1.0.0       *          255.255.0.0   U       0
➥0        0 ath0
default    192.168.0.1 0.0.0.0           UG      0
➥0        0 eth0
```

Here you indicated the wireless card with dev ath0,
and then specified the netmask as 255.255.0.0 so routing would occur correctly. If you later want to remove
that route, you'd use the following:

```
# route
Kernel IP routing table
Destination Gateway       Genmask         Flags Metric
➥Ref    Use Iface
192.168.0.0 *             255.255.255.0 U       0
➥0        0 eth0
10.1.0.0       *          255.255.0.0   U       0
➥0        0 ath0
default    192.168.0.1 0.0.0.0           UG      0
➥0        0 eth0
```

```
# route del -net 10.1.0.0 netmask 255.255.0.0 dev
➥eth0
# route
Kernel IP routing table
Destination Gateway     Genmask        Flags Metric
➥Ref    Use Iface
192.168.0.0 *           255.255.255.0 U     0
➥0       0 eth0
default     192.168.0.1 0.0.0.0        UG    0
➥0       0 eth0
```

Everything is the same, except you use del instead of add. Now that's easy!

Troubleshooting Network Problems

Linux distributions nowadays usually "just work" when it comes to networking, but you might still experience an issue. Following are some basic tips for trouble-shooting network problems.

If your network interface appears to be up and running, but you can't get on the Internet, first try pinging your localhost device, at 127.0.0.1. If that doesn't work, stop and go no further, because you have a seriously damaged system. If that works, ping your machine's external IP address. If that doesn't work, make sure networking is enabled on your machine. If it does work, now try pinging other machines on your network, assuming you have any. If you're not successful, it's your interface (assuming your router is okay). Make sure that your cables are plugged in (seriously). Use ifconfig (or iwconfig if it's wireless) to verify the status of your interface and use ifup to turn the interface on, if necessary. Then try ping again.

If your attempt to ping another local computer was successful, next try pinging your router. If you can get to other machines on your network, but you can't get to your router, time to check your routing tables with `route` (refer to "Display Your IP Routing Table"). If you're missing items from your routing table, add them, as detailed in "Change Your IP Routing Table."

NOTE: It's much easier to diagnose and fix problems if you have a baseline from which to work. After you know a machine's networking is correct, run `route` and save the results, so you have a stored blueprint if the routing table goes bonkers and you need to restore something later.

If you can get to your router, try pinging a machine you know will be up and running out on the Internet, like www.google.com or www.apple.com. If that doesn't work, try pinging that same machine's IP address. Yes, that means that you need to have some IP addresses on a sticky note or in a text file on your computer for just such an occasion as this. Here are a few that are good right now; of course, they could change, so you really should look these up yourself.

Site	IP Address
www.google.com	72.14.203.99
www.apple.com	17.254.0.91
www.ubuntu.com	82.211.81.166
www.ibm.com	129.42.16.99
www.granneman.com	216.23.180.5

NOTE: How do you get those IP addresses? You can ping the machine using its domain name, and `ping` gives you the IP address, or you can get the same info with traceroute. A quicker method is with the host command, covered earlier in "Perform DNS Lookups."

If you can get to the IP address, but can't get to the domain name, you have a DNS problem. If you're using DHCP, it's time to run dhclient (refer to "Grab a New Address Using DHCP") to try to renew the DNS information provided by your DHCP server. If you're not using DHCP, find the DNS information you need by looking on your router or asking your administrator or ISP, and then add it manually as root to /etc/resolv.conf so that it looks like this, for example:

```
nameserver 24.217.0.5
nameserver 24.217.0.55
```

That's nameserver (a required word), followed by an IP address you're supposed to use for the DNS. If your router can handle it, and you know its IP address (192.168.0.1, let's say), you can always try this first:

```
nameserver 192.168.0.1
```

Try ifdown and then ifup and see if you're good to go. If you're still having problems, time to begin again, starting always with hardware. Is everything seated correctly? Is everything plugged in? After you're sure of that, start checking your software. The worst-case scenario is that your hardware just doesn't have drivers to work with Linux. It's rare, and growing rarer all the time, but it still happens.

Wireless cards, however, can be wildly incompatible with Linux thanks to close-mouthed manufacturers who don't want to help Linux developers make their hardware work. To prevent headaches, it's a good idea to check online to make sure a wireless card you're thinking about purchasing will be copasetic with Linux. Good sites to review include Hardware Supported by Madwifi (http://madwifi.org/wiki/Compatibility); Linux Wireless LAN Support (http://linux-wless.passys.nl/), which is a bit outdated but still useful; and my constantly updated list of bookmarks relating to Linux and wireless connectivity (http://del.icio.us/rsgranne/wireless). When it comes to specific hardware, I can wholeheartedly recommend the Netgear WG511T wireless PCMCIA card. I simply inserted it into my laptop running the latest K/Ubuntu, and it worked immediately.

Oh, and to finish our troubleshooting: If you can successfully ping both the IP address and the domain name, stop reading this—you're online! Go have fun!

Conclusion

You've covered a wide selection of networking tools in this chapter. Many of them, such as `ifconfig`, `iwconfig`, and `route`, can perform double duty, both informing you about the status of your connectivity and allowing you to change the parameters of your connections. Others are used more for diagnostic purposes, such as `ping`, `traceroute`, and `host`. Finally, some govern your ability to connect to a network at all: `dhclient`, `ifup`, and `ifdown`. If you're serious about Linux, you're going to need to learn all of them. There's nothing more frustrating than a network connection that won't work, but often the right program can fix that problem in a matter of seconds. Know your tools well, and you can fix issues quickly and efficiently as they arise.

15

Working on the Network

Many of the commands in this chapter are so rich in features and power that they deserve books of their own. This book can't begin to cover all of the awesome stuff you can do with ssh, rsync, wget, and curl, for instance, but it can get you started. The best thing to do with these commands is to try them, get comfortable with the basics, and then begin exploring the areas that interest you. There's enough to keep you busy for a long time, and after you start using your imagination, you'll discover a world of cool applications for the programs you're going to read about in this chapter.

Securely Log In to Another Computer

ssh

Because Unix was built with networking in mind, it's no surprise that early developers created programs that would allow users to connect to other machines so they could run programs, view files, and access resources. For a long time, telnet was the program to use, but it had a huge problem; it was completely insecure. Everything you send using telnet—your username, password, and all commands and data—is sent without any encryption at all. Anyone listening in can see everything, and that's just not good.

To combat this problem, ssh (secure shell) was developed. It can do everything telnet can, and then a lot more. Even better, all ssh traffic is encrypted, making it even more powerful and useful. If you need to connect to another machine, whether that computer is on the other side of the globe or in the next room, use ssh.

Let's say you want to use the ssh command from your laptop (named pound, and found at 192.168.0.15) to your desktop (named eliot, and located at 192.168.0.25) so you can look at a file. Your username on the laptop is ezra, but on the desktop it's tom. To SSH to eliot, you'd enter the following (you could also use domain names such as hoohah.granneman.com if one existed):

```
$ ssh tom@192.168.0.25
tom@192.168.0.25's password:
Linux eliot 2.6.12-10-386 #1 Mon Jan 16 17:18:08 UTC
➥ 2006 i686 GNU/Linux
Last login: Mon Feb 6 22:40:31 2006
➥from 192.168.0.15
[Listing truncated for length]
```

You're prompted for a password after you connect. Type it in (you won't see what you're typing, in order to prevent someone from "shoulder surfing" and discovering your password), press Enter, and if it's accepted, you see some information about the machine to which you just connected, including its name, kernel, date and time, and the last time you logged in. You can now run any command you're authorized to run on that machine as though you were sitting right in front of it. From the perspective of ssh and eliot, it doesn't matter where on earth you are—you're logged in and ready to go.

If this were the first time you'd ever connected to eliot, however, you would have seen a different message:

```
$ ssh tom@192.168.0.25
The authenticity of host '192.168.0.25
➡(192.168.0.25)' can't be established.
RSA key fingerprint is 54:53:c3:1c:9a:07:22:0c:82:
➡7b:38:53:21:23:ce:53.
Are you sure you want to continue connecting
➡(yes/no)?
```

Basically, ssh is telling you that it doesn't recognize this machine, and it's asking you to verify the machine's identity. Type in **yes**, press Enter, and you get another message, along with the password prompt:

```
Warning: Permanently added '192.168.0.25' (RSA)
➡to the list of known hosts.1
tom@192.168.0.25's password:
```

From here things proceed normally. You only see this message the first time you connect to eliot because ssh stores that RSA key fingerprint it mentioned in a file on pound located at ~/.ssh/known_hosts. Take a look at that file, and you see a line has been added to it. Depending on whether the HashKnownHosts option has been enabled in your /etc/ssh/ssh_config file, that line appears in one of two formats. If HashKnownHosts is set to no, it looks something like this:

```
192.168.0.25 ssh-rsa SkxPUQLYqXSzknsstN6Bh2MHK5AmC6E
➥pg4psdNL69R5pHbQi3kRWNNNNO3AmnP1lp2RNNNNOVjNN9mu5FZe
➥l6zKOiKfJBbLh/Mh9KOhBNtrX6prfcxO9vBEAHYITeLTMmYZLQHB
➥xSr6ehj/9xFxkCHDYLdKFmxaffgA6Ou2ZUX5NzP6Rct4cfqAY69E
➥5cUoDv3xEJ/gj2zv0bh630zehrGc=
```

You can clearly see the IP address as well as the
encryption hash, but that's nothing compared to what
you'd see if HashKnownHosts is set to yes:

```
NNNNO3AmnP1lp2RNNNNOVjNNNVRNgaJdxOt3GIrhOOlPD6KBIU1k
➥aT6nQoJUMVTx2tWb5KiF/LLD4Zwbv2Z/j/OczCZIQNPwDUf6YiKU
➥FFC6eagqpLDDB4T9qsOajOPLNinRZpcQoPlXf1u6j1agfJzqUJUY
➥E+Lwv8yzmPidCvOuCZOLQH4qfkVNXEQxmyy6iz6b2wp=?
```

Everything is hashed, even the machine's IP address or
domain name. This is good from a security standpoint,
but it's a problem if the OS on eliot should ever
change. In other words, if you ever need to reinstall
Linux on eliot, the next time you log in from pound
you'll see this dire warning:

```
@@@@@@@@@@@@@@@@@@@@@@@@@@@@@@@@@@@@@@@@@@@@@@@@@@@@@@@
@ WARNING: REMOTE HOST IDENTIFICATION HAS CHANGED! @
@@@@@@@@@@@@@@@@@@@@@@@@@@@@@@@@@@@@@@@@@@@@@@@@@@@@@@@
IT IS POSSIBLE THAT SOMEONE IS DOING SOMETHING NASTY
Someone could be eavesdropping on you right now
➥(man-in-the-middle attack)!
It is also possible that the RSA host key has just
➥been changed.
The fingerprint for the RSA key sent by the remote
➥host is
19:85:59:5c:6a:24:85:53:07:7a:dc:34:37:c6:72:1b.
Please contact your system administrator.
Add correct host key in /home/pound/.ssh/
➥known_hosts to get rid of this message.
```

```
Offending key in /home/pound/.ssh/known_hosts:8
RSA host key for 192.168.0.125 has changed and you
➥have requested strict checking.
Host key verification failed.
```

The problem is that the ssh key on eliot has changed since the OS has been reinstalled, and when ssh checks the key for eliot it has stored in pound's known_hosts file with the new key, it sees that there's a mismatch and warns you. To fix this, simply delete the line in pound's known_hosts that corresponds to eliot, save the file, and reconnect. To ssh, this is the first time you've connected, so it asks if you want to accept the key. Say yes, and things are good again.

If eliot is the only machine you ever SSH to, finding the correct line to delete in known_hosts is easy because it's the only one. But if you connect to several machines, you're going to have a hard time. Quick, which one of these represents hoohah.granneman.com?

- AAAAB3NzaC1yc2EAAAABIwAAAIEAtnWqkBg3TVeuO0yCQ6XO
  VH1xnG6aDbWHZIGk2gJo5XvS/YYQ4Mjoi2M/w/OpmPMVDACj
  QHs6LvXHSSP6rntdcYQQO4G9dfBnwBCYAvaEMcpDbCyKs1h6
  w1ntsWmdHWHLR+Yji8lmzCvqPiBhPMOYDU4dsxIAKRDkzll6
  vm6o2jc=

- NNNNO3AmnP1lp2RNNNNOVjNNNNVRNgaJdxOt3GIrhOOlPD6KB
  IU1kaT6nQoJUMVTx2tWb5KiF/LLD4Zwbv2Z/j/OczCZIQNPw
  DUf6YiKUFFC6eagqpLDDB4T9qsOajOPLNinRZpcQoPlXf1u6
  j1agfJzqUJUYE+Lwv8yzmPidCvOuCZOLQH4qfkVNXEQxmyy6
  iz6b2wp=

- AAAAB3NzaC1yc2EAAAABIwAAAIEAtnWqkBg3TVeuO0yCQ6XO
  VH1xnG6aDbWHZIGk2gJo5XvS/YYQ4Mjoi2M/w/OpmPMVDACj
  QHs6LvXHSSP6rntdcYQQO4G9dfBnwBCYAvaEMcpDbCyKs1h6
  w1ntsWmdHWHLR+Yji8lmzCvqPiBhPMOYDU4dsxIAKRDkzll6
  vm6o2jc=

Hard to tell, eh? Because you can't tell, you really have no choice but to delete every line, which means that you have to re-accept the key every time you log in to a machine. In order to avoid this, it might be easier just to edit /etc/ssh/ssh_config as root and set HashKnownHosts to no.

Securely Log In to Another Machine Without a Password

`ssh`

The name of this section might appear to be a misnomer, but it's entirely possible to log in to a machine via ssh, but without providing a password. If you log in every day to a particular computer (and there are some boxes that I might log in to several times a day), the techniques in this section will make you very happy.

Let's say you want to make it possible to log in to eliot (username: tom) from pound (username: ezra) without requiring that you type a password. To start with, create an ssh authentication key on pound using the following command:

```
$ ssh-keygen -t dsa
Generating public/private dsa key pair.
Enter file in which to save the key
➥(/home/ezra/.ssh/id_dsa):
Enter passphrase (empty for no passphrase):
Enter same passphrase again:
Your identification has been saved in
➥/home/ezra/.ssh/id_dsa.
Your public key has been saved in
➥/home/ezra/.ssh/id_dsa.pub.
```

```
The key fingerprint is:
30:a4:a7:31:27:d1:61:82:e7:66:ae:ed:6b:96:3c:24
➥ezra@pound
```

Accept the default location in which to save the key by
pressing Enter, and leave the passphrase field blank as
well by pressing Enter twice when asked. You just created a private key at ~/.ssh/id_dsa and a public key at
~/.ssh/id_dsa.pub.

Now you need to transfer the public key—not the private key!—from pound to eliot. The developers behind
ssh are way ahead of you, and have created a program
that makes this as easy as falling off a log. To automatically copy your public key from pound to eliot, just
enter the following on pound:

$ **ssh-copy-id -i ~/.ssh/id_dsa.pub tom@192.168.0.25**
Now try logging into the machine, with ssh 'tom@
192.168.0.25', and check in .ssh/authorized_keys to
make sure you haven't added extra keys that you
weren't expecting.

You're done (although if you want to follow the advice
given by ssh-copy-id, go right ahead). Watch what happens when you use the ssh command from pound to
eliot now:

```
$ ssh tom@192.168.0.25
Linux eliot 2.6.12-10-386 #1 Mon Jan 16 17:18:08 UTC
➥ 2006 i686 GNU/Linux
Last login: Mon Feb 6 22:40:31 2006 from
➥192.168.0.15
```

Notice that you weren't asked to enter a password,
which is exactly what you wanted.

Some of you are wondering about the security of this
trick. No passwords? Freely exchanging keys? It's true,

but think about it for a moment. True, if someone gets
on pound, he can now connect to eliot without a password. But that simply means that you need to practice
good security on pound. If pound is compromised, you
have enormous problems whether or not the attacker
realizes that he can also get to eliot. On top of that,
you shoot passwords around the Internet all the time. If
an attacker acquires your password, he can do major
damage as well. Isn't your private key as important as a
password? And aren't you going to back it up and safe-
guard it? When you think about it in those terms,
exchanging keys via ssh is at least as secure as passwords, and in most ways much more secure.

Nonetheless, if you prefer to keep using passwords,
that's certainly your prerogative. That's what open
source and Linux is all about: choice.

Securely Transfer Files Between Machines

sftp

In the same way that ssh is a far better choice than
telnet, SFTP is far better than FTP. Like telnet, FTP
sends your name and password, as well as all the data
being transferred, in the clear so that anyone sniffing
packets can listen in. SFTP, on the other hand, uses ssh
to encrypt everything: username, passwords, and traffic.
Other than the fact it's about a million times more
secure, it's remarkably similar to FTP in its commands,
which should make it easy to learn and use.

If you can access a machine via ssh, you can also SFTP to
it. To use the sftp command from pound (192.168.0.15;

username ezra) to eliot (192.168.0.25; username tom),
just use this command:

```
$ sftp tom@192.168.0.25
Connecting to 192.168.0.25...
tom@192.168.0.25's password:
sftp>
```

If you've read the previous section, "Securely Log In to
Another Machine Without a Password," you might be
wondering why you were prompted for a password.
You're correct: The preceding example was taken
before a connection that didn't require a password was
set. After you've done that, you would instead see a
login that looks like this:

```
$ sftp tom@192.168.0.25
Connecting to 192.168.0.25...
sftp>
```

After you're logged in via sftp, the commands you can
run are pretty standard. Table 15.1 lists some of the more
common commands; for the full list, look at man sftp.

Table 15.1 Useful SFTP Commands

Command	Meaning
cd	Change directory
exit	Close the connection to the remote SSH server
get	Copy the specified file to the local machine
help	Get help on commands
lcd	Change the directory on the local machine
lls	List files on the local machine

Table 15.1   **Continued**

Command	Meaning
ls	List files in the working directory on the remote SSH server
put	Copy the specified file to the remote SSH server
rm	Remove the specified file from the remote SSH server

Securely Copy Files Between Hosts

scp

If you're in a hurry and you need to copy a file securely from one machine to another, scp (secure copy) is what you want. In essence, here's the basic pattern for using scp:

```
scp user@host1:file1 user@host2:file2
```

This is basically the same syntax as good ol' cp, but now extended to the network. An example will make things clearer. Let's say you want to copy backup.sh from pound (192.168.0.15; username ezra) to /home/tom/bin on eliot (129.168.0.25; username tom) using scp:

```
$ pwd
/home/ezra
$ ls ~/bin
backup.sh
$ scp ~/bin/backup.sh tom@192.168.0.25/home/tom/bin
backup.sh                  100% 8806        8.6KB/s    00:00
$
```

You weren't prompted for a password because you set things up earlier in "Securely Log In to Another Machine Without a Password" so ssh doesn't require passwords to connect from pound to eliot, and because scp relies on ssh, you don't need a password here, either. If you hadn't done that, you would have been asked to enter tom's password before continuing.

Let's say you have several JPEGs you want to transfer from pound to eliot. No problem—just use a wildcard:

```
$ ls -1 ~/covers
earth_wind_&_fire.jpg
handel_-_chamber_music.jpg
smiths_best_1.jpg
strokes_-_is_this_it.jpg
u2_pop.jpg
$ scp *.jpg tom@192.168.0.25:/home/tom/album_covers
earth_wind_&_fire.jpg           100%   44KB   43.8KB/s
handel_-_chamber_music.jpg      100%   12KB   12.3KB/s
smiths_best_1.jpg               100%   47KB   47.5KB/s
strokes_-_is_this_it.jpg        100%   38KB   38.3KB/s
u2_pop.jpg                      100%   9222
9.0KB/sQ
```

Now let's say you want to go the other direction. You're still on pound, and you want to copy several pictures of Libby from eliot to pound, and into a different directory than the one in which you currently are in:

```
$ scp tom@192.168.0.25:/home/tom/pictures/dog/libby*
➡ ~/pix/libby
libby_in_window_1.20020611.jpg 100%   172KB 172.4KB/s
libby_in_window_2.20020611.jpg 100%   181KB 180.8KB/s
libby_in_window_3.20020611.jpg 100%   197KB 196.7KB/s
libby_in_window_4.20020611.jpg 100%   188KB 187.9KB/s
```

The scp command is really useful when you need to securely copy files between machines. If you have many files to copy, however, you'll find that scp can quickly grow tiresome. In cases like that, you might want to look at SFTP or a mounted Samba share (which is covered in "Mount a Samba Filesystem," found in Chapter 16, "Windows Networking").

Securely Transfer and Back Up Files

`rsync -v`

rsync is one of the coolest, most useful programs ever invented, and many people rely on it every day (like me!). What does it do? Its uses are myriad (here we go again into "you could write a book about this command!"), but let's focus on one very powerful, necessary feature: its capability to back up files effectively and securely, with a minimum of network traffic.

Let's say you intend to back up 2GB of files every night from a machine named coleridge (username: sam) to another computer named wordsworth (username: will). Without rsync, you're looking at a transfer of 2GB every single night, a substantial amount of traffic, even on a fast network connection. With rsync, however, you might be looking at a transfer that will take a few moments at most. Why? Because when rsync backs up those 2GB, it transfers only the differences between all the files that make up those 2GB of data. If only a few hundred kilobytes changed in the past 24 hours, that's all that rsync transfers. If instead it was 100MB, that's what rsync copies over. Either way, it's much less than 2GB.

Here's a command that, run from coleridge, transfers the entire content of the documents directory to a backup drive on wordsworth. Look at the command, look at the results, and then you can walk through what those options mean (the command is given first with long options instead of single letters for readability, and then with single letters, if available, for comparison).

```
$ rsync --verbose --progress --stats --recursive
➥--times --perms --links --compress --rsh=ssh
➥--delete /home/sam/documents/
➥will@wordsworth:/media/backup/documents

$ rsync -v --progress --stats -r -t -p -l -z -e ssh
➥--delete /home/sam/documents/
➥will@wordsworth:/media/backup/documents
```

Of course, you could also run the command this way, if you wanted to combine all the options:

```
$ rsync -vrtplze ssh --progress --stats --delete
➥/home/sam/documents/
➥will@wordsworth:/media/backup/documents
```

Upon running rsync using any of the methods listed, you'd see something like this:

```
building file list ...
107805 files to consider
deleting clientele/Linux_Magazine/do_it_yourself/13/
➥gantt_chart.txt~
deleting Security/diebold_voting/black_box_voting/
➥bbv_chapter-9.pdf


deleting E-commerce/Books/20050811 eBay LIL ABNER
➥DAILIES 6 1940.txt
```

```
Security/electronic_voting/diebold/black_box_voting/
➥bbv_chapter-9.pdf
legal_issues/free_speech/Timeline A history of free
➥speech.txt
E-commerce/2005/Books/20050811 eBay LIL ABNER
➥DAILIES 6 1940.txt

connectivity/connectivity_info.txt
[Results greatly truncated for length]
Number of files: 107805
Number of files transferred: 120
Total file size: 6702042249 bytes
Total transferred file size: 15337159 bytes

File list size: 2344115

Total bytes sent: 2345101
Total bytes received: 986
sent 2345101 bytes  received 986 bytes  7507.48
➥bytes/sec
total size is 6702042249  speedup is 2856.69
```

Take a look at those results. rsync first builds a list of all files that it must consider—107,805 in this case—and then deletes any files on the target (wordsworth) that no longer exist on the source (coleridge). In this example, three files are deleted: a backup file (the ~ is a giveaway on that one) from an article for *Linux Magazine*, a PDF on electronic voting, and then a text receipt for a purchased book.

After deleting files, rsync copies over any that have changed, or if it's the same file, just the changes to the file, which is part of what makes rsync so slick. In this case, four files are copied over. It turns out that the PDF was actually moved to a new subdirectory, but to rsync it's a new file, so it's copied over in its entirety.

The same is true for the text receipt. The A history of free speech.txt file is an entirely new file, so it's copied over to wordsworth as well.

After listing the changes it made, rsync gives you some information about the transfer as a whole. 120 files were transferred, 15337159 bytes (about 14MB) out of 6702042249 bytes (around 6.4GB). Other data points are contained in the summation, but those are the key ones.

Now let's look at what you asked your computer to do. The head and tail of the command are easy to understand: the command rsync at the start, then options, and then the source directory you're copying from (/home/sam/documents/, found on coleridge), followed by the target directory you're copying to (/media/backup/documents, found on wordsworth). Before going on to examine the options, you need to focus on the way the source and target directories are designated because there's a catch in there that will really hurt if you don't watch it.

You want to copy the contents of the documents directory found on coleridge, but not the directory itself, and that's why you use documents/ and not documents. The slash after documents in /home/sam/documents/ tells rsync that you want to copy the *contents* of that directory into the documents directory found on wordsworth; if you instead used documents, you'd copy the directory *and* its contents, resulting in /media/backup/documents/ documents on wordsworth.

NOTE: The slash is only important on the source directory; it doesn't matter whether you use a slash on the target directory.

There's one option that wasn't listed previously but is still a good idea to include when you're figuring out how your rsync command will be structured: -n (or --dry-run). If you include that option, rsync runs, but doesn't actually delete or copy anything. This can be a lifesaver if your choices would have resulted in the deletion of important files. Before committing to your rsync command, especially if you're including the --delete option, do yourself a favor and perform a dry run first!

Now on to the options you used. The -v (or --verbose) option, coupled with --progress, orders rsync to tell you in detail what it's doing at all times. You saw that in the results shown earlier in this section, in which rsync tells you what it's deleting and what it's copying. If you're running rsync via an automated script, you don't need this option, although it doesn't hurt; if you're running rsync interactively, this is an incredibly useful display of information to have in front of you because you can see what's happening.

The metadata you saw at the end of rsync's results—the information about the number and size of files transferred, as well as other interesting data—appeared because you included the --stats option. Again, if you're scripting rsync, this isn't needed, but it's sure nice to see if you're running the program manually.

You've seen the -r (or --recursive) option many other times with other commands, and it does here what it does everywhere else. Instead of stopping in the current directory, it tunnels down through all subdirectories, affecting everything in its path. Because you want to copy the entire documents directory and all of its contents, you want to use -r.

The -t (or --times) option makes rsync transfer the files' modification times along with the files. If you don't include this option, rsync cannot tell what it has previously transferred, and the next time you run the command, all files are copied over again. This is probably not the behavior you want, as it completely obviates the features that make rsync so useful, so be sure to include -t.

Permissions were discussed in Chapter 7, "Ownerships and Permissions," and here they reappear again. The -p (or --perms) option tells rsync to update permissions on any files found on the target so they match what's on the source. It's part of making the backup as accurate as possible, so it's a good idea.

When a soft link is found on the source, the -l (or --links) option re-creates the link on the target. Instead of copying the actual file, which is obviously not what the creator of a soft link intended, the link to the file is copied over, again preserving the original state of the source.

Even over a fast connection, it's a good idea to use the -z (or --compress) option, as rsync then uses gzip compression while transferring files. On a slow connection, this option is mandatory; on a fast connection, it saves you that much more time.

In the name of security, you're using the -e (or --rsh=ssh) option, which tells rsync to tunnel all of its traffic using ssh. Easy file transfers, and secure as well? Sign me up!

NOTE: If you're using ssh, why didn't you have to provide a password? Because you used the technique displayed in "Securely Log In to Another Machine Without a Password" to remove the need to do so.

We've saved the most dangerous for last: --delete. If you're creating a mirror of your files, you obviously want that mirror to be as accurate as possible. That means deleted files on the source need to be deleted on the target as well. But that also means you can accidentally blow away stuff you wanted to keep. If you're going to use the --delete option—and you probably will—be sure to use the -n (or --dry-run) option that was discussed at the beginning of your look at rysnc's options.

rsync has many other options and plenty of other ways to use the command (the man page identifies eight ways it can be used, which is impressive), but the setup discussed in this section will definitely get you started. Open up man rsync on your terminal, or search Google for "rsync tutorial," and you'll find a wealth of great information. Get to know rsync: When you yell out "Oh no!" upon deleting a file, but then follow it with "Whew! It's backed up using rsync!" you'll be glad you took the time to learn this incredibly versatile and useful command.

TIP: If you want to be really safe with your data, set up rsync to run with a regular cron job. For instance, create a file titled backup.sh (~/bin is a good place for it) and type in the command you've been using:

```
$ rsync --verbose --progress --stats
➥--recursive --times --perms --links
➥--compress --rsh=ssh --delete
➥/home/sam/documents/ will@wordsworth:
➥/media/backup/documents
```

Use chmod to make the file executable:

```
$ chmod 744 /home/scott/bin/backup.sh
```

Then add the following lines to a file named cronfile (I put mine in my ~/bin directory as well):

```
# backup documents every morning at 3:05 am
05 03 * * * /home/scott/bin/backup.sh
```

The first line is a comment explaining the purpose of the job, and the second line tells cron to automatically run /home/scott/bin/backup.sh every night at 3:05 a.m.

Now add the job to cron:

```
$ crontab /home/scott/bin/cronfile
```

Now you don't need to worry about your backups ever again. It's all automated for you—just make sure you leave your computers on overnight!

(For more on cron, see man cron or "Newbie: Intro to cron" at www.unixgeeks.org/security/newbie/unix/cron-1.html.)

Download Files Non-interactively

wget

The Net is a treasure trove of pictures, movies, and music that are available for downloading. The problem is that manually downloading every file from a collection of 200 MP3s quickly grows tedious, leading to mind rot and uncontrollable drooling. The wget command is used to download files and websites without any interference; you set the command in motion and it happily downloads whatever you specified, for hours on end.

The tricky part, of course, is setting up the command. wget is another super-powerful program that really deserves a book all to itself, so we don't have space to show you everything it can do. Instead, you're going to focus on doing two things with wget: downloading a whole mess of files, which is looked at here, and downloading entire websites, which is covered in the next section.

Here's the premise: You find a wonderful website called "The Old Time Radio Archives." On this website are a large number of vintage radio shows, available for download in MP3 format—365 MP3s, to be exact, one for every day of the year. It would sure be nice to grab those MP3s, but the prospect of right-clicking on every MP3 hyperlink, choosing Save Link As, and then clicking OK to start the download isn't very appealing.

Examining the directory structure a bit more, you notice that the MP3s are organized in a directory structure like this:

```
http://www.oldtimeradioarchives.com/mp3/
    season_10/
    season_11/

    ...
    season_20/

    ...
    season_3/
    season_4/
    ...
    season_9/
```

NOTE: The directories are not sorted in numerical order, as humans would do it, but in alphabetical order, which is how computers sort numbers unless told otherwise. After all, "ten" comes before "three" alphabetically.

Inside each directory sit the MP3s. Some directories have just a few files in them, and some have close to 20. If you click on the link to a directory, you get a web page that lists the files in that directory like this:

```
[BACK] Parent Directory        19-May-2002 01:03      -
[SND]  1944-12-24_532.mp3      06-Jul-2002 13:54    6.0M
[SND]  1944-12-31_533.mp3      06-Jul-2002 14:28    6.5M
[SND]  1945-01-07_534.mp3      06-Jul-2002 20:05    6.8M
```

[SND] is a GIF image of musical notes that shows up in front of every file listing.

So the question is, how do you download all of these MP3s that have different filenames and exist in different directories? The answer is wget!

Start by creating a directory on your computer into which you'll download the MP3 files.

```
$ mkdir radio_mp3s
```

Now use the cd command to get into that directory, and then run wget:

```
$ cd radio_mp3s
$ wget -r -l2 -np -w 5 -A.mp3 -R.html,.gif
➥http://www.oldtimeradioarchives.com/mp3/`
```

Let's walk through this command and its options.

wget is the command you're running, of course, and at the far end is the URL that you want wget to use: http://www.oldtimeradioarchives.com/mp3. The important stuff, though, lies in between the command and the URL.

The -r (or --recursive) option for wget follows links and goes down through directories in search of files. By telling wget that it is to act recursively, you ensure that wget will go through every season's directory, grabbing all the MP3s it finds.

The -l2 (or --level=[#]) option is important yet tricky. It tells wget how deep it should go in retrieving files recursively. The lowercase l stands for *level* and the number is the depth to which wget should descend. If you specified -l1 for level one, wget would look in the /mp3 directory only. That would result in a download of...nothing. Remember, the /mp3 directory contains other subdirectories: season_10, season_11, and so on, and those are directories that contain the MP3s you want. By specifying -l2, you're asking wget to first enter /mp3 (which would be level one), and then go into each season_# directory in turn and grab anything in it. You need to be very careful with the level you specify. If you aren't careful, you can easily fill your hard drive in very little time.

One of the ways to avoid downloading more than you expected is to use the -np (or --no-parent) option, which prevents wget from recursing into the parent directory. If you look back at the preceding list of files, you'll note that the very first link is the parent directory. In other words, when in /season_10, the parent is /mp3. The same is true for /season_11, /season_12, and so on. You don't want wget to go *up*, however, you want it to go *down*. And you certainly don't need to waste time by going up into the same directory—/mp3— every time you're in a season's directory.

This next option isn't required, but it would sure be polite of you to use it. The -w (or --wait=[#]) option introduces a short wait between each file download. This helps prevent overloading the server as you hammer it continuously for files. By default, the number is interpreted by wget as seconds; if you want, you can also specify minutes by appending m after the number, or hours with h, or even days with d.

Now it gets very interesting. The -A (or --accept) option emphasizes to wget that you only want to download files of a certain type and nothing else. The A stands for *accept*, and it's followed by the file suffixes that you want, separated by commas. You only want one kind of file type, MP3, so that's all you specify: -A.mp3.

On the flip side, the -R (or --reject) option tells wget what you don't want: HTML and GIF files. By refusing those, you don't get those little musical notes represented by [SND] shown previously. Separate your list of suffixes with a comma, giving you -R.html,.gif.

Running wget with those options results in a download of 365 MP3s to your computer. If, for some reason, the transfer was interrupted—your router dies, someone trips over your Ethernet cable and yanks it out of your box, a backhoe rips up the fiber coming in to your business—just repeat the command, but add the -c (or --continue) option. This tells wget to take over from where it was forced to stop. That way you don't download everything all over again.

Here's another example that uses wget to download files. A London DJ released two albums worth of MP3s consisting of mash-ups of The Beatles and The Beastie Boys, giving us The Beastles, of course. The MP3s are listed, one after the other, on www.djbc.net/beastles.

The following command pulls the links out of that web page, writes them to a file, and then starts downloading those links using wget:

```
$ dog --links http://www.djbc.net/beastles/ | grep
➥mp3 > beastles ; wget -i beastles
--12:58:12--  http://www.djbc.net/beastles/
➥webcontent/djbc-holdittogethernow.mp3
           => `djbc-holdittogethernow.mp3'
Resolving www.djbc.net... 216.227.209.173
Connecting to www.djbc.net|216.227.209.173|:80...
➥connected.
HTTP request sent, awaiting response... 200 OK
Length: 4,533,083 (4.3M) [audio/mpeg]
100%[==========>] 4,533,083    203.20K/s    ETA 00:00
12:58:39 (166.88 KB/s) - `djbc-holdittogethernow.
➥mp3' saved [4533083/4533083]
```

In Chapter 5, "Viewing Files," you learned about cat, which outputs files to STDOUT. The "Concatenate Files and Number the Lines" section mentioned a better cat, known as dog (which is true because dogs *are* better than cats). If you invoke dog with the --links option and point it at a URL, the links are pulled out of the page and displayed on STDOUT. You pipe those links to grep, asking grep to filter out all but lines containing mp3, and then redirect the resulting MP3 links to a text file named beastles (piping and redirecting are covered in Chapter 4, "Building Blocks," and the grep command is covered in Chapter 9, "Finding Stuff: Easy").

The semicolon (covered in the "Run Several Commands Sequentially" section in Chapter 4) ends that command and starts a new one: wget. The -i (or --input-file) option tells wget to look in a file for the URLs to download, instead of STDIN. If you have many links, put them all in a file and use the -i option

with wget. In this case, you point wget to the beastles
file you just created via dog and grep, and the MP3s
begin to download, one after the other.

Now really, what could be easier? Ah, the power of the
Linux command line!

Download Websites
Non-interactively

wget

If you want to back up your website or download
another website, look to wget. In the previous section
you used wget to grab individual files, but you can use
it to obtain entire sites as well.

NOTE: Please be reasonable with wget. Don't download
enormous sites, and keep in mind that someone creates and
owns the sites that you're copying. Don't copy a site
because you want to "steal" it.

Let's say you're buzzing around a site at www.neato.
com and you find yourself at www.neato.com/articles/
index.htm. You'd like to copy everything in the
/articles section, but you don't want anything else on
the site. The following command does what you'd like:

```
$ wget -E -r -k -p -w 5 -np
➥http://www.neato.com/articles/index.htm
```

You could have combined the options this way, as well:

```
$ wget -Erkp -w 5 -np
➥http://www.neato.com/articles/index.htm
```

As in the previous section, the command begins with wget and ends with the URL you want to use. You looked at the -w (or --wait=[#]) option before, and that's the same, as well as -np (or --no-parent) and -r (or --recursive). Let's examine the new options that have been introduced in this example.

When you download a site, some of the pages might not end with .htm or .html; instead, they might end with .asp, .php, .cfm, or something else. The problem comes in if you try to view the downloaded site on your computer. If you're running a web server on your desktop, things might look just fine, but more than likely you're not running Apache on your desktop. Even without a web server, however, pages ending in .htm or .html will work on your box if you open them with a web browser. If you use the -E (or --html-extension) option, wget converts every page so that it ends with .html, thus enabling you to view them on your computer without any special software.

Downloading a site might introduce other issues, however, which you can fortunately get around with the right wget options. Links on the pages you download with wget might not work after you open the pages on your computer, making it impossible to navigate from page to page. By specifying the -k (or --convert-links) option, you order wget to rewrite links in the pages so they work on your computer. This option fixes not only links to pages, but also links to pictures, Cascading Style Sheets, and files. You'll be glad you used it.

Speaking of Cascading Style Sheets (CSS) and images, they're why you want to use the -p (or --page-requisites) option. In order for the web page to display correctly, the web developer might have specified images, CSS, and JavaScript files to be used along with the page's HTML. The -p option requires that wget download any files needed to display the web pages that you're grabbing. With it, looking at the page after it's on your machine duplicates what you saw on the Web; without it, you might end up with an unreadable file.

The man page for wget is enormously long and detailed, and it's where you will ultimately end up if you want to use wget in a more sophisticated way. If you think wget sounds interesting to you, start reading. You'll learn a lot.

Download Sequential Files and Internet Resources

`curl`

At first blush, wget and curl seem similar: Both download files non-interactively. They each have one large difference distinguishing them, however, among many smaller ones: curl supports sequences and sets in specifying what to download, which wget does not, while wget supports recursion, a feature missing from curl.

NOTE: The programs have plenty of other differences. The full list of curl's features can be seen at "Features—What Can curl Do" (http://curl.haxx.se/docs/features.html), while some of wget's are listed at "Overview" (www.gnu.org/software/wget/manual/html_node/Overview.html#Overview). The cURL site has a chart comparing curl to other, similar programs at "Compare cURL Features with Other FTP+HTTP Tools" (http://curl.haxx.se/docs/comparison-table.html); while informative, the chart is (unsurprisingly) a bit biased toward curl.

Here's an example that uses curl's capability to support sequences in specifying what to download. The excellent National Public Radio show *This American Life* makes archives of all of its shows available for download on its parent website in Real Audio format (why they chose Real and not a more open format is a mystery). If you want to download 10 of these Real Audio files, just use the following:

```
$ curl -O http://www.wbez.org/ta/[1-10].rm
[1/10]: http://www.wbez.org/ta/1.rm --> 1.rm
--_curl_--http://www.wbez.org/ta/1.rm
```

Notice how you used [1-10].rm to specify that you wanted to download 1.rm, 2.rm, 3.rm, and so on. If WBEZ had instead named the files one.rm, two.rm, and three.rm, for example, you could have used a part set instead:

```
$ curl -O http://www.wbez.org/ta/{one,two,three}.rm
```

The -O (or --remote-name) option is absolutely required. If you don't use it, curl writes the output of the download to STDOUT, which means that your terminal will quickly fill with unusable goobledygook. The -O asks curl to write out what it downloads to a file, and to use the name of the file being downloaded as the local filename as well.

We've barely scratched the surface of curl. Its man page, while not as long as wget's, is also full of useful information that you need to read if you're going to maximize your use of curl. Consider it required reading.

Conclusion

The commands in this chapter are some of my personal favorites, as they allow me to accomplish tasks that would otherwise be overly tedious, unsafe, or difficult. All of them make the network just another avenue for your data, your programs, and your imagination, and that's really where Linux shines. By making tools as powerful as ssh, rsync, wget, and curl freely available to users, Linux encourages innovation and safety in a way that's just not possible on another operating system that many people are forced to use. Jump in and learn ssh so you can securely connect to other computers, master rsync for safe and automated backups, and rely on wget and curl to specifically download needed content in as efficient a manner as possible. You'll be glad you did!

16

Windows Networking

Samba is one of the most important open-source projects in the world because it makes it possible for Linux (and other Unix machines, such as Mac OS X) to use Server Message Block (SMB), the networking protocol used on all Microsoft Windows machines. With Samba, Unix machines can connect to and mount shares on Windows machines, and print to shared printers connected to Windows machines. Unix machines can also set up Samba-based printer and file shares that Windows machines can connect to and use. In fact, Samba is so useful that you don't even need Windows machines in the equation. You might choose to implement Samba for file and printer sharing on a network of Linux machines because it works so well.

Many good books cover how to set up Samba on a server, so we're not going to cover administrative commands such as smbd, smbcacls, or smbpasswd (which, it is true, can be run by normal users to change their own passwords, but in practice is almost always run by the Samba server admin), or how to configure smb.conf. Instead, this chapter assumes you already have SMB shares set up on a Windows, Linux, or Mac OS X machine. You're instead going to focus on the client end of things: how to find out where those shares are, how to connect to those shares, and how to mount shares on your hard drive.

TIP: Some good books on setting up and administering Samba include

- *Sams Samba Unleashed*, ISBN: 0672318628; by Steve Litt
- *Sams Teach Yourself Samba in 24 Hours, 2nd Edition*, ISBN: 0672322692; by Gerald Carter
- *The Official Samba-3 HOWTO and Reference Guide* at http://samba.org/samba/docs/man/Samba-HOWTO-Collection/ is excellent.

Discover the Workgroup's Master Browsers

```
nmblookup -M [Master Browser]
nmblookup -S [NetBIOS name]
nmblookup -A [IP address]
```

A Samba server actually uses two daemons: smbd, which makes the shares available, and nmbd, which maps the NetBIOS names that identify machines using SMB to their IP addresses, thus making it possible to find and browse SMB shares. You're going to focus for now on commands that communicate with nmbd, used to gain some overall information about the Windows workgroup you're querying.

NOTE: The following examples assume you're using a Windows workgroup, and not a domain. A *workgroup* is

essentially a small group of machines that choose to identify themselves as belonging together by self-identifying
as members of the workgroup. A *domain* uses a central
server—or several servers in a large network—to authenti-
cate computers and users who want to join the network.
Domains are large, hairy, complicated beasts, and you're
best referred to the books referenced in this chapter's
introduction if you want to learn more about them.

In a Windows workgroup, you need a machine that
keeps track of the other members of the workgroup—
what their SMB names and IP addresses are, for
instance. That machine is known as the Master Browser.
But which computer in a workgroup is the Master? The
one that is elected, based on the operating system it's
running. The latest and greatest OS always wins, so XP
will always beat 2000, which will always beat 98.

When setting up a Samba server, however, it's possible
to configure things so the server always stays out of any
such election, letting other machines duke it out, or set
things up so that the server always wins any election.
You could go ahead and start connecting to Samba
shares if you knew about them, but it helps to know
where your Master Browsers are in case you have any
issues.

To query your network for a Master Browser, run
nmblookup with the -M (or --master-browser) option,
followed by a - at the end, which basically means "find
me a Master Browser." The problem is that you can't
use a - on the command line, or the shell thinks it's the
start of an option. So you need to preface it with
-- first, which tells the shell that the following - is in
fact a -, and not part of an option.

```
$ nmblookup -M -- -
querying __MSBROWSE__ on 192.168.1.255
192.168.1.151 __MSBROWSE__<01>
192.168.1.104 __MSBROWSE__<01>
```

This isn't good. In your case, you appear to have two Master Browsers on one network, which can be a real problem because different Masters might know about different machines at different times, causing mass confusion to users. One minute a user can get to a machine, and the next it's gone. Why? Because one Master knows about the machine, but the other doesn't. Try explaining that to Bob in Accounting. Yipes.

To get more information about the Master, use nmblookup with the -S (or --status) option, which returns the SMB names the host uses.

```
$ nmblookup -S 192.168.1.151
querying 192.168.1.151 on 192.168.1.255
name_query failed to find name 192.168.1.151
```

That didn't work because -S expects a NetBIOS name instead of an IP address. Unfortunately, you don't know the machine's NetBIOS name, only its IP address. Actually, that's not a problem. You simply add the -A (or --lookup-by-ip) option, which tells nmblookup that you're giving it an IP address instead of a NetBIOS name.

```
$ nmblookup -SA 192.168.1.151
Looking up status of 192.168.1.151
        JANSMAC          <00> -        B <ACTIVE>
        JANSMAC          <03> -        B <ACTIVE>
        JANSMAC          <20> -        B <ACTIVE>
        .._MSBROWSE__. <01> - <GROUP> B <ACTIVE>
```

```
        MILTON              <00> - <GROUP> B <ACTIVE>
        MILTON              <1d> -         B <ACTIVE>
        MILTON              <1e> - <GROUP> B <ACTIVE>

        MAC Address = 00-00-00-00-00-00
```

Now you know that the machine at 192.168.1.151
identifies itself as JANSMAC (it must be a Mac OS box)
and is the Master for the MILTON workgroup. What
about the other IP address?

```
$ nmblookup -SA 192.168.1.104
Looking up status of 192.168.1.104
        ELIOT               <00> -         B <ACTIVE>
        ELIOT               <03> -         B <ACTIVE>
        ELIOT               <20> -         B <ACTIVE>
        ..__MSBROWSE__. <01> - <GROUP> B <ACTIVE>
        TURING              <00> - <GROUP> B <ACTIVE>
        TURING              <1d> -         B <ACTIVE>
        TURING              <1e> - <GROUP> B <ACTIVE>

        MAC Address = 00-00-00-00-00-00
```

The computer found at 192.168.1.104 has a NetBIOS
name of ELIOT, and is the Master for the TURING workgroup. So actually you have nothing to worry about, as
the two machines are each a Master for a separate
Workgroup. Machines that self-identify as members of
MILTON look to JANSMAC for information, while those
that consider themselves part of TURING use ELIOT for
the same purpose.

NOTE: For more information about what the output in
these examples means, see http://support.microsoft.com/
kb/q163409/ in Microsoft's Knowledge Base.

Query and Map NetBIOS Names and IP Addresses

```
nmblookup -T
```

You can use nmblookup as a quick way to find any machines that are sharing files and printers via Samba. Append the -T option to the command, followed by "*" (and yes, you *must* include the quotation marks to tell the shell that you're not using the * as a wildcard representing the files in your current working directory).

```
$ nmblookup -T "*"
querying * on 192.168.1.255
192.168.1.151 *<00>
192.168.1.104 *<00>
192.168.1.10 *<00>
```

Three machines are on this LAN with Samba shares. To find out which of those are Master Browsers, see the previous section; to produce a list of the shares offered by each computer, proceed to the next section.

List a Machine's Samba Shares

```
smbclient
```

So you know that a machine has Samba shares on it, thanks to the commands outlined in the previous section, but you don't know what those shares are. The smbclient command is a versatile tool that can be used to connect to shares and work with them; at a more simple level, however, it can also list the shares available on a computer. Just use the -L (or --list) option, followed by the NetBIOS name or IP address. When prompted for a password, simply press Enter.

```
$ smbclient -L ELIOT
Password:
Anonymous login successful
Domain=[TURING] OS=[Unix] Server=[Samba 3.0.14a-
➥Ubuntu]
Sharename Type Comment

print$     Disk Printer Drivers
documents  Disk Shared presentations and other files
IPC$       IPC  IPC Service (eliot server (Samba,
➥Ubuntu))
ADMIN$     IPC  IPC Service (eliot server (Samba,
➥Ubuntu))
Anonymous login successful
Domain=[TURING] OS=[Unix] Server=[Samba 3.0.14a-
➥Ubuntu]
```

In this case, you can see all of the shares that are available either to an anonymous logon or have been marked as being able to be browsed in the server's smb.conf file. To see the shares available to you if you were to log on, add the -U (or --user) option, followed by your Samba username as found on the Samba server.

NOTE: Your Samba username might or might not be the same as your Linux (or Windows or Mac OS X) username on the Samba server. You need to look on the Samba server to make sure.

```
$ smbclient -L ELIOT -U scott
Password:
Domain=[ELIOT] OS=[Unix] Server=[Samba 3.0.14a-
```

```
➥Ubuntu]
Sharename  Type  Comment

print$     Disk  Printer Drivers
documents  Disk  Shared presentations and other files
IPC$       IPC   IPC Service (eliot server (Samba,
➥Ubuntu))
ADMIN$     IPC   IPC Service (eliot server (Samba,
➥Ubuntu))
scott      Disk  Home Directories
Domain=[ELIOT] OS=[Unix] Server=[Samba 3.0.14a-
➥Ubuntu]
```

When you log in, you now see a new share, scott—the home directory of this user. This also tells you that you *can* log in, which brings you to the next section, in which you log in and actually use the stuff you find on the share.

TIP: If you want to test the shares you just created on a Samba server, an excellent method is to open a shell on that box, and then enter the following:

`$ smbclient -L localhost`

When prompted for a password, press Enter. This way you can quickly see if the new share you added is available. Of course, if you didn't make the share open to browsing, you'll need to log on as a user who can view that share using the -U option.

Access Samba Resources with an FTP-Like Client

`smbclient`

After you know the shares available on a Samba server, you can log in and start using them. Use the `smbclient` command, but in this format:

```
smbclient //server/share -U username
```

You can't just log in to a server; instead, you need to log in to a share on that server. To access password-protected items (and it's certainly advisable to password-protect your shares), you need to specify a user. To access the documents share on the server ELIOT, you'd use the following:

```
$ smbclient //eliot/documents -U scott
Password:
Domain=[ELIOT] OS=[Unix] Server=[Samba 3.0.14a-
➥Ubuntu]
smb: \>
```

You'll know you were successful because you'll be at the Samba prompt, which looks like smb: \>. Notice that you're prompted for a password. Assuming that the password for the scott user was 123456 (a very bad password, but this is just hypothetical), you could have entered this command instead, and you wouldn't be prompted for a password:

```
$ smbclient //eliot/documents -U scott%123456
```

This is a terrible idea, however, because anyone looking at either your .bash_history file (discussed in the "View Your Command-Line History" section in Chapter 11, "Your Shell") or the list of running processes with ps (see "View All Currently Running Processes" in Chapter 12, "Monitoring System Resources") could see your password. Never append your password onto your username. It's just good security practice to enter it when prompted.

TIP: If you're writing a script and you need to log in without interaction, you still shouldn't append the password onto the username. Instead, use the -A (or --authentication-file=[filename]) option, which references a credentials file. Using the scott user, that file would contain the following:

```
username = scott
password = 123456
```

Make sure you use chmod (see Chapter 7, "Ownerships and Permissions") to set the permissions on that file so it isn't readable by the world.

After you're connected to a Samba share, you can use many of the commands familiar to those who have ever used FTP on the command line (see Table 16.1).

Table 16.1   Important smbclient Commands

Command	Meaning
cd	Change directory
exit	Close the connection to the Samba server
get	Copy the specified file to the local machine
help	Get help on commands
lcd	Change the directory on the local machine
ls	List files in the working directory on the Samba server
mget	Copy all files matching a pattern to the local machine

Table 16.1   Continued

Command	Meaning
mkdir	Create a new directory on the Samba server
mput	Copy all files matching a pattern to the Samba server
put	Copy the specified file to the Samba server
rm	Remove the specified file from the Samba server

You can view other commands by simply typing **help** after you've logged in to the Samba server, but Table 16.1 contains the basics. When you're finished, simply type **exit**, and you log out of the server and are back on your own machine.

Mount a Samba Filesystem

smbmount
smbumount

It's cool that you can use smbclient to access Samba shares, but it's also a pain if you want to use a GUI, or if you want to do a lot of work on the share. In those cases, you should use smbmount, which mounts the Samba share to your local filesystem as though it was part of your hard drive. After it's mounted, you can open your favorite file manager and access files on the share easily, and you can even open programs such as word processors and open the files directly with a minimum of fuss.

To mount a Samba share on your filesystem, you must create a mount point onto which Linux will graft the share. For instance, if you were going to mount the documents share from ELIOT, you might create a directory like this:

```
$ mkdir /home/scott/eliot_documents
```

Now you run the smbmount command, along with a whole host of options.

```
$ smbmount //eliot/documents /home/scott/eliot_
➥documents -o credentials=/home/scott/bin/
➥credentials_eliot,fmask=644,dmask=755,uid=1001,
➥gid=1001,workgroup=TURING
smbmnt must be installed suid root for direct user
➥mounts (1000,1000)
smbmnt failed: 1
```

Before looking at the option, let's talk about why smbmount failed. The second line tells you why: smbmnt, which smbmount calls, can only be run by root. This can be a problem if you want your non-root users to be able to mount Samba shares. The way around that is to set smbmnt as suid root (you learned about suid in Chapter 7's "Set and Then Clear suid").

NOTE: Yes, you're giving ordinary users the ability to use smbmnt as though they were root, but it's not really a big problem. It's certainly better than giving them the root password, or requiring your participation every time they want to mount a Samba share.

Here's how to set smbmnt as suid root.

NOTE: In order to save space, some of the details you'd normally see with ls -l have been removed.

```
# ls /usr/bin/smbmnt
-rwxr-xr-x  1 root root /usr/bin/smbmnt
# chmod u+s /usr/bin/smbmnt
# ls -l /usr/bin/smbmnt
-rwsr-xr-x  1 root root /usr/bin/smbmnt
```

Now let's try smbmount again.

```
$ smbmount //eliot/documents /home/scott/eliot_
➥documents -o redentials=/home/scott/
➥credentials_eliot,fmask=644,dmask=755,uid=1001,
➥gid=1001,workgroup=TURING
$ ls -F /home/scott/eliot_documents
presentations/  to_print/
```

Let's walk through the command you used. After
smbmount, //eliot/documents specifies the Samba server
and Samba share to which you're connecting. Then
comes the path to your mount point, /home/scott/
eliot_documents. The -o option indicates that options
are coming next.

Instead of credentials=/home/scott/credentials_eliot,
you could have used any of the following:

- username=scott,password=123456

- username=scott%123456

- username=scott

The first and second choices are completely unsafe
because the password would now show up in .bash_
history and ps. Don't do that! The final choice prompts
you for a password, which would be safe because the
password wouldn't appear in either .bash_history or ps.
But you're trying to automate the process of mounting
the Samba share, so the last choice wouldn't work,
either.

That leaves you with `credentials=/home/scott/`
`credentials_eliot`. This tells `smbmount` that the username and password are stored in a file, in this format:

```
username = scott
password = 123456
```

This is just like the credentials file discussed previously
in "Access Samba Resources with an FTP-Like
Client," and as in that example, use `chmod` after you create a credentials file to tightly limit who can view that
file. If you don't care about automating the logon
process, by all means, use `username=scott` and get
prompted to enter the password, which is certainly the
safest option.

The `fmask` and `dmask` options respectively control the
default permissions for any new files and directories
that you create in the mounted Samba share. `644` would
produce `rw-r--r--` for files, while `755` would end up
with `rwxr-xr-x` for directories.

NOTE: Don't recall what we're talking about? Take a look
back at "Understand the Basics of Permissions" in Chapter 7.

Remember that all usernames and group names are really references to numbers, which you can see in `/etc/`
`passwd` and `/etc/group`, respectively. Your user ID number
on your current machine might be 1000, but on the
Samba server, 1000 could be a completely different user,
with the same problem for your group ID. With
`uid=1001` and `gid=1001`, you tell the Samba server who
you are *on the Samba server*. In other words, you need to
look those numbers up in `/etc/passwd` and `/etc/group`
on the Samba server, not on your local machine. If you
don't, you may create files and directories, only to find

that you don't really own them and can't use them the
way you want.

Finally, workgroup=TURING specifies the workgroup,
which is obvious enough.

After the share is mounted, you can open your file
manager and start browsing the contents of eliot_
documents, start OpenOffice.org and directly open a file
inside eliot_documents/presentations/, or open a PDF
in eliot_documents/to_print and send it to the printer.
If you place the following lines in your machine's
/etc/fstab file, the share is mounted automatically.

```
//eliot/documents /home/scott/eliot_documents smbfs
➥credentials=/home/scott/credentials_eliot,fmask=644,
➥dmask=755,uid=1001,gid=1001,workgroup=TURING 0 0
```

CAUTION: Be very careful changing your /etc/fstab file
because mistakes can render your system unbootable. Sure,
you can fix that problem (see my book *Hacking Knoppix* for
some tips) but it's still a pain that would be better to avoid
with caution and prudence. For more on the fstab file, see
man fstab on your system.

If you decide that you don't want to access the Samba
share at eliot_documents any longer, you can unmount
it with smbumount (notice that's *u*mount , not *un*mount).

```
$ smbumount eliot_documents
smbumount must be installed suid root
```

How frustrating! You need to set smbumount as suid
root, too.

```
$ ls -l /usr/bin/smbumount
-rwxr-xr-x  1 root root /usr/bin/smbumount
$ sudo chmod u+s /usr/bin/smbumount
$ ls -l /usr/bin/smbumount
-rwsr-xr-x  1 root root /usr/bin/smbumount
```

Now the user that mounted eliot_documents—and only that user—can unmount eliot_documents. Root can unmount it, too, because root can do whatever it wants.

```
$ smbumount eliot_documents
```

And that's it. If you want to verify that smbumount worked, try ls eliot_documents, and there shouldn't be anything in there. You're disconnected from that Samba share.

Conclusion

Much as Linux users would like to pretend that Microsoft doesn't exist, you have to realize that (for now) you live in a Windows world. Samba makes coexistence that much easier because it allows Linux users to access resources on Windows machines, and even makes resources available on a Linux box to users of other operating systems. Microsoft might not like it very much, but Samba is a mature, stable, powerful technology, and thanks to its open-source nature, it has helped bring the entire world of computing more closely together. Samba helps you reduce the need for Windows servers in homes and businesses, and that, as a certain doyenne might say, is a good thing.

Index

How can we make this index more useful? Email us at indexes@samspublishing.com

375

INDEX